The Life, Studies, and Works of Benjamin West, Esq.

John Galt, Esq.

Contents

PART I	7
CHAPTER I	8
CHAPTER II	19
CHAPTER III	28
CHAPTER IV	35
CHAPTER V	43
CHAPTER VI	52
CHAPTER VII	61
CHAPTER VIII	69
PART II	84
CHAPTER I	87
CHAPTER II	92
CHAPTER III	96
CHAPTER IV	101
CHAPTER V	107
CHAPTER VI	113
CHAPTER VII	119
CHAPTER VIII	125
CHAPTER IX	130
CHAPTER X	135
CHAPTER XI	143
CHAPTER XII	154
CHAPTER XIII	167
CHAPTER XIV	172
APPENDIX No. I.	180
APPENDIX No. II.	186

THE LIFE, STUDIES, AND WORKS OF BENJAMIN WEST, ESQ.

by

John Galt, Esq.

To
Alexander Gordon, Esq.
This little work
Is respectfully inscribed
By the Author.

Part I

PREFACE

THE professional life of Mr. West constitutes an important part of an historical work, in which the matter of this volume could only have been introduced as an episode, and, perhaps, not with much propriety even in that form. It was my intention, at one time, to have prepared the whole of his memoirs, separately, for publication; but a careful review of the manuscript convinced me, that the transactions in which he has been engaged, subsequently to his arrival in England, are so much of a public nature, and belong so immediately to the history of the Arts, that such a separation could not be effected without essentially impairing the interest and unity of the main design; and that the particular nature of this portion of his memoirs admitted of being easily detached and arranged into a whole, complete within itself.

I do not think that there can be two opinions with respect to the utility of a work of this kind. Mr. West, in relating the circumstances by which he was led to approximate, without the aid of an instructor, to those principles and rules of art, which it is the object of schools and academies to disseminate, has conferred a greater benefit on young Artists than he could possibly have done by the most ingenious and eloquent lectures on the theories of his profession; and it was necessary that the narrative should appear in his own time, in order that the authenticity of the incidents might not rest on the authority of any biographer.

April 25,1816.   John Galt.

CHAPTER I

The Birth and Paternal Ancestry of Mr. West —His Maternal Family —His Father —The Origin of the Abolition of Slavery by the Quakers —The Progress of the Abolition —The Education of the Negroes —The Preaching of Edmund Peckover —His Admonitory Prediction to the Father of West —The first Indication of Benjamin's Genius —State of Society in Pennsylvania —The Indians give West the Primary Colours —The Artist's first Pencils —The Present of a Box of Colours and Engravings —His first Painting

Benjamin West, the subject of the following Memoirs, was the youngest son of John West and Sarah Pearson, and was born near Springfield, in Chester County, in the State of Pennsylvania, on the 10th of October, 1738.

The branch of the West family, to which he belongs, has been traced in an unbroken series to the Lord Delawarre, who distinguished himself in the great wars of King Edward the Third, and particularly at the battle of Cressy, under the immediate command of the Black Prince. In the reign of Richard the Second, the ancestors of Mr. West settled at Long Crandon in Buckinghamshire. About the year 1667 they embraced the tenets of the Quakers; and Colonel James West, the friend and companion in arms of the celebrated Hampden, is said to have been the first proselyte of the family. In 1699 they emigrated to America.

Thomas Pearson, the maternal grandfather of the Artist, was the confidential friend of William Penn, and accompanied him to America. On their first landing, the venerable Founder of the State of Pennsylvania said to him, "Providence has brought us safely hither; thou hast been the companion of my perils, what wilt thou that I should call this place?" Mr, Pearson replied, that "since he had honoured him so far as to desire him to give that part of the country a name, he would, in remembrance of his native City, call it Chester." The exact spot where these patriarchs of the new world first landed, is still pointed out with reverence by the inhabitants. Mr. Pearson built a house and formed a plantation in the neighbourhood, which he called Springfield, in consequence of discovering a large spring of water in the first field cleared for cultivation; and it was near this place that Benjamin West was born.

When the West family emigrated, John, the father of Benjamin, was left to complete his education at the great school of the Quakers at Uxbridge, and did not join his relations in America till the year 1714. Soon after his arrival he married the mother of the Artist; and of the worth and piety of his character we have a remarkable proof in the following transactions, which, perhaps, reflect more real glory on his family than the achievements of all his heroic ancestors.

As a part of the marriage portion of Mrs. West he received a negro slave, whose diligence and fidelity very soon obtained his full confidence. Being engaged in trade, he had occasion to make a voyage in the West Indies, and left this young black to superintend the plantation in his absence, During his residence in Barbadoes, his feelings were greatly molested, and his principles shocked, by the cruelties to which he saw the negroes subjected in that island; and the debasing effects were forcibly contrasted in his mind with the morals and intelligence of his own slave. Conversing on this subject with Doctor Gammon, who was then at the head of the community of Friends in Barbadoes, the Doctor convinced him that it was contrary to the laws of God and Nature that any man should retain his fellow-creatures in slavery. This conviction could not rest long inactive in a character framed like that of Mr. West. On his return to America he gave the negro his freedom, and retained him as a hired servant.

Not content with doing good himself, he endeavoured to make others follow his example, and in a short time his arguments had such an effect on his neighbours, that it was agreed to discuss publicly the general question of Slavery. This was done accordingly; and, after debating it at many meetings, it was resolved by a considerable majority THAT IT WAS THE DUTY OF CHRISTIANS TO GIVE FREEDOM

TO THEIR SLAVES. The result of this discussion was soon afterwards followed by a similar proposal to the head meeting of the Quakers in the township of Goshen in Chester County; and the cause of Humanity was again victorious. Finally, about the year 1753, the same question was agitated in the annual general assembly at Philadelphia, when it was ultimately established as one of the tenets of the Quakers, that no person could remain a member of their community who held a human creature in slavery. This transaction is perhaps the first example in the history of communities, of a great public sacrifice of individual interest, not originating from considerations of policy or the exigences of public danger, but purely from moral and religious principles.

The benevolent work of restoring their natural rights to the unfortunate Negroes, did not rest even at this great pecuniary sacrifice. The Society of Friends went farther, and established Schools for the education of their children; and some of the first characters among themselves volunteered to superintend the course of instruction.

In the autumn of 1738, Edmund Peckover, a celebrated Orator among the Quakers, came to the neighbourhood of Springfield, and on the 28th of September preached in a meeting-house erected by the father of Mrs. West at the distance of about a mile and a half from his residence. Mrs. West was then the mother of nine children, and far advanced in her pregnancy with Benjamin.—Peckover possessed the most essential qualities of an impressive speaker, and on this occasion the subject of his address was of extraordinary interest to his auditors. He reviewed the rise and progress of society in America, and with an enthusiastic eloquence which partook of the sublimity and vehemence of the prophetic spirit, he predicted the future greatness of the country. He described the condition of the European nations, decrepid in their institutions, and corrupt in their morality, and contrasted them with the young and flourishing establishments of the New World. He held up to their abhorrence the licentious manners and atheistical principles of the French, among whom God was disregarded or forgotten; and, elevated by the importance of his subject, he described the Almighty as mustering his wrath to descend on that nation, and disperse it as chaff in a whirlwind. He called on them to look towards their home of England, and to see with what eager devotion the inhabitants worshiped the golden image of Commerce, and laid the tribute of all their thoughts on its altars; believing that with the power of the idol alone, they should be able to withstand all calamities. "The day and the hour are, however, hastening on, when the image shall be shaken from its pedestal by the tempest of Jehovah's descending vengeance, its altars overturned, and the worshipers terribly convinced that without the favour of the Almighty God there is no wisdom in man! But," continued this impassioned orator, "from the woes and the crimes of Europe let us turn aside our eyes; let us turn from the worshipers of Commerce, clinging round their idols of gold and silver, and, amidst the wrath, the storm, and the thunder, endeavouring to hold them up; let us not look at the land of blasphemies; for in the crashing of engines, the gushing of blood, and the shrieking of witnesses more to be pitied than the victims, the activity of God's purifying displeasure will be heard; while turning our eyes towards the mountains of this New World, the forests shall be seen fading away, cities rising along the shores, and the terrified nations of Europe flying out of the smoke and the burning to find refuge here."—All his auditors were deeply affected, particularly Mrs. West, who was taken with the pains of labour on the spot. The meeting was broken up; the women made a circle round her as they carried her home, and such was the agitation into which she was thrown, that the consequences had nearly proved fatal both to the mother and the infant, of which she was prematurely delivered.

This occurrence naturally excited much attention, and became the subject of general conversation. It made a deep impression on the mind of Mr. West, who could not divest himself of a feeling that it indicated something extraordinary in the future fortunes of his child; and when Peckover, soon afterwards, on his leaving that part of the country, paid him a farewell visit, he took an opportunity of introducing the subject. The warm imagination of the Preacher eagerly sympathised with the feelings of his friend. He took him by the hand, and, with emphatic solemnity, said that a child sent into the world under such remarkable circumstances would prove no ordinary man; and he charged him to watch over the boy's character with the utmost degree of paternal solicitude. It will appear in the sequel, that this singular admonition was not lost on Mr. West.

The first six years of Benjamin's life passed away in calm uniformity; leaving only the placid remembrance of enjoyment. In the month of June 1745, one of his sisters, who had been married some time before, and who had a daughter, came with her infant to spend a few days at her father's. When the child was asleep in the cradle, Mrs. West invited her daughter to gather flowers in the garden, and committed the infant to the care of Benjamin during their absence; giving him a fan to flap away the flies from molesting his little charge. After some time the child happened to smile in its sleep, and its beauty attracted his attention. He looked at it with a pleasure which he had never before experienced, and observing some paper on a table, together with pens and red and black ink, he seized them with agitation, and endeavoured to delineate a portrait: although at this period he had never seen an engraving or a picture, and was only in the seventh year of his age.

Hearing the approach of his mother and sister, he endeavoured to conceal what he had been doing; but the old lady observing his confusion, enquired what he was about, and requested him to show her the paper. He obeyed, entreating her not to be angry. Mrs. West, after looking some time at the drawing with evident pleasure, said to her daughter, "I declare he has made a likeness of little Sally," and kissed him with much fondness and satisfaction. This encouraged him to say, that if it would give her any pleasure, he would make pictures of the flowers which she held in her hand; for the instinct of his genius was now awakened, and he felt that he could imitate the forms of those things which pleased his sight.

This curious incident deserves consideration in two points of view. The sketch must have had some merit, since the likeness was so obvious, indicating how early the hand of the young artist possessed the power of representing the observations of his eye. But it is still more remarkable as the birth of the fine arts in the New World, and as one of the few instances in the history of art, in which the first inspiration of genius can be distinctly traced to a particular circumstance. The drawing was shown by Mrs. West to her husband, who, remembering the prediction of Peckover, was delighted with this early indication of talent in his son. But the fact, though in itself very curious, will appear still more remarkable, when the state of the country at that period, and the peculiar manners of the Quakers, are taken into consideration.

The institutions of William Penn had been sacredly preserved by the descendants of the first settlers, with whom the remembrance of the causes which had led their ancestors to forsake their native country, was cherished like the traditions of religion, and became a motive to themselves, for indulging in the exercise of those blameless principles, which had been so obnoxious to the arrogant spirit of the Old World. The associates of the Wests and the Pearsons, considered the patriarchs of Pennsylvania as having been driven from England, because their endeavours to regulate their conduct by the example of Jesus Christ, mortified the temporal pretensions of those who satisfied themselves with attempting to repeat his doctrines; and they thought that the asylum in America was chosen, to facilitate the enjoyment of that affectionate intercourse which their tenets enjoined, free from the military predilections and political jealousies of Europe. The effect of this opinion tended to produce a state of society more peaceful and pleasing than the World had ever before exhibited. When the American Poets shall in future times celebrate the golden age of their country, they will draw their descriptions from the authentic history of Pennsylvania in the reign of King George the Second.

From the first emigration in 1681, the colony had continued to thrive with a rapidity unknown to the other European Settlements. It was blessed in the maxims upon which it had been founded, and richly exhibited the fruits of their beneficent operation. At the birth of Benjamin West it had obtained great wealth, and the population was increasing much more vigorously than the ordinary reproduction of the human species in any other part of the world. In the houses of the principal families, the patricians of the country, unlimited hospitality formed a part of their regular economy. It was the custom among those who resided near the highways, after supper and the last religious exercise of the evening, to make a large fire in the hall, and to set out a table with refreshments for such travellers as might have occasion to pass during the night; and when the families assembled in the morning they seldom found that their tables had been unvisited. This was particularly the case at Springfield. Poverty was never heard of in the land. The disposition to common charity having no objects, was blended with the domestic affections, and rendered the ties of friendship and kindred stronger and dearer. Acts of liberality were frequently performed to an extent that would have beggared the munificence of the Old World. With all these delightful indications of a better order of things, society in Pennsylvania retained, at this time, many of those respectable prejudices which gave a venerable grace to manners, and are regarded by the practical philosopher as little inferior in dignity to the virtues. William Penn was proud of his distinguished parentage, and many of his friends traced their lineage to the antient and noble families of England. In their descendants the pride of ancestry was so tempered with the meekness of their religious tenets, that it lent a kind of patriarchal dignity to their benevolence.

In beautiful contrast to the systematic morality of the new inhabitants, was the simplicity of the Indians, who mingled safe and harmless among the Friends. In the annual visits which they were in the practice of paying to the Plantations, they raised their huts in the fields and orchards without asking leave, nor were they ever molested. Voltaire has observed, that the treaty which was concluded between the Indians and William Penn was the first public contract which connected the inhabitants of the Old and New World together, and, though not ratified by oaths, and without invoking the Trinity, is still the only treaty that has never been broken. It may be further said, that Pennsylvania is the first country which has not been subdued by the sword, for the inhabitants were conquered by the force of Christian benevolence.

When the great founder of the State marked out the site of Philadelphia in the woods, he allotted a piece of ground for a public library. It was his opinion, that although the labour of clearing the country would long employ the settlers, hours of relaxation would still be requisite; and, with his usual sagacity, he judged that the reading of books was more conducive to good morals and to the formation of just sentiments, than any other species of amusement. The different counties afterwards instituted libraries, which the townships have also imitated: where the population was insufficient to establish a large collection of books, the neighbouring families formed themselves into societies for procuring the popular publications. But in these arrangements for cultivating the powers of the understanding, no provision was made, during the reign of George the Second, for improving the faculties of taste. The works of which the libraries then consisted, treated of useful and practical subjects. It was the policy of the Quakers to make mankind wiser and better; and they thought that, as the passions are the springs of all moral evil when in a state of excitement, whatever tends to awaken them is unfavourable to that placid tenour of mind which they wished to see diffused throughout the world. This notion is prudent, perhaps judicious; but works of imagination may be rendered subservient to the same purpose. Every thing in Pennsylvania was thus unpropitious to the fine arts. There were no cares in the bosoms of individuals to require public diversions, nor any emulation in the expenditure of wealth to encourage the ornamental manufactures. In the whole Christian world no spot was apparently so unlikely to produce a painter as Pennsylvania. It might, indeed, be supposed, according to a popular opinion, that a youth, reared among the concentrating elements of a new state, in the midst of boundless forests, tremendous waterfalls, and mountains whose summits were inaccessible to "the lightest foot and wildest wing," was the most favourable situation to imbibe the enthusiasm either of poetry or of painting, if scenery and such accidental circumstances are to be regarded as every thing, and original character as nothing. But it may reasonably be doubted if ever natural scenery has any assignable influence on the productions of genius. The idea has probably arisen from the impression which the magnificence of nature makes on persons of cultivated minds, who fall into the mistake of considering the elevated emotions arising in reality from their own associations, as being naturally connected with the objects that excite them. Of all the nations of Europe the Swiss are the least poetical, and yet the scenery of no other country seems so well calculated as that of Switzerland to awaken the imagination; and Shakespeare, the greatest of all modern Poets, was brought up in one of the least picturesque districts of England.

Soon after the occurrence of the incident which has given rise to these observations, the young Artist was sent to a school in the neighbourhood. During his hours of leisure he was permitted to draw with pen and ink; for it did not occur to any of the family to provide him with better materials. In the course of the summer a party of Indians came to pay their annual visit to Springfield, and being amused with the sketches of birds and flowers which Benjamin shewed them, they taught him to prepare the red and yellow colours with which they painted their ornaments. To these his mother added blue, by giving him a piece of indigo, so that he was thus put in possession of the three primary colours. The fancy is disposed to expatiate on this interesting fact; for the mythologies of antiquity furnish no allegory more beautiful; and a Painter who would embody the metaphor of an Artist instructed by Nature, could scarcely imagine any thing more picturesque than the real incident of the Indians instructing West to prepare the prismatic colours. The Indians also taught him to be an expert archer, and he was sometimes in the practice of shooting birds for models, when he thought that their plumage would look well in a picture.

His drawings at length attracted the attention of the neighbours; and some of them happening to regret that the Artist had no pencils, he enquired what kind of things these were, and they were described to him as small brushes made of camels' hair fastened in a quill. As there were, however, no camels in America, he could not think of any substitute, till he happened to cast his eyes on a black cat, the favourite of his father; when, in the tapering fur of her tail, he discovered the means of supplying what he wanted. He immediately armed himself with his mother's scissors, and, laying hold of Grimalkin with all due caution, and a proper attention to her feelings, cut off the fur at the end of her tail, and with this made his first pencil. But the tail only furnished him with one, which did not last long, and he soon stood in need of a further supply. He then had recourse to the animal's back, his depredations upon which were so frequently repeated, that his father observed the altered appearance of his favourite, and lamented it as the effect of disease. The Artist, with suitable marks of contrition, informed him of the true cause; and the old gentleman was so much amused with his ingenuity, that if he rebuked him, it was certainly not in anger.

Anecdotes of this kind, trifling as they may seem, have an interest independent of the insight they afford into the character to which they relate. It will often appear, upon a careful study of authentic biography, that the means of giving body and effect to their conceptions, are rarely withheld from men of genius. If the circumstances of Fortune are unfavourable, Nature instructs them to draw assistance immediately from herself, by endowing them with the faculty of perceiving a fitness and correspondence in things which no force of reasoning, founded on the experience of others, could enable them to discover. This aptness is, perhaps, the surest indication of the possession of original talent. There are minds of a high class to which the world, in the latitude of its expressions, often ascribes genius, but which possess only a superior capacity for the application of other men's notions, unconnected with any unusual portion of the inventive faculty.

In the following year Mr. Pennington, a merchant of Philadelphia, who was related to the West family, came to pay a visit to Mr. West. This gentleman was also a member of the Society of Friends, and, though strictly attentive to the peculiar observances of the sect, was a man of pleasant temper and indulgent dispositions. He noticed the drawings of birds and flowers round the room, unusual ornaments in the house of a Quaker; and heard with surprise that they were the work of his little cousin. Of their merit as pictures he did not pretend to judge, but he thought them wonderful productions for a boy only entering on his eighth year, and being told with what imperfect materials they had been executed, he promised to send the young Artist a box of paints and pencils from the city. On his return home he fulfilled his engagement, and at the bottom of the box placed several pieces of canvass prepared for the easel, and six engravings by Grevling.

The arrival of the box was an aera in the history of the Painter and his art. It was received with feelings of delight which only a similar mind can justly appreciate. He opened it, and in the colours, the oils, and the pencils, found all his wants supplied, even beyond his utmost conceptions. But who can describe the surprise with which he beheld the engravings; he who had never seen any picture but his own drawings, nor knew that such an art as the Engraver's existed! He sat over the box with enamoured eyes; his mind was in a flutter of joy; and he could not refrain from constantly touching the different articles, to ascertain that they were real. At night he placed the box on a chair near his bed, and as often as he was overpowered by sleep, he started suddenly and stretched out his hand to satisfy himself that the possession of such a treasure was not merely a pleasing dream. He rose at the dawn of day, and carried the box to a room in the garret, where he spread a canvass, prepared a pallet, and immediately began to imitate the figures in the engravings. Enchanted by his art he forgot the school hours, and joined the family at dinner without mentioning the employment in which he had been engaged. In the afternoon he again retired to his study in the garret; and for several days successively he thus withdrew and devoted himself to painting. The schoolmaster, observing his absence, sent to ask the cause of it. Mrs. West, affecting not to take any particular notice of the message, recollected that she had seen Benjamin going up stairs every morning, and suspecting that the box occasioned his neglect of the school, went to the garret, and found him employed on the picture. Her anger was appeased by the sight of his performance, and changed to a very different feeling. She saw, not a mere copy, but a composition from two of the engravings. With no other guide than that delicacy of sight which renders the Painter's eye, with respect to colours, what the Musician's ear is with respect to sounds, he had formed a picture as complete, in the scientific arrangement of the tints, notwithstanding the necessary imperfection of the pencilling, as the most skilful Artist could have painted, assisted by the precepts of Newton. She kissed him with transports of affection, and assured him that she would not only intercede with his father to pardon him for having absented himself from school, but would go herself to the master, and beg that he might not be punished. The delightful encouragement which this well-judged kindness afforded to the young Painter may be easily imagined; but who will not regret that the mother's over-anxious admiration would not suffer him to finish the picture, lest he should spoil what was already in her opinion perfect, even with half the canvass bare? Sixty-seven years afterwards the writer of these Memoirs had the gratification to see this piece in the same room with the sublime painting of "Christ Rejected," on which occasion the Painter declared to him that there were inventive touches of art in his first and juvenile essay, which, with all his subsequent knowledge and experience, he had not been able to surpass.

CHAPTER II

The Artist visits Philadelphia —His second Picture —Williams the Painter gives him the works of Fresnoy and Richardson —Anecdote of the Taylor's Apprentice —The Drawings of the Schoolboys —Anecdote relative to Wayne —Anecdote relative to Mr. Flower —Anecdote relative to Mr. Ross —Anecdote of Mr. Henry —The Artist's first Historical Picture —Origin of his Acquaintance with Dr. Smith of Philadelphia —The friendship of Dr. Smith, and the character of the early companions of West —Anecdote of General Washington

IN the course of a few days after the affair of the painting, Mr. Pennington paid another visit to Mr. West; and was so highly pleased with the effect of his present, and the promising talents of his young relation, that he entreated the old gentleman to allow Benjamin to accompany him for a few days to Philadelphia. This was cheerfully agreed to, and the Artist felt himself almost, as much delighted with the journey as with the box of colours. Every thing in the town filled him with astonishment; but the view of the shipping, which was entirely new, particularly attracted his eye, and interested him like the imaginary spectacles of magic.

When the first emotions of his pleasure and wonder had subsided, he applied to Mr. Pennington to procure him materials for painting. That gentleman was desirous of getting possession of the first picture, and had only resigned what he jocularly alleged were his just claims, in consideration of the mother's feelings, and on being assured that the next picture should be purposely painted for him. The materials were procured, and the Artist composed a landscape, which comprehended a picturesque view of a river, with vessels on the water, and cattle pasturing on the banks. While he was engaged in this picture, an incident occurred which, though trivial in itself, was so much in unison with the other circumstances that favoured the bent of his genius, that it ought not to be omitted.

Samuel Shoemaker[1], an intimate friend of Mr. Pennington, one of the principal merchants of Philadelphia, happened to meet in the street with one Williams, a Painter, carrying home a picture. Struck by the beauty of the performance, he enquired if it was intended for sale, and being told that it was already disposed of, he ordered another to be painted for himself. When the painting was finished, he requested the Artist to carry it to Mr. Pennington's house, in order that it might be shewn to young West. It was very well executed, and the boy was so much astonished at the sight of it, that his emotion and surprise attracted the attention of Williams, who was a man of observation, and judged correctly in thinking that such an uncommon manifestation of sensibility in so young a boy, indicated something extraordinary in his character. He entered into conversation with him, and enquired if he had read any books, or the lives of great men, The little amateur told him that he had read the Bible, and was well acquainted with the history of Adam, Joseph, David, Solomon, and the other great and good men whose actions are recorded in the Holy Scriptures. Williams was much pleased with the simplicity of the answer; and it might have occurred to him that histories more interesting have never been written, or written so well. Turning to Mr. Pennington, who was present, he asked if Benjamin was his son; advising him at the same time to indulge him in whatever might appear to be the bent of his talents, assuring him that he was no common boy.

This interview was afterwards much spoken of by Williams, who in the mean time lent him the works of Fresnoy and Richardson on Painting, and invited him to see his pictures and drawings. The impression which these books made on the imagination of West finally decided his destination. He was allowed to carry them with him into the country; and his father and mother, soon perceiving a great change in his conversation, were referred to the books for an explanation of the

---

1 This gentleman was afterwards introduced by Mr. West to the King, at Windsor, as one of the American Loyalists.

cause. They read them for the first time themselves, and treasuring in their minds those anecdotes of the indications of the early symptoms of talent with which both works abound, they remembered the prophetic injunction of Edmund Peckover.

The effect of the enthusiasm inspired by Richardson and Fresnoy may be conceived from the following incident. Soon after the young Artist had returned to Springfield, one of his schoolfellows, on a Saturday's half holiday, engaged him to give up a party at trap-ball to ride with him to one of the neighbouring plantations. At the time appointed the boy came, with the horse saddled. West enquired how he was to ride; "Behind me," said the boy; but Benjamin, full of the dignity of the profession to which he felt himself destined, answered, that he never would ride behind any body. "O! very well then," said the good-natured boy, "you may take the saddle, and I will get up behind you." Thus mounted, they proceeded on their excursion; and the boy began to inform his companion that his father intended to send him to be an apprentice. "In what business?" enquired West; "A taylor," answered the boy. "Surely," said West, "you will never follow that trade;" animadverting upon its feminine character. The other, however, was a shrewd, sound-headed lad, and defended the election very stoutly, saying that his father had made choice of it for him, and that the person with whom he was to learn the business was much respected by all his neighbours. "But what do you intend to be, Benjamin?" West answered, that he had not thought at all on the subject, but he should like to be a painter. "A painter!" exclaimed the boy, "what sort of a trade is a painter? I never heard of such a thing." "A painter," said West, "is a companion for Kings and Emperors." "Surely you are mad," replied the boy, "for there are no such people in America." "Very true," answered Benjamin, "but there are plenty in other parts of the world." The other, still more amazed at the apparent absurdity of this speech, reiterated in a tone of greater surprise, "You are surely quite mad." To this the enthusiast replied by asking him if he really intended to be a taylor. "Most certainly," answered the other. "Then you may ride by yourself, for I will no longer keep your company," said West, and, alighting, immediately returned home.

The report of this incident, with the affair of the picture, which had occasioned his absence from school, and visit to Philadelphia, made a great impression on the boys in the neighbourhood of Springfield. All their accustomed sports were neglected, and their play-hours devoted to drawing with chalk and oker. The little president was confessedly the most expert among them, but he has often since declared, that, according to his recollection, many of his juvenile companions evinced a degree of taste and skill in this exercise, that would not have discredited the students of any regular academy.

Not far from the residence of Mr. West a cabinet-maker had a shop, in which Benjamin sometimes amused himself with the tools of the workmen. One day several large and beautiful boards of poplar tree were brought to it; and he happening to observe that they would answer very well for drawing on, the owner gave him two or three of them for that purpose, and he drew figures and compositions on them with ink, chalk, and charcoal. Mr. Wayne, a gentleman of the neighbourhood, having soon after occasion to call at his father's, noticed the boards in the room, and was so much pleased with the drawings, that he begged the young Artist to allow him to take two or three of them home, which, as but little value was set on them, was thought no great favour, either by the painter or his father. Next day Mr. Wayne called again, and after complimenting Benjamin on his taste and proficiency, gave him a dollar for each of the boards which he had taken away, and was resolved to preserve. Doctor Jonathan Moris, another neighbour, soon after, also made him a present of a few dollars to buy materials to paint with. These were the first public patrons of the Artist; and it is at his own request that their names are thus particularly inserted.

About twelve months after the visit to Philadelphia, Mr. Flower, one of the Justices of the county of Chester, who possessed some taste in painting, requested Mr, West to allow Benjamin to spend a few weeks at his house. A short time before, this gentleman had met with a severe domestic misfortune in the loss of a wife, to whom he was much attached; and he resolved to shew his respect to her memory by devoting his attention exclusively to the improvement of his children: for this purpose he had sent to England for a governess qualified to undertake the education of his daughters, and he had the good fortune to obtain a lady eminently fitted for the trust. She arrived a few days only before the young Artist, and her natural discernment enabled her to appreciate that original bias of mind which she had heard ascribed to him, and of which she soon perceived the determination and the strength. Finding him unacquainted with any other books than the Bible, and the works of Richardson and Fresnoy, she frequently invited him to sit with her pupils, and, during the intervals of their tasks, she read to him the most striking and picturesque passages from translations of the antient historians and poetry, of which Mr. Flower had a choice and extensive collection. It was from this intelligent woman that he heard, for the first time, of the Greeks and Romans; and the impression which the story of those illustrious nations made on his mind, was answerable to her expectations.

Among the acquaintance of Mr. Flower was a Mr. Ross, a lawyer in the town of Lancaster, a place at that time remarkable for its wealth, and which had the reputation of possessing the best and most intelligent society to be then found in America. It was chiefly inhabited by Germans, who of all people in the practice of emigrating, carry along with them the greatest stock of knowledge and accomplishments. The society of Lancaster, therefore, though it could not boast of any very distinguished character, yet comprehended many individuals who were capable of appreciating the merit of essays in art, and of discriminating the rude efforts of real genius from the more complete productions of mere mechanical skill. It was exactly in such a place that such a youth as Benjamin West was likely to meet with that flattering attention which is the best stimulus of juvenile talent. The wife of Mr. Ross was greatly admired for her beauty, and she had several children who were so remarkable in this respect as to be objects of general notice. One day when Mr. Flower was dining with them, he advised his friend to have their portraits taken; and mentioned that they would be excellent subjects for young West. Application was in consequence made to old Mr. West, and permission obtained for the little Artist to go to Lancaster for the purpose of taking the likenesses of Mrs. Ross and her family. Such was the success with which he executed this task, that the sphere of his celebrity was greatly enlarged; and so numerous were the applications for portraits, that it was with difficulty he could find time to satisfy the demands of his admirers.

Among those who sent to him in this early stage of his career, was a person of the name of William Henry. He was an able mechanic, and had acquired a handsome fortune by his profession of a gunsmith. Henry was, indeed, in several respects, an extraordinary man, and possessed the power generally attendant upon genius under all circumstances, that of interesting the imagination of those with whom he conversed. On examining the young Artist's performance, he observed to him, that, if he could paint as well, he would not waste his time on portraits, but would devote himself to historical subjects; and he mentioned the Death of Socrates as affording one of the best topics for illustrating the moral effect of the art of painting. The Painter knew nothing of the history of the Philosopher; and, upon confessing his ignorance, Mr. Henry went to his library, and, taking down a volume of the English translation of Plutarch, read to him the account given by that writer of this affecting story.

The suggestion and description wrought upon the imagination of West, and induced him to make a drawing, which he shewed to Mr. Henry, who commended it as a perspicuous delineation of the probable circumstances of the event, and requested him to paint it. West said that he would he happy to undertake the task, but, having hitherto painted only faces and men cloathed, he should be unable to do justice to the figure of the slave who presented the poison, and which he thought ought to be naked. Henry had among his workmen a very handsome young man, and, without waiting to answer the objection, he sent for him into the room. On his entrance he pointed him out to West, and said, "There is your model." The appearance of the young man, whose arms and breast were naked, instantaneously convinced the Artist that he had only to look into nature for the models which would impart grace and energy to his delineation of forms.

When the death of Socrates was finished, it attracted much attention, and led to one of those fortunate acquaintances by which the subsequent career of the Artist has been so happily facilitated. About this period the inhabitants of Lancaster had resolved to erect a public grammar-school; and Dr. Smith, the Provost of the College at Philadelphia, was invited by them to arrange the course of instruction, and to place the institution in the way best calculated to answer the intention of the founders. This gentleman was an excellent classical scholar, and combined with his knowledge and admiration of the merits of the antients that liberality of respect for the endeavours of modern talent, with which the same kind of feeling is but rarely found connected. After seeing the picture and conversing with the Artist, he offered to undertake to make him to a certain degree acquainted with classical literature; while at the same time he would give him such a sketch of the taste and character of the spirit of antiquity, as would have all the effect of the regular education requisite to a painter. When this liberal proposal was communicated to old Mr. West, he readily agreed that Benjamin should go for some time to Philadelphia, in order to take advantage of the Provost's instructions; and accordingly, after returning home for a few days, Benjamin went to the capital, and resided at the house of Mr. Clarkson, his brother-in-law, a gentleman who had been educated at Leyden, and was much respected for the intelligence of his conversation, and the propriety of his manners.

Provost Smith introduced West, among other persons, to four young men, pupils of his own, whom he particularly recommended to his acquaintance, as possessing endowments of mind greatly superior to the common standard of mankind. One of these was Francis Hopkins, who afterwards highly distinguished himself in the early proceedings of the Congress of the United States. Thomas Godfrey, the second, died after having given the most promising indications of an elegant genius for pathetic and descriptive poetry. He was an apprentice to a watchmaker, and had secretly written a poem, which he published anonymously in the Philadelphia newspaper, under the title of "The Temple of Fame." The attention which it attracted, and the encomiums which the Provost in particular bestowed on it, induced West, who was in the Poet's confidence, to mention to him who was the author. The information excited the alert benevolence of Smith's character, and he lost no time until he had procured the release of Godfrey from his indenture, and a respectable employment for him in the government of the state; but this he did not live long to enjoy: being sent on some public business to Carolina, he fell a victim to the climate.

It is pleasant to redeem from oblivion the memory of early talent thus prematurely withdrawn from the world. Many of Godfrey's verses were composed under a clump of pines which grew near the upper ferry of the river Schuylkill, to which spot he sometimes accompanied West and their mutual friends to angle. In the heat of the day he used to stretch himself beneath the shade of the trees, and repeat to them his verses as he composed them. Reid was the name of the other young man, and the same person who first opposed the British troops in their passing through Jersey, when the rebellion of the Provinces commenced. Previous to the revolution, he was bred to the bar, and practised with distinction in the courts of Philadelphia. He was afterwards elected a Member of Congress, and is the same person who was appointed to meet Lord Carlisle on his mission from the British Court.

Provost Smith was himself possessed of a fluent vein of powerful eloquence, and it happened that many of his pupils who distinguished themselves in the great struggle of their country, appeared to have imbibed his talent; but none of them more than Jacob Duchey, another of the four youths whom he recommended to the Artist. He became a Clergyman, and was celebrated throughout the whole of the British Provinces in America as a most pathetic and persuasive preacher. The publicity of his character in the world was, however, chiefly owing to a letter which he addressed to General Washington, soon after the appointment of that chief to the command of the army. The purport of this letter was to persuade the General to go over to the British cause. It was carried to him by a Mrs. Ferguson, a daughter of Doctor Graham, a Scottish Physician in Philadelphia. Washington, with his army, at that time lay at Valley-forge, and this lady, on the pretext of paying him a visit, as they were previously acquainted, went to the camp. The General received her in his tent with much respect, for he greatly admired the masculine vigour of her mind. When she had delivered the letter he read it attentively, and, rising from his seat, walked backwards and forwards upwards of an hour, without speaking. He appeared to be much agitated during the greatest part of the time; but at length, having decided with himself, he stopped, and addressed her in nearly the following words: "Madam, I have always esteemed your character and endowments, and I am fully sensible of the noble principles by which you are actuated on this occasion; nor has any man in the whole continent more confidence in the integrity of his friend, than I have in the honour of Mr. Duchey. But I am here entrusted by the people of America with sovereign authority. They have placed their lives and fortunes at my disposal, because they believe me to be an honest man. Were I, therefore, to desert their cause, and consign them again to the British, what would be the consequence? to myself perpetual infamy; and to them endless calamity. The seeds of everlasting division are sown between the two countries; and, were the British again to become our masters, they would have to maintain their dominion by force, and would, after all, retain us in subjection only so long as they could hold their bayonets to our breasts. No, Madam, the proposal of Mr. Duchey, though conceived with the best intention, is not framed in wisdom. America and England must be separate states; but they may have common interests, for they are but one people. It will, therefore, be the object of my life and ambition to establish the independence of America in the first place; and in the second, to arrange such a community of interests between the two nations as shall indemnify them for the calamities which they now suffer, and form a new aera in the history of nations. But, Madam, you are aware that I have many enemies; Congress may hear of your visit, and of this letter, and I should be suspected were I to conceal it from them. I respect you truly, as I have said; and I esteem the probity and motives of Mr. Duchey, and therefore you are free to depart from the camp, but the letter will be transmitted without delay to Congress."

Mrs. Ferguson herself communicated the circumstances of this interesting transaction to Mr. West, after she came to England; for she, as well as Mr. Duchey, were obliged to quit the country. It is painful to add, that Duchey came to England, and was allowed to pine unnoticed by the Government, and was heard of no more.

CHAPTER III

The course of instruction adopted by Provost Smith —The Artist led to the discovery of the Camera —His Father becomes anxious to place him in business —Extraordinary proceedings of the Quakers in consequence —The Speech of Williamson the Preacher in defence of the Fine Arts —Magnanimous Resolution of the Quakers —Reflections on this singular transaction

THERE was something so judicious in the plan of study which Provost Smith had formed for his pupil, that it deserves to be particularly considered. He regarded him as destined to be a Painter; and on this account did not impose upon him those grammatical exercises of language which are usually required from the young student of the classics, but directed his attention to those incidents which were likely to interest his fancy, and to furnish him at some future time with subjects for the easel. He carried him immediately to those passages of antient history which make the most lasting impression on the imagination of the regular-bred scholar, and described the picturesque circumstances of the transactions with a minuteness of detail that would have been superfluous to a general student.

In the midst of this course of education the Artist happened to be taken ill of a slight fever, and when it had subsided, he was in so weak a state as to be obliged to keep his bed, and to have the room darkened. In this situation he remained several days, with no other light than what was admitted by the seams and fissures in the window-shutters, which had the usual effect of expanding the pupil of his eyes to such a degree that he could distinctly see every object in the room, which to others appeared in complete obscurity. While he was thus lying in bed, he observed the apparitional form of a white cow enter at the one side of the roof, and walking over the bed, gradually vanish at the other. The phenomenon surprised him exceedingly, and he feared that his mind was impaired by his disease, which his sister also suspected, when on entering to inquire how he felt himself, he related to her what he had seen. Without, however, saying any thing, she went immediately and informed her husband, who accompanied her back to the apartment; and as they were standing near the bed, West repeated the story, exclaiming in his discourse that he saw, at the very moment in which he was then speaking, several little pigs running along the roof. This confirmed them in the apprehension of his delirium, and they sent for a physician. But the doctor could discover no symptoms of fever; the pulse was regular, the skin moist and cool, the thirst was abated, and indeed every thing about the patient indicated convalescence. Still the Painter persisted in his story, and assured them that he then saw the figures of several of their mutual friends passing on the roof, over the bed; and that he even saw fowls pecking, and the very stones of the street. All this seemed to them very extraordinary, for their eyes, not accustomed to the gloom of the chamber, could discern nothing; and the learned physician himself, in despite of the symptoms, began to suspect that the convalescent was really delirious. Prescribing, therefore, a composing mixture, which the Painter submitted to swallow, he took his fee and leave, requesting Mrs. Clarkson and her husband to come away and not disturb the patient. After they had retired, curiosity overcame the influence of the drug, and the Artist got up, determined to find out the cause of the strange apparitions which had so alarmed them all. In a short time he discovered a diagonal knot-hole in one of the window-shutters, and upon placing his hand over it, the visionary paintings on the roof disappeared. This confirmed him in an opinion that he began to form, that there must be some simple natural cause for what he had seen; and, having thus ascertained the way in which it acted, he called his sister and her husband into the room and explained it to them. When able to go down stairs, Mr. Clarkson gave him permission to perforate one of the parlour window-shutters horizontally, in order to obtain a representation on the wall of the buildings of the opposite side of the street. The effect was as he expected, but, to his astonishment, the objects appeared inverted. Without attempting to remedy this with the aid of glasses, as a mathematical genius would perhaps have done, he was delighted to see in it the means of studying the pictural appearance of Nature, and he hailed the discovery as a revelation to promote his improvement in the art of painting. On his return soon after to his father's, he had a box made with one of the sides perforated; and, adverting to the reflective power of the mirror, he contrived, without ever having heard of the instrument, to invent the *Camera*. Thus furnishing another proof, that although the faculty which enables a man to excel in any particular art or science is a natural endowment, it is seldom unaccompanied with a general superiority of observation. It will, however, not be disputed, that a boy under sixteen, who had thus, by the guidance of his own unassisted judgment, found out a method of ascertaining the colour and outline of natural objects as they should appear in painting, possessed no ordinary mind. Observations of this nature mark the difference between innate talent and instructed habits; and, whether in painting, or in poetry, in art, or in science, constitute the source of that peculiarity of intellect which is discriminated from the effects of education by the name of original talent. The self-educated man of genius, when his mind is formed, differs but little in the method of expressing his notions, from the most mechanical disciple of the schools; but the process by which he attains that result, renders his history interesting by its incidents, and valuable by the hints which it furnishes for the study of human character. It is, perhaps, also, one great cause of his own distinguishing features of mind, as the very contrivances to which he has recourse have the effect of taking, as it were, something extraneous into the matter of his experiments which tinges the product with curious and singular effects.—West, on afterwards mentioning his discovery to Williams the painter, was surprised to find himself anticipated, that Artist having received a complete Camera some time before from England.

In this favourable state of things he attained his sixteenth year, when his father became anxious to see him settled in some established business. For, though reluctant to thwart the bias of a genius at once so decided and original, and to which the injunction of Peckover had rendered him favourable and indulgent, the old gentleman was sensible that the profession of a painter was not only precarious, but regarded by the religious association to which he belonged, as adverse to their tenets, by being only ornamental; and he was anxious, on his son's account and on his own, to avoid those animadversions to which he was exposed by the freedom he had hitherto granted to the predilections of Benjamin. He, therefore, consulted several of his neighbours on the subject; and a meeting of the Society of Friends in the vicinity was called, to consider, publicly, what ought to be the destiny of his son.

The assembly met in the Meeting-house near Springfield, and after much debate, approaching to altercation, a man of the name of John Williamson rose, and delivered a very extraordinary speech upon the subject. He was much respected by all present, for the purity and integrity of his life, and enjoyed great influence in his sphere on account of the superiority of his natural wisdom, and, as a public preacher among the Friends, possessed an astonishing gift of convincing eloquence. He pointed to old Mr. West and his wife, and expatiated on the blameless reputation which they had so long maintained, and merited so well. "They have had," said he, "ten children, whom they have carefully brought up in the fear of God, and in the Christian religion; and the youth, whose lot in life we are now convened to consider, is Benjamin, their youngest child. It is known to you all that God is pleased, from time to time, to bestow upon some men extraordinary gifts of mind, and you need not be told by how wonderful an inspiration their son has been led to cultivate the art of painting. It is true that our tenets deny the utility of that art to mankind. But God has bestowed on the youth a genius for the art, and can we believe that Omniscience bestows His gifts but for great purposes? What God has given, who shall dare to throw away? Let us not estimate Almighty wisdom by our notions; let us not presume to arraign His judgment by our ignorance, but in the evident propensity of the young man, be assured that we see an impulse of the Divine hand operating towards some high and beneficent end."

The effect of this argument, and the lofty commanding manner in which it was delivered, induced the assembly to agree that the Artist should be allowed to indulge the predilections of his genius; and a private meeting of the Friends was appointed to be holden at his father's house, at which the youth himself was requested to be present, in order to receive, in form, the assent and blessing of the Society. On the day of meeting, the great room was put in order, and a numerous company of both sexes assembled. Benjamin was placed by his father, and the men and women took their respective forms on each side. After sitting some time in silence, one of the women rose and addressed the meeting on the wisdom of God, and the various occasions on which He selected from among His creatures the agents of His goodness. When she had concluded her exhortation, John Williamson also rose, and in a speech than which, perhaps, the porticos of Athens never resounded with a more impressive oratory, he resumed the topic which had been the subject of his former address. He began by observing that it was fixed as one of their indisputable maxims, that things merely ornamental were not necessary to the well-being of man, and that all superfluous things should be excluded from the usages and manners of their society. "In this proscription, we have included," said he, "the study of the fine arts, for we see them applied only to embellish pleasures, and to strengthen our inducements to gratify the senses at the expense of our immortal claims. But, because we have seen painting put to this derogatory use, and have, in consequence, prohibited the cultivation of it among us, are we sure that it is not one of those gracious gifts which God has bestowed on the world, not to add to the sensual pleasures of man, but to facilitate his improvement as a social and a moral being? The fine arts are called the offspring and the emblems of peace. The Christian religion itself is the doctrine of good will to man. Can those things which only prosper in peace be contrary to the Christian religion? But, it is said, that the fine arts soften and emasculate the mind. In what way? is it by withdrawing those who study them from the robust exercises which enable nations and people to make war with success? Is it by lessening the disposition of mankind to destroy one another, and by taming the audacity of their animal fierceness? Is it for such a reason as this, that we who profess to live in unison and friendship, not only among ourselves, but with all the world that we should object to the cultivation of the fine arts, of those arts which disarm the natural ferocity of man? We may as well be told that the doctrine of peace and life ought to be proscribed in the world because it is pernicious to the practice of war and slaughter, as that the arts which call on man to exercise his intellectual powers more than his physical strength, can be contrary to Christianity, and adverse to the benevolence of the Deity. I speak not, however, of the fine arts as the means of amusement, nor the study of them as pastime to fill up the vacant hours of business, though even as such, the taste for them deserves to be regarded as a manifestation of Divine favour, in as much as they dispose the heart to kind and gentle inclinations. For, I think them ordained by God for some great and holy purpose. Do we not know that the professors of the fine arts are commonly men greatly distinguished by special gifts of a creative and discerning spirit? If there be any thing in the usual course of human affairs which exhibits the immediate interposition of the Deity, it is in the progress of the fine arts, in which it would appear he often raises up those great characters, the spirit of whose imaginations have an interminable influence on posterity, and who are themselves separated and elevated among the generality of mankind, by the name of men of genius. Can we believe that all this is not for some useful purpose? What that purpose is, ought we to pretend to investigate? Let us rather reflect that the Almighty God has been pleased among us, and in this remote wilderness, to endow, with the rich gifts of a peculiar spirit, that youth who has now our common consent to cultivate his talents for an art, which, according to our humble and human judgment, was previously thought an unnecessary ministration to the sensual propensities of our nature. May it be demonstrated by the life and works of the Artist, that the gift of God has not been bestowed on him in vain, nor the motives of the beneficent inspiration which induces us to suspend our particular tenets, prove barren of religious or moral effect. On the contrary, let us confidently hope that this occurrence has been for good, and that the consequences which may arise in the society of this new world, from the example which Benjamin West will be enabled to give, will be such a love of the arts of peace as shall tend to draw the ties of affection closer, and diffuse over a wider extent of community the interests and blessing of fraternal love."

At the conclusion of this address, the women rose and kissed the young Artist, and the men, one by one, laid their hands on his head and prayed that the Lord might verify in his life the value of the gift which had induced them, in despite of their religious tenets, to allow him to cultivate the faculties of his genius.

The history of no other individual affords an incident so extraordinary. This could not be called a presentiment, but the result of a clear expectation, that some important consequence would ensue. It may be added that a more beautiful instance of liberality is not to be found in the records of any religious society. Hitherto, all sects, even of Christians, were disposed to regard, with jealousy and hatred, all those members who embraced any pursuit that might tend to alienate them from their particular modes of discipline. The Quakers have, therefore, the honour of having been the first to allow, by a public act, that their conception of the religious duties of man was liable to the errors of the human judgment, and was not to be maintained on the presumption of being actually according to the will of God. There is something at once simple and venerable in the humility with which they regarded their own peculiar principles, especially contrasted with the sublime view they appeared to take of the wisdom and providence of the Deity. But, with whatever delightful feelings strangers and posterity may contemplate this beautiful example of Christian magnanimity, it would be impossible to convey any idea of the sentiments with which it affected the youth who was the object of its exercise. He must have been less than man had he not endeavoured, without ceasing, to attain an honourable eminence in his profession; or, had he forgotten, in the honours which he has since received from all polished nations, that he was authorized by his friends and his religion, to cultivate the art by which he obtained such distinctions, not for his own sake, but as an instrument chosen by Providence to disseminate the arts of peace in the world.

CHAPTER IV

Reflections on the Eccentricities of Young Men of Genius with respect to pecuniary matters —The Death of the Artist's Mother —The Embodying of the Pennsylvanian Militia; an Anecdote of General Wayne —The Artist elected Commandant of a corps of Volunteer boys —The circumstances which occasioned the Search for the Bones of Bradock's army —The Search —The Discovery of the Bones of the Father and Brother of Sir Peter Halket —The Artist proposed afterwards to paint a Picture of the Discovery of the Bones of the Halkets —He commences regularly as a Painter —He copies a St. Ignatius —He is induced to attempt Historical Portraiture —His Picture of the Trial of Susannah —Of the merits of that Picture

THERE is a regardless independence about minds of superior endowment, which, in similar characters, manifests itself differently according to the circumstances in which they happen to be placed. Devoted to the contemplation of the means of future celebrity, the man of genius frequently finds himself little disposed to set a proper value on the common interests of of life. When bred in affluence, and exempted from the necessity of considering the importance of money to the attainment of his object, he is often found, to a blameful degree, negligent of pecuniary concerns; and, on the contrary, when his situation is such that he may only hope for distinction by the practice of the most parsimonious frugality, he will as often appear in the social and propelling season of youth enduring voluntary privations with an equanimity which the ostentatious fanatic or contrite penitent would in vain attempt to surpass. This peculiar feature of the self-sustained mind of genius has often been misunderstood, and seldom valued as it ought to be. The presumptuous weak who mistake the wish of distinction for the workings of talent, admire the eccentricities of the gifted youth who is reared in opulence, and, mistaking the prodigality which is only the effect of his fortune, for the attributes of his talents, imitate his errors, and imagine that, by copying the blemishes of his conduct, they possess what is illustrious in his mind. Such men are incapable of appreciating the self-denial which Benjamin West made it a duty to impose upon himself on entering the world; but to those who are truly conscious of possessing the means of attracting the admiration of their contemporaries and posterity, the voluntary abstinence of a youth of genius will afford them delight in the contemplation, even though they may be happily free from the obligation of practising it themselves.

When it was determined among the Friends that Benjamin West should be allowed to cultivate the art of Painting, he went to Lancaster, but he was hastily recalled by a severe domestic misfortune. His mother was seized by a dangerous illness, and being conscious that she could not live long, she requested that he might be sent for home. Benjamin hastily obeyed the summons, but, before he reached the house, her strength was exhausted, and she was only able to express by her look the satisfaction with which she saw him approach the bed, before she expired. Her funeral, and the distress which the event naturally occasioned to her family, by all of whom she was very tenderly beloved, detained the young Artist some time at his father's. About the end of August, in 1756, however, he took his final departure, and went to Philadelphia. But, before proceeding with the narrative of his professional career, it is necessary to advert to some of the public transactions of that period, by which his sensibility was powerfully excited. Indeed it will appear throughout the whole of these singular memoirs, that the subject of them was, perhaps, more immediately affected by the developement of national events, than usually falls to the lot of any individual so little connected with public men, and so far remote from the great thoroughfare of political occurrences.

After the destruction of General Braddock's army, the Pennsylvanians being alarmed at the defenceless state in which they were placed by that calamity, the Assembly of the Province resolved to embody a militia force; and Mr, Wayne, who has been already mentioned, was appointed Colonel of the Regiment raised in Chester County. This defensive measure announced that the golden age of the country was past, and the change felt by the peaceful Quakers indicated an alteration in their harmless manners. West, among others, went to view the first muster of the troops under the command of Colonel Wayne, and the sight of men in arms, their purpose and array, warmed his lively imagination with military enthusiasm. In conjunction with a son of the Colonel, a boy of his own age, with whom he had become acquainted, he procured a gun, and determined also to be a soldier. Young Wayne was drilled by the diciplinarians of his father's corps, and he, in turn, exercised West, who, being more alert and active, soon obtained a decided superiority; but what different destinies were attached to them! West has attained, in the intellectual discipline of the arts of peace, an enviable reputation; and Wayne, who was inferior to him in the manual of the soldier, became an illustrious commander, and partook, as the companion in arms of Washington, of the glory of having established the independence of America.

The martial preparations inspired all the youths of Pennsylvania with the love of arms, and diffused the principles of that military spirit which was afterwards exerted with so much effect against the erroneous policy of the mother country. West, soon after his drilling under young Wayne, visited Lancaster; and the boys of that town having formed themselves into a little corps, made choice of him for their commandant. Among others who caught the spirit of the time, was his brother Samuel, who possessed a bold character and an enterprising disposition. He was about six years older than the Artist, and, being appointed a Captain in Colonel Wayne's regiment, joined the troops under the command of General Forbes, who was sent to repair the disasters which had happened to the unfortunate Bradock.

After the taking of Fort Duane, to which the new name of Pittsburgh was given, in compliment to the minister of the day, General Forbes resolved to search for the relics of Bradock's army. As the European soldiers were not so well qualified to explore the forests, Captain West was appointed, with his company of American sharpshooters, to assist in the execution of this duty; and a party of Indian warriors, who had returned to the British interests, were requested to conduct him to the places where the bones of the slain were likely to be found. In this solemn and affecting duty several officers belonging to the 42d regiment accompanied the detachment, and with them Major Sir Peter Halket, who had lost his father and a brother in the fatal destruction of the army. It might have been thought a hopeless task that he should be able to discriminate their remains from the common relics of the other soldiers; but he was induced to think otherwise, as one of the Indian warriors assured him that he had seen an officer fall near a remarkable tree, which he thought he could still discover; informing him at the same time, that the incident was impressed on his memory by observing a young subaltern, who, in running to the officer's assistance, was also shot dead on his reaching the spot, and fell across the other's body. The Major had a mournful conviction in his own mind that the two officers were his father and brother, and, indeed, it was chiefly owing to his anxiety on the subject, that this pious expedition, the second of the kind that History records, was undertaken.

Captain West and his companions proceeded through the woods and along the banks of the river towards the scene of the battle. The Indians regarded the expedition as a religious service, and guided the troops with awe, and in profound silence. The soldiers were affected with sentiments not less serious; and as they explored the bewildering labyrinths of those vast forests, their hearts were often melted with inexpressible sorrow; for they frequently found skeletons lying across the trunks of fallen trees, a mournful proof to their imaginations that the men who sat there, had perished of hunger, in vainly attempting to find their way to the plantations. Sometimes their feelings were raised to the utmost pitch of horror by the sight of sculls and bones scattered on the ground—a certain indication that the bodies had been devoured by wild beasts; and in other places they saw the blackness of ashes amidst the relics,—the tremendous evidence of atrocious rites.

At length they reached a turn of the river not far from the principal scene of destruction, and the Indian who remembered the death of the two officers, stopped; the detachment also halted. He then looked around in quest of some object which might recall, distinctly, his recollection of the ground, and suddenly darted into the wood. The soldiers rested their arms without speaking. A shrill cry was soon after heard; and the other guides made signs for the troops to follow them towards the spot from which it came. In the course of a short time they reached the Indian warrior, who, by his cry, had announced to his companions that he had found the place where he was posted on the day of battle. As the troops approached, he pointed to the tree under which the officers had fallen. Captain West halted his men round the spot, and with Sir Peter Halket and the other officers, formed a circle, while the Indians removed the leaves which thickly covered the ground. The skeletons were found, as the Indian expected, lying across each other. The officers having looked at them some time, the Major said, that as his father had an artificial tooth, he thought he might be able to ascertain if they were indeed his bones and those of his brother. The Indians were, therefore, ordered to remove the skeleton of the youth, and to bring to view that of the old officer. This was immediately done, and after a short examination, Major Halket exclaimed, "It is my father!" and fell back into the arms of his companions. The pioneers then dug a grave, and the bones being laid in it together, a highland plaid was spread over them, and they were interred with the customary honours.

When Lord Grosvenor bought the picture of the death of Wolfe, Mr. West mentioned to him the finding of the bones of Bradock's army as a pictorial subject capable of being managed with great effect. The gloom of the vast forest, the naked and simple Indians supporting the skeletons, the grief of the son on recognizing the relics of his father, the subdued melancholy of the spectators, and the picturesque garb of the Pennsylvanian sharpshooters, undoubtedly furnished topics capable of every effect which the pencil could bestow, or the imagination require in the treatment of so sublime a scene. His Lordship admitted, that in possessing so affecting an incident as the discovery of the bones of the Halkets, it was superior even to that of the search for the remains of the army of Varus; the transaction, however, being little known, and not recorded by any historian, he thought it would not be interesting to the public. Other engagements have since prevented Mr. West from attempting it on his own account. But it is necessary that the regular narrative should be resumed; for the military history of the Artist terminated when he was recalled home by the last illness of his mother, although the excitement which the events that led to it occasioned never lost its influence on his mind, especially that of the incident which has been described, and which has ever been present to his imagination as one of the most affecting occurrences, whether considered with respect to the feelings of the gentlemen most immediately interested in it, or with respect to the wild and solemn circumstances under which the service was performed.

On his return to Philadelphia, he again resided with Mr. Clarkson, his brother-in-law; and Provost Smith, in the evenings, continued to direct his attention to those topics of literature which were most suitable to cherish the expansion of his mind, and to enrich his imagination with ideas useful to his profession. While his leisure hours were thus profitably employed, his reputation as a portrait painter was rapidly extended. His youth, and the peculiar incidents of his history, attracted many sitters, and his merits verified the recommendations of his friends. This constancy of employment, no doubt materially tended to his improvement in the manipulation of his art; for whatever may be the native force of talent, it is impossible that the possessor can attain excellence by any other means than practice. Facility to express the conceptions of the mind must be acquired before the pen or the pencil can embody them appropriately, and the author who does not execute much, however little he may exhibit, can never expect to do justice to the truth and beauty of his own ideas. West was very soon duly impressed with the justness of this observation; and, while in the execution of his portraits, he was assiduous to acquire a ready knowledge of those characteristic traits which have since enabled him to throw so much variety into his compositions; he felt conscious that, without seeing better pictures than his own, he could neither hope to attain distinction, nor to appreciate his own peculiar powers. It was this consideration that induced him to adopt a most rigid system of frugality. He looked forward to a period when he might be enabled, by the fruits of his own industry, to visit the great scenes of the fine arts in Europe; and the care with which he treasured the money that he received for his portraits was rewarded even at the time with the assurance of realizing his expectations. The prices which he first fixed for his portraits, were two guineas and a half for a head, and five guineas for a half length.

After what has already been mentioned of the state of Society in Pennsylvania, it is needless to say that at the period to which these memoirs refer, there were but few pictures in the British Plantations; indeed, without any other explanation, all that should be contended for by any person who might imagine it necessary to advocate the pretensions of Benjamin West to be placed in the list of original and self-instructed artists, would be readily granted, upon stating the single fact, that he was born in Pennsylvania, and did not leave America till the year 1760. At the same time, it might be construed into an injudicious concealment, if it were not mentioned that Governor Hamilton, who at that period presided with so much popularity over the affairs of the province, possessed a few pictures, consisting, however, chiefly of family portraits. Among them was a St. Ignatius, which was found in the course of the preceding war on board a Spanish prize, and which Mr. Pennington obtained leave for West to copy. The Artist had made choice of it himself, without being aware of its merits as a work of art, for it was not until several years after that he discovered it to be a fine piece of the Morillo school, and in the best style of the master.

This copy was greatly admired by all who saw it, and by none more than his valuable friend Provost Smith, to whom it suggested the notion that portrait-painting might be raised to something greatly above the exhibition of a mere physical likeness; and he in consequence endeavoured to impress upon the mind of his pupil, that characteristic painting opened a new line in the art, only inferior in dignity to that of history, but requiring, perhaps, a nicer discriminative tact of mind. This judicious reflection of Dr. Smith was however anticipated by Sir Joshua Reynolds, who had already made the discovery, and was carrying it into effect with admirable success. The Provost, however, was unacquainted with that circumstance, and induced West to make an experiment by drawing his portrait in the style and attitude of the St. Ignatius.

While he was thus employed on portraits, a gentleman of the name of Cox called on him to agree for a likeness of his daughter; and the picture of Dr. Smith attracted his attention. It indeed appeared to him to evince such a capacity for historical composition, that, instead of then determining any thing respecting his daughter's portrait, he gave an order for an historical picture, allowing the Artist himself to choose the subject. This task had peculiar charms; for the Painter in the course of reading the Bible to his mother some time before, had been led to think that the Trial of Susannah was a fine subject, and he was thus enabled, by the liberality of Mr. Cox, to embody the conceptions of his imagination while they were yet in all the freshness and vigour of original formation. He made his canvas about the size of a half length portrait, on which he introduced not fewer than forty figures. In the execution he followed the rule which he had adopted in painting the Death of Socrates, and drew the principal figures from living models.—It is not known what has become of the Trial of Susannah. In the rebellion of the Colonies, Mr. Cox adhered to the British interest; and his daughter, the last person into whose possession the picture has been traced, having married a British officer, came to England during the war, and the Artist has not heard where she has since resided.

In point of composition, Mr. West is of opinion that the Trial of Susannah was superior to the Death of Socrates. In this he is probably correct; for during the interval between the execution of the one and the other, his mind had been enlarged in knowledge by reading, his eye improved by the study of pictorial outline and perspective in the *Camera*, and his touch softened by the portraits which he painted, and particularly by his careful copy of the St. Ignatius. In point of drawing, both pictures were no doubt greatly inferior to many of his subsequent works; but his son, long after he had acquired much celebrity, saw the picture of the Death of Socrates; and was of opinion that it was not surpassed by any of them in variety of composition, and in that perspicuity of narrative which is the grand characteristic of the Artist's genius.

CHAPTER V

Motives which induced him to visit New York —State of Society in New York —Reflections on the sterility of American talent —Considerations on the circumstances which tend to produce Poetical feelings —The causes which produced the peculiarities in the state of Society in New York —The Accident which led the Artist to discover the method of colouring Candle-light and Fire effects after Nature —He copies Strange's engraving of Belisarius, by Salvador Rosa —The occurrence which hastened his Voyage to Italy, with the Anecdote of his obligations to Mr. Kelly —Reflections on Plutarch, occasioned by reference to the effect which his works had on the mind of West —The Artist embarks; occurrence at Gibraltar —He arrives at Leghorn —Journey to Rome

BUT although West found himself in possession of abundant employment in Philadelphia, he was sensible that he could not expect to increase his prices with effect, if he continued constantly in the same place. He also became sensible that to view life in various lights was as necessary to his improvement as to exercise his pencil on different subjects. And, beyond all, he was profoundly sensible, by this time, that he could not hope to attain eminence in his profession, without inspecting the great master-pieces of art in Europe, and comparing them with his own works in order to ascertain the extent of his powers. This philosophical view of his situation was doubtless partly owing to the excellent precepts of Provost Smith, but mainly to his own just perception of what was necessary to the successful career of an Artist: indeed the principle upon which the notion was formed is universal, and applies to all intellectual pursuits. Accordingly, impressed with these considerations, he frugally treasured the earnings of his pencil, that he might undertake, in the first place, a professional journey from Philadelphia, as preparatory to acquiring the means of afterwards visiting Europe, and particularly Rome. When he found that the state of his funds enabled him to undertake the journey, he went to New York.

The Society of New York was much less intelligent in matters of taste and knowledge than that of Philadelphia. In the latter city the institutions of the college and library, and the strict moral and political respectability of the first settlers, had contributed to form a community, which, though inferior in the elegancies of living, and the etiquettes of intercourse, to what is commonly found in the European capitals, was little behind them in point of practical and historical information. Dr. Smith, the Provost of the college, had largely contributed to elevate the taste, the sentiment and the topics of conversation in Philadelphia. He was full of the best spirit of antiquity, and there was a classical purity of mind and splendour of imagination sometimes met with in the families which he frequented, that would have done honour to the best periods of polished society.

It would be difficult to assign any reason why it has so happened that no literary author of any general celebrity, with the exception of Franklin, has yet arisen in America. That men of learning and extensive reading, capable of vying with the same description of persons in Europe, are to be found in the United States, particularly in Philadelphia, is not to be denied; but of that class, whose talents tend to augment the stock of intellectual enjoyment in the world, no one, with the single exception already alluded to, has yet appeared.

Poetry is the art of connecting ideas of sensible objects with moral sentiments; and without the previous existence of local feelings, there can be no poetry. America to the first European settlers had no objects interesting to the imagination, at least of the description thus strictly considered as poetical; for although the vigour and stupendous appearances of Nature were calculated to fill the mind with awe, and to exalt the contemplations of enthusiasm, there was nothing connected with the circumstances of the scene susceptible of that colouring from the memory, which gives to the ideas of local resemblance the peculiar qualities of poetry. The forests, though interminable, were but composed of trees; the mountains and rivers, though on a larger scale, were not associated in the mind with the exertions of patriotic valour, and the achievements of individual enterprize, like the Alps or the Danube, the Grampians or the Tweed. It is impossible to tread the depopulated and exhausted soil of Greece without meeting with innumerable relics and objects, which, like magical talismans, call up the genius of departed ages with the long-enriched roll of those great transactions, that, in their moral effect, have raised the nature of man, occasioning trains of reflection which want only the rythm of language to be poetry. But in the unstoried solitudes of America, the traveller meets with nothing to awaken the sympathy of his recollective feelings. Even the very character of the trees, though interesting to scientific research, chills, beneath the spaciousness of their shade, every poetical disposition. They bear little resemblance to those which the stranger has left behind in his native country. To the descendants of the first settlers, they wanted even the charm of those accidental associations which their appearance might have recalled to the minds of their fathers. Poetry is, doubtless, the first of the intellectual arts which mankind cultivate. In its earliest form it is the mode of expressing affection and admiration; but, before it can be invented, there must be objects beloved and admired, associated with things in nature endowed with a local habitation and a name. In America, therefore, although there has been no lack of clever versifiers, nor of men who have respectably echoed the ideas current in the old world, the country has produced nothing of any value descriptive of the peculiar associations connected with its scenery. Among some of the Indian tribes a vein of original poetry has, indeed, been discovered; but the riches of the mine are unexplored, and the charge of sterility of fancy, which is made by the Europeans against the citizens of the United States, still remains unrefuted. Since the period, however, to which these memoirs chiefly refer, events of great importance have occurred, and the recollections connected with them, no doubt, tend to imbue the American climate with the elements of poetical thought; but they are of too recent occurrence for the purposes either of the epic or the tragic muse. The facts of history in America are still seen too much in detail for the imagination to combine them with her own creation. The fields of battle are almost too fresh for the farmer to break the surface; and years must elapse before the ploughshare shall turn up those eroded arms of which the sight will call into poetical existence the sad and dreadful incidents of the civil war.

In New York Mr. West found the society wholly devoted to mercantile pursuits. A disposition to estimate the value of things, not by their utility, or by their beauty, but by the price which they would bring in the market, almost universally prevailed. Mercantile men are habituated by the nature of their transactions to overlook the intrinsic qualities of the very commodities in which they deal; and though of all the community they are the most liberal and the most munificent, they set the least value on intellectual productions. The population of New York was formed of adventurers from all parts of Europe, who had come thither for the express purpose of making money, in order, afterwards, to appear with distinction at home. Although West, therefore, found in that city much employment in taking likenesses destined to be transmitted to relations and friends, he met with but few in whom he found any disposition congenial to his own; and the eleven months which he passed there, in consequence, contributed less to the improvement of his mind than might have been expected from a city so flourishing. Still, the time was not altogether barren of occurrences which tended to advance his progress in his art, independent of the advantage arising from constant practice.

He happened, during his residence there, to see a beautiful Flemish picture of a hermit praying before a lamp, and he was resolved to paint a companion to it, of a man reading by candle-light. But before he discovered a method of producing, in day-light, an effect on his model similar to what he wished to imitate, he was frequently baffled in his attempts. At length, he hit on the expedient of persuading his landlord to sit with an open book before a candle in a dark closet; and he found that, by looking in upon him from his study, the appearance was exactly what he wished for. In the schools and academies of Europe, tradition has preserved the methods by which all the magical effects of light and shadow have been produced, with the exception, however, of Rembrandt's method, and which the author of these sketches ventures to suggest was attained, in general, by observing the effect of sunshine passing through chinks into a dark room. But the American Artist was as yet unacquainted with any of them, and had no other guides to the essential principles of his art but the delicacy of his sight, and that ingenious observation of Nature to which allusion has been already so often made.

The picture of the Student, or man reading by candle-light, was bought by a Mr.

Myers, who, in the revolution, continued to adhere to the English cause. The same gentleman also bought a copy which West made about the same time of Belisarius, from the engraving by Strange, of Salvator Rosa's painting. It is not known what has now become of these pictures; but when the Artist long afterwards saw the original of Salvator Rosa, he was gratified to observe that he had instinctively coloured his copy almost as faithfully as if it had been painted from the picture instead of the engraving.

In the year 1759 the harvest in Italy fell far short of what was requisite for the ordinary consumption of the population, and a great dearth being foreseen, Messrs. Rutherford and Jackson, of Leghorn, a house of the first consequence then in the Mediterranean trade, and well known to all travellers for the hospitality of the partners, wrote to their correspondent Mr. Allen, at Philadelphia, to send them a cargo of wheat and flour. Mr. Allen was anxious that his son, before finally embarking in business, should see something of the world; and Provost Smith, hearing his intention of sending him to Leghorn with the vessel, immediately waited on the old gentleman, and begged him to allow West to accompany him, which was cheerfully acceded to, and the Provost immediately wrote to his pupil at New York on the subject. In the mean time, West had heard that there was a vessel at Philadelphia loading for Italy, and had expressed to Mr. William Kelly, a merchant, who was then sitting to him for his portrait, a strong desire to avail himself of this opportunity to visit the fountain-head of the arts. Before this period, he had raised his terms for a half-length to ten guineas, by which he acquired a sum of money adequate to the expenses of a short excursion to Italy. When he had finished Mr. Kelly's portrait, that gentleman, in paying him, requested that he would take charge of a letter to his agents in Philadelphia, and deliver it to them himself on his return to that city, which he was induced to do immediately, on receiving Dr. Smith's letter, informing him of the arrangement made with Mr. Allen. When this letter was opened, an instance of delicate munificence appeared on the part of Mr. Kelly, which cannot be too highly applauded. It stated to the concern to which it was addressed, that it would be delivered by an ingenious young gentleman, who, he understood, intended to visit Rome for the purpose of studying the fine arts, and ordered them to pay him fifty guineas as a present from him towards furnishing his stores for the voyage.

While waiting till the vessel was clear to sail, West had the gratification to see, in Philadelphia, his old friend Mr. Henry, for whom he had painted the Death of Socrates. Towards him he always cherished the most grateful affection. He was the first who urged him to attempt historical composition; and, above all, he was the first who had made him acquainted with the magnanimous tales of Plutarch; perhaps, the greatest favour which could be conferred on a youthful mind, susceptible of impressions from the sublime and beautiful of human actions, which no author has better illustrated than that celebrated Biographer, who may indeed be regarded, almost without hyperbole, as the recorder of antient worth, and the tutor of modern genius. In his peculiar class, Plutarch still stands alone, at least no author in any of the living languages appears to be yet truly sensible of the secret cause by which his sketches give that direct impulse to the elements of genius, by which the vague and wandering feelings of unappropriated strength are converted into an uniform energy, endowed with productive action. Plutarch, like the sculptors of antiquity, has selected only the great and elegant traits of character; and hence his lives, like those statues which are the models of art, possess, with all that is graceful and noble in human nature, the particular features of individuals. He had no taste for the blemishes of mankind. His mind delighted in the contemplation of moral vigour; and he seems justly to have thought that it was nearly allied to virtue: hence many of those characters whose portraitures in his works furnish the youthful mind with inspiring examples of true greatness, more authentic historians represent in a light far different. It is the aim of all dignified art to exalt the mind by exciting the feelings as well as the judgment; and the immortal lessons of Plutarch would never have awakened the first stirrings of ambition in the innumerable great men who date their career from reading his pages, had he been actuated by the minute and invidious spirit of modern biography. These reflections have occurred the more forcibly at this juncture, as the subject of this narrative was on the point of leaving a country in which were men destined to acquire glory in such achievements as Plutarch would have delighted to record; and of parting from early associates who afterwards attained a degree of eminence in the public service that places them high in the roll of those who have emulated the exploits and virtues of the Heroes of that great Biographer.

The Artist having embarked with young Allen had a speedy and pleasant passage to Gibraltar; where, in consequence of the war then raging, the ship stopped for convoy. As soon as they came to anchor, Commodore Carney and another officer came on board to examine the vessel's papers. It happened that some time before, the British Government had, on account of political circumstances, prohibited the carrying of provisions into Italy, by which prohibition the ship and cargo would have been forfeited had she been arrested in attempting to enter an Italian port, or, indeed, in proceeding with such an intention. But Captain Carney had scarcely taken his pen to write the replies to the questions which he put to the Master, as to the owners of the vessel and her destination, when he again threw it down, and, looking the other officer full in the face, said, "I am much affected by the situation in which I am now placed. This valuable ship is the property of some of my nearest relations, and the best friends that I have ever had in the world!" and he refrained from asking any more questions. There was, undoubtedly, much generosity in this conduct, for by the indulgence of the crown, all prizes taken in war become the property of the captors; and Captain Carney, rather than enrich himself at the expence of his friends, chose to run the hazard of having his own conduct called in question for the non-performance of his official duty. It perhaps deserves also to be considered as affording a favourable example of that manly confidence in the gentlemanly honour of each other which has so long distinguished the British officers. On the mind of West it tended to confirm that agreeable impression by which so many previous incidents had made him cherish a liberal opinion of mankind. In other respects, Captain Carney happening to be the officer who came on board, was a fortunate circumstance; for on learning that young Allen was in the ship, he invited the passengers to dine on board his frigate; and the company, consisting of the Governor, his staff, and principal officers in the garrison, tended to raise the consideration of the Artist, and his companion in the estimation of the fleet with which their vessel was to proceed to Leghorn. Indeed, throughout his whole life, Mr. West was, in this respect, singularly fortunate; for although the condescensions of rank do not in themselves confer any power on talent, they have the effect of producing that complacency of mind in those who are the objects of them, which is at once the reward and the solace of intellectual exertion, at the same time that they tend to mollify the spirit of contemporary invidiousness. The day after, the fleet sailed; and when they had passed the rock, the captains of the two men of war [Footnote: The two frigates, the Shannon, Captain Meadow, since Lord Manvers, whose intimacy still continues with Mr. West, and the Favourite sloop of war, Captain Pownell.] who had charge of the convoy, came on board the American, and invited Mr. Allen and Mr. West to take their passage in one of the frigates; this, however, they declined, but every day, when the weather was favourable, they were taken on board the one ship or the other, to dine; and when the weather did not permit this to be done with pleasure to the strangers, the officers sent them presents from their stock.

After touching at several parts of the coast of Spain, the ship arrived safely at Leghorn, where mercantile enquiries detained Mr. Allen some time, and West being impatient to proceed to Rome, bade him adieu. Prior to his departure from Philadelphia, he had paid into the hands of old Mr. Allen the money which he thought would be requisite for his expenses in Italy, and had received from him a letter of credit on Messrs. Jackson and Rutherford. When they were made acquainted with the object of his voyage, and heard his history, they showed him a degree of attention beyond even their general great hospitality, and presented him with letters to Cardinal Albani, and several of the most distinguished characters for erudition and taste in Rome; and as he was unacquainted with French or Italian, they recommended him to the care of a French Courier, who had occasion to pass that way.

When the travellers had reached the last stage of their journey, while their horses were baiting, West walked on alone. It was a beautiful morning; the air was perfectly placid, not a speck of vapour in the sky, and a profound tranquillity seemed almost sensibly diffused over the landscape. The appearance of Nature was calculated to lighten and elevate the spirits; but the general silence and nakedness of the scene touched the feelings with solemnity approaching to awe. Filled with the idea of the metropolitan city, the Artist hastened forward till he reached an elevated part of the high road, which afforded him a view of a spacious champaign country, bounded by hills, and in the midst of it the sublime dome of St. Peter's. The magnificence of this view of the Campagna excited, in his imagination, an agitated train of reflections that partook more of the nature of feeling than of thought. He looked for a spot to rest on, that he might contemplate at leisure a scene at once so noble and so interesting; and, near a pile of ruins fringed and trellissed with ivy, he saw a stone that appeared to be part of a column. On going towards it, he perceived that it was a mile-stone, and that he was then only eight miles from the Capitol. In looking before him, where every object seemed by the transparency of the Italian atmosphere to be brought nearer than it was in reality, he could not but reflect on the contrast between the circumstances of that view and the scenery of America; and his thoughts naturally adverted to the progress of civilization. The sun seemed, to his fancy, the image of truth and knowledge, arising in the East, continuing to illuminate and adorn the whole earth, and withdrawing from the eyes of the old world to enlighten the uncultivated regions of the new. He thought of that remote antiquity when the site of Rome itself was covered with unexplored forests; and passing with a rapid reminiscence over her eventful story, he was touched with sorrow at the solitude of decay with which she appeared to be environed, till he adverted to the condition of his native country, and was cheered by the thought of the greatness which even the fate of Rome seemed to assure to America. For he reflected that, although the progress of knowledge appeared to intimate that there was some great cycle in human affairs, and that the procession of the arts and sciences from the East to the West demonstrated their course to be neither stationary nor retrograde; he could not but rejoice, in contemplating the skeleton of the mighty capital before him, that they had improved as they advanced, and that the splendour which would precede their setting on the shores of Europe, would be the gorgeous omen of the glory which they would attain in their passage over America.

While he was rapt in these reflections, he heard the drowsy tinkle of a pastoral bell behind him, and on turning round, he saw a peasant dressed in shaggy skins, driving a few goats from the ruins. The appearance and physiognomy of this peasant struck him as something more wild and ferocious than any thing about the Indians; and, perhaps, the observation was correctly philosophical. In the Indian, Nature is seen in that primitive vigour and simplicity, in which the actions are regulated by those feelings that are the elements of the virtues; but in the Italian bandit, for such he had reason afterwards to think was the real character of the goat-herd, he saw man in that second state of barbarity, in which his actions are instigated by wants that have often a vicious origin.

CHAPTER VI

State of the stationary Society of Rome —Causes which rendered the City a delightful temporary residence —Defects of the Academical methods of study —His introduction to Mr. Robinson —Anecdote of Cardinal Albani —The Cardinal's method of finding Resemblances, and curious mistake of the Italians —The Artist's first visit to the Works of Art

DURING the pontificate of Pope Rezzonico, the society of Rome had attained a pitch of elegance and a liberality of sentiment superior to that of any other city of Christendom. The theocratic nature of the government induced an exterior decorum in the public form of politeness, which, to strangers who took no interest in the abuses of the state, was so highly agreeable, that it tended even to appease their indignation against the laxity of private morals. If the traveller would forget that the name of Christianity was employed in supporting a baneful administration to the vices, or could withdraw his thoughts from the penury and suffering which such an administration necessarily entailed on the people, he had opportunities of access at Rome to the most various and delightful exercises of the faculties of memory, taste, and judgment, in the company of persons distinguished for their knowledge and genius. For, with all the social intercourse for which Paris was celebrated in the reign of Louis XV. the local objects at Rome gave a higher and richer tone to conversation there; even the living vices were there less offensive than at Paris, the rumours of them being almost lost in the remembrance of departed virtue, constantly kept awake by the sight of its monuments and vouchers. Tyranny in Rome was exercised more intellectually than in the French Capital. Injustice and oppression were used more in the form of persuasion; and though the crosier was not less pernicious than the bayonet, it inflicted a less irritating injury. The virtuous endured with patience the wrongs that their misguided judgment led them to believe were salutary to their eternal welfare. But it ought to be observed, that the immorality of the Romans was greatly exaggerated. Individuals redeemed by their merits the reproach of universal profligacy; and strangers, by being on their guard against the moral contagion, suffered a less dangerous taint than in the Atheistical coteries of Paris. Many, in consequence, who came prepared to be disgusted with the degenerated Romans, often bade them adieu with sentiments of respect, and remembered their urbanity and accomplishments with delightful satisfaction.

It was not, however, the native inhabitants of Rome who constituted the chief attractions of society there, but the number of accomplished strangers of all countries and religions, who, in constant succession, came in pilgrimage to the shrine of antiquity; and who, by the contemplation of the merits and glories of departed worth, often felt themselves, as it were, miraculously endowed with new qualities. The collision of minds fraught with learning, in that high state of excitement which the genius of the place produced on the coldest imaginations, together with those innumerable brilliant and transitory topics which were never elicited in any other city, made the Roman conversations a continual exercise of the understanding. The details of political intrigue, and the follies of individuals, excited but little interest among the strangers in Rome. It seemed as if by an universal tacit resolution, national and personal peculiarities and prejudices were forgotten, and that all strangers simultaneously turned their attention to the transactions and affairs of former ages, and of statesmen and authors now no more. Their mornings were spent in surveying the monuments raised to public virtue, and in giving local features in their minds to the knowledge which they had acquired by the perusal of those works that have perpetuated the dignity of the Roman character. Their evenings were often allotted to the comparison of their respective conjectures, and to ascertain the authenticity and history of the relics which they had collected of ancient art. Sometimes the day was consumed in the study of those inestimable ornaments of religion, by which the fraudulent disposition of the priesthood had, in the decay of its power, rendered itself venerable to the most enlightened minds;

and the night was devoted to the consideration of the causes which contribute to the developement of genius, or of the events which tend to stifle and overwhelm its powers. Every recreation of the stranger in Rome was an effort of the memory, of abstraction, and of fancy.—Society, in this elevated state of enjoyment, surrounded by the greatest works of human creation, and placed amidst the monuments of the most illustrious of mankind,—and that of the Quakers of Pennsylvania, employed in the mechanical industry of felling timber, and amid the sobriety of rural and commercial oeconomy, were like the extremes of a long series of events, in which, though the former is the necessary consequence of the latter, no resemblance can be traced in their respective characteristics. In America all was young, vigorous, and growing,—the spring of a nation, frugal, active, and simple. In Rome all was old, infirm, and decaying,—the autumn of a people who had gathered their glory, and were sinking into sleep under the disgraceful excesses of the vintage. On the most inert mind, passing from the one continent to the other, the contrast was sufficient to excite great emotion; on such a character as that of Mr. West, who was naturally disposed to the contemplation of the sublime and beautiful, both as to their moral and visible effect, it made a deep and indelible impression. It confirmed him in the wisdom of those strict religious principles which denied the utility of art when solely employed as the medium of amusement; and impelled him to attempt what could be done to approximate the uses of the pencil to those of the pen, in order to render Painting, indeed, the sister of Eloquence and Poetry.

But the course of study in the Roman schools was not calculated to enable him to carry this grand purpose into effect; for the principles by which Michael Angelo and Raphael had attained their excellence, were no longer regarded. The study of Nature was deserted for that of the antique; and pictures were composed according to rules derived from other paintings, without respect to what the subject required, or what the circumstances of the scene probably appeared to be. It was, therefore, not one of the least happy occurrences in his life that he went to Rome when society was not only in the most favourable state for the improvement of his mind, and for convincing him of the deleterious influence of the arts when employed as the embellishments of voluptuousness and luxury; but also when the state of the arts was so mean, that the full effect of studying the antique only, and of grouping characters by academical rules, should appear so striking as to satisfy him that he could never hope for any eminence, if he did not attend more to the phenomena of Nature, than to the productions of the greatest genius. The perusal of the works of other painters, he was sensible, would improve his taste; but he was convinced, that the design which he had formed for establishing his own fame, could not be realised, if, for a single moment, he forgot that their works, however exquisite, were but the imitations and forms of those eternal models to which he had been instinctively directed.

It was on the 10th of July, 1760, that he arrived at Rome. The French Courier conducted him to a hotel, and, having mentioned in the house that he was an American, and a Quaker, come to study the fine arts, the circumstance seemed so extraordinary, that it reached the ears of Mr. Robinson, afterwards Lord Grantham, who immediately found himself possessed by an irresistible desire to see him; and who, before he had time to dress or refresh himself, paid him a visit, and insisted that he should dine with him. In the course of dinner, that gentleman inquired what letters of introduction the Artist had brought with him; and West having informed him, he observed it was somewhat remarkable that the whole of them should be addressed to his most particular friends, adding, that as he was engaged to meet them at a party in the evening, he expected West would accompany him. This attention and frankness was acknowledged as it deserved to be, and is remembered by the Artist among those fortunate incidents which have rendered the recollection of his past life so pleasant, as scarcely to leave a wish for any part of it to have been spent otherwise than it was. At the hour appointed, Mr. Robinson conducted him to the house of Mr. Crispigne, an English gentleman who had long resided at Rome, where the evening party was held.

Among the distinguished persons whom Mr. West found in the company, was the celebrated Cardinal Albani. His eminence, although quite blind, had acquired, by the exquisite delicacy of his touch, and the combining powers of his mind, such a sense of antient beauty, that he excelled all the virtuosi then in Rome, in the correctness of his knowledge of the verity and peculiarities of the smallest medals and intaglios. Mr. Robinson conducted the Artist to the inner apartment, where the Cardinal was sitting, and said, "I have the honour to present a young American, who has a letter of introduction to your eminence, and who has come to Italy for the purpose of studying the fine arts." The Cardinal fancying that the American must be an Indian, exclaimed, "Is he black or white?" and on being told that he was very fair, "What as fair as I am?" cried the Cardinal still more surprised. This latter expression excited a good deal of mirth at the Cardinal's expence, for his complexion was of the darkest Italian olive, and West's was even of more than the usual degree of English fairness. For some time after, if it be not still in use, the expression of "as fair as the Cardinal" acquired proverbial currency in the Roman conversations, applied to persons who had any inordinate conceit of their own beauty.

The Cardinal, after some other short questions, invited West to come near him, and running his hands over his features, still more attracted the attention of the company to the stranger, by the admiration which he expressed at the form of his head. This occasioned inquiries respecting the youth; and the Italians concluding that, as he was an American, he must, of course, have received the education of a savage, became curious to witness the effect which the works of Art in the Belvidere and Vatican would produce on him. The whole company, which consisted of the principal Roman nobility, and strangers of distinction then in Rome, were interested in the event; and it was arranged in the course of the evening that on the following morning they should accompany Mr. Robinson and his protege to the palaces.

At the hour appointed, the company assembled; and a procession, consisting of upwards of thirty of the most magnificent equipages in the capital of Christendom, and filled with some of the most erudite characters in Europe, conducted the young Quaker to view the master-pieces of art. It was agreed that the Apollo should be first submitted to his view, because it was the most perfect work among all the ornaments of Rome, and, consequently, the best calculated to produce that effect which the company were anxious to witness. The statue then stood in a case, enclosed with doors, which could be so opened as to disclose it at once to full view. West was placed in the situation where it was seen to the most advantage, and the spectators arranged themselves on each side. When the keeper threw open the doors, the Artist felt himself surprised with a sudden recollection altogether different from the gratification which he had expected; and without being aware of the force of what he said, exclaimed, "My God, how like it is to a young Mohawk warrior." The Italians, observing his surprise, and hearing the exclamation, requested Mr. Robinson to translate to them what he said; and they were excessively mortified to find that the god of their idolatry was compared to a savage. Mr. Robinson mentioned to West their chagrin, and asked him to give some more distinct explanation, by informing him what sort of people the Mohawk Indians were. He described to him their education; their dexterity with the bow and arrow; the admirable elasticity of their limbs; and how much their active life expands the chest, while the quick breathing of their speed in the chace, dilates the nostrils with that apparent consciousness of vigour which is so nobly depicted in the Apollo. "I have seen them often," added he, "standing in that very attitude, and pursuing, with an intense eye, the arrow which they had just discharged from the bow." This descriptive explanation did not lose by Mr. Robinson's translation. The Italians were delighted, and allowed that a better criticism had rarely been pronounced on the merits of the statue. The view of the other great works did not awaken the same vivid feelings. Those of Raphael, in the Vatican, did not at first particularly interest him; nor was it until he had often visited them alone, and studied them by himself, that he could appreciate the fulness of their excellence. His first view of the works of Michael Angelo, was still less satisfactory: indeed, he continued always to think, that, with the single exception of the Moses, that Artist had not succeeded in giving a probable character to any of his subjects, notwithstanding the masterly hand and mind which pervade the weakest of his productions.

Among the first objects which particularly interested Mr. West, and which he never ceased to re-visit day after day with increasing pleasure, were the celebrated statues ascribed to Phidias, on the Monte Cavallo. The action of the human figure appeared to him so majestic, that it seemed to throw, as it were, a visible kind of awe into the very atmosphere, and over all the surrounding buildings. But the smallness of the horse struck him as exceedingly preposterous. He had often examined it before the idea occurred to him that it was probably reduced according to some unknown principle of antient art; and in this notion he was confirmed, by observing something of the same kind in the relative proportion of human figures and animals, on the different gems and bas-reliefs to which his attention was subsequently directed. The antient sculptors uniformly seemed to consider the human figure as the chief object, and sacrificed, to give it effect, the proportions of inferior parts. The author of the group on the Monte Cavallo, in the opinion of Mr. West, represented the horse smaller than the natural size, in order to augment the grandeur of the man. How far this notion, as the principle of a rule, may be sound, it would be unnecessary, perhaps impertinent, to inquire here; but its justness as applicable to the sculptures of antiquity, is abundantly verified by the bas-reliefs brought from the Parthenon of Athens. It is, indeed, so admitted a feature of antient art, as to be regarded by some critics as having for its object the same effect in sculpture, which is attained by light and shadow in painting.—In a picture, the Artist, by a judicious obscurity, so veils the magnitude of the car in which he places a victor, that notwithstanding its size, it may not appear the principal object; but this artifice is denied to the sculptor, who is necessitated to diminish the size of those things which are of least importance, in order to give dignity to the predominant figures. Raphael, in making the boat so small in the miraculous draught of fishes, is thought to have injudiciously applied this rule of antient sculpture; for he ought to have accomplished, by foreshortening, the same effect which he meant to produce by diminishing the size. It should, however, be observed, that great doubts are entertained if the statues on the Monte Cavallo were originally integral parts of the same group; but although this doubt may be well founded, it will not invalidate the supposed general principle of the antient sculptors, corroborated, as it is, by innumerable examples.

In the evening, after visiting the palaces, Mr. Robinson carried Mr. West to see a grand religious ceremony in one of the churches. Hitherto he was acquainted only with the simple worship of the Quakers. The pomp of the papal ceremonies was as much beyond his comprehension, as the overpowering excellence of the music surpassed his utmost expectations. Undoubtedly, in all the spectacles and amusements of Rome, he possessed a keener sense of enjoyment, arising from the simplicity of his education, than most other travellers. That same sensibility to the beauty of forms and colours which had awakened his genius for painting, was, probably, accompanied with a general superior susceptibility of the other organs as well as the sight; for it is observed that a taste for any one of the fine arts is connected with a general predilection for them all. But neither the Apollo, the Vatican, nor the pomp of the Catholic ritual, excited his feelings to so great a degree as the spectacle which presented itself to his view around the portico of the church. Bred in the universal prosperity of Pennsylvania, where the benevolence of the human bosom was only employed in acts of hospitality and mutual kindness, he had never witnessed any spectacle of beggary, nor had he ever heard the name of God uttered to second an entreaty for alms. Here, however, all the lazars and the wretched in Rome were collected together; hundreds of young and old in that extreme of squalor, nakedness, and disease which affrights the English traveller in Italy, were seen on all sides; and their importunities and cries, for the love of God, and the mercy of Christ, to relieve them, thrilled in his ears, and smote upon his heart to such a degree, that his joints became as it were loosened, and his legs scarcely able to support him. Many of the beggars knew Mr. Robinson, and seeing him accompanied by a stranger, an Englishman, as they concluded the Artist to be from his appearance, surrounded them with confidence and clamours.

* * * * *

As they returned from the church, a woman somewhat advanced in life, and of a better appearance than the generality of the beggars, followed them, and Mr. West gave her a small piece of copper money, the first Roman coin which he had received in change, the relative value of which to the other coins of the country was unknown to him. Shortly afterwards they were joined by some of the Italians, whom they had seen in the morning, and while they were conversing together, he felt some one pull his coat, and turned round. It was the poor woman to whom he had given the piece of copper money. She held out in her hand several smaller pieces, and as he did not understand her language, he concluded that she was chiding him for having given her such a trifle, and coloured deeply with the idea. His English friend, observing his confusion, inquired what he had given her, and he answered that he did not know, but it was a piece of money which he had received in change. Robinson, after a short conversation with the beggar, told Mr. West that she had asked him to give her a farthing. "But as you gave her a two-penny piece," said he, "she has brought you the change." This instance of humble honesty, contrasted with the awful mass of misery with which it was united, gave him a favourable idea of the latent sentiments of the Italians. How much, indeed, is the character of that people traduced by the rest of Europe! How often is the traveller in Italy, when he dreads the approach of robbers, and prepares against murder, surprised at the bountiful disposition of the common Italians, and made to blush at having applied the charges against a few criminals to the character of a whole people—without reflecting that the nation is only weak because it is subdivided.

CHAPTER VII

Anecdote of a famous Impoverisatore —West the subject of one of his finest effusions —Anecdote of Cardinal Albani —West introduced to Mengs —Satisfactory result of Wests's first essay in Rome —Consequences of the continual excitement which the Artist's feelings endured —He goes to Florence for advice —He accompanies Mr. Matthews in a tour —Singular instance of liberality towards the Artist from several Gentlemen of Philadelphia

IT was not, however, the novelty, variety, and magnificence of the works of art and antiquity in Rome, that kept Mr. West in a constant state of high excitement; the vast difference in the manners of the people from those of the inhabitants of America, acted also as an incessant stimulus on his feelings and imagination: even that difference, great as it happened to be, was rendered particularly interesting to him by incidents arising out of his own peculiar situation. One night, soon after his arrival in Rome, Mr. Gavin Hamilton, the painter, to whom he had been introduced by Mr. Robinson, took him to a coffee-house, the usual resort of the British travellers. While they were sitting at one of the tables, a venerable old man, with a guitar suspended from his shoulder, entered the room, and coming immediately to their table, Mr. Hamilton addressed him by the name of Homer.— He was the most celebrated Improvisatore in all Italy, and the richness of expression, and nobleness of conception which he displayed in his effusions, had obtained for him that distinguished name. Those who once heard his poetry, never ceased to lament that it was lost in the same moment, affirming, that it often was so regular and dignified, as to equal the finest compositions of Tasso and Ariosto.—It will, perhaps, afford some gratification to the admirers of native genius to learn, that this old man, though led by the fine frenzy of his imagination to prefer a wild and wandering life to the offer of a settled independence, which had been often made to him in his youth, enjoyed in his old age, by the liberality of several Englishmen, who had raised a subscription for the purpose, a small pension, sufficient to keep him comfortable in his own way, when he became incapable of amusing the public.

After some conversation, Homer requested Mr. Hamilton to give him a subject for a poem. In the mean time, a number of Italians had gathered round them to look at Mr. West, who they had heard was an American, and whom, like Cardinal Albani, they imagined to be an Indian. Some of them, on hearing Homer's request, observed, that he had exhausted his vein, and had already said and sung every subject over and over. Mr. Hamilton, however, remarked that he thought he could propose something new to the bard, and pointing to Mr. West, said, that he was an American come to study the fine arts in Rome; and that such an event furnished a new and magnificent theme. Homer took possession of the thought with the ardour of inspiration. He immediately unslung his guitar, and began to draw his fingers rapidly over the strings, swinging his body from side to side, and striking fine and impressive chords. When he had thus brought his motions and his feelings into unison with the instrument, he began an extemporaneous ode in a manner so dignified, so pathetic, and so enthusiastic, that Mr. West was scarcely less interested by his appearance than those who enjoyed the subject and melody of his numbers. He sung the darkness which for so many ages veiled America from the eyes of Science. He described the fulness of time when the purposes for which it had been raised from the deep were to be manifested. He painted the seraph of knowledge descending from heaven, and directing Columbus to undertake the discovery; and he related the leading incidents of the voyage. He invoked the fancy of his auditors to contemplate the wild magnificence of mountain, lake, and wood, in the new world; and he raised, as it were, in vivid perspective, the Indians in the chase, and at their horrible sacrifices. "But," he exclaimed, "the beneficent spirit of improvement is ever on the wing, and, like the ray from the throne of God which inspired the conception of the Virgin, it has descended on this youth, and the hope which ushered in its new miracle, like the star that guided the magi to Bethlehem, has led him to Rome. Methinks I behold in him an instrument chosen by heaven, to raise in America the taste for those arts which elevate the nature of man,—an assurance that his country will afford a refuge to science and knowledge, when in the old age of Europe they shall have forsaken her shores. But all things of heavenly origin, like the glorious sun, move Westward; and Truth and Art have their periods of shining, and of night. Rejoice then, O venerable Rome, in thy divine destiny, for though darkness overshadow thy seats, and though thy mitred head must descend into the dust, as deep as the earth that now covers thy antient helmet and imperial diadem, thy spirit, immortal and undecayed, already spreads towards a new world, where, like the soul of man in Paradise, it will be perfected in virtue and beauty more and more." The highest efforts of the greatest actors, even of Garrick himself delivering the poetry of Shakespeare, never produced a more immediate and inspiring effect than this rapid burst of genius. When the applause had abated, Mr. West being the stranger, and the party addressed, according to the common practice, made the bard a present. Mr. Hamilton explained the subject of the ode: though with the weakness of a verbal translation, and the imperfection of an indistinct echo, it was so connected with the appearance which the author made in the recital, that the incident has never been obliterated from Mr. West's recollection.

While the Artist was gratifying himself with a cursory view of the works of art, and of the curiosities, Mr. Hope, of Amsterdam, the father of the gentlemen who have since become so well known in London for their taste in the arts, and their superb collections of pictures and marbles, arrived in Rome. Mr. West being introduced to him, accompanied him to Cardinal Albani, to whom he had letters of introduction, and witnessed a proof of the peculiar skill of his Eminence. The Cardinal requested Mr. Hope to come near him, and according to his usual custom with strangers, drew his hands over his face, observing that he was a German. In doing the same thing to Mr. West, he recognized him as the young American.

At this time Mengs was in the zenith of his popularity, and West was introduced to him at the Cardinal's villa. He appeared to be as much struck as every other person, with the extraordinary circumstance of an American coming to study the fine arts; and begged that Mr. West would show him a specimen of his proficiency in drawing. In returning home, our Artist mentioned to Mr. Robinson that as he had never learnt to draw, he could not produce any sketch like those made by the other students; but that he could paint a little, and if Mr. Robinson would take the trouble to sit, he would execute his portrait to shew Mengs. The proposal was readily acceded to, and it was also agreed, that except to two of their most intimate acquaintances, the undertaking should be kept a profound secret. When the picture was finished, it was so advantageous to the Artist, that it tended to confirm the opinion which was entertained of his powers, founded only on the strength of the curiosity which had brought him from America. But, before shewing it to Mengs, it was resolved that the taste and judgment of the public with respect to its merits should be ascertained.

Mr. Crespigne, one of the two friends in the secret, lived as a Roman gentleman, and twice a year gave a grand assembly at his house, to which all the nobility and strangers in Rome, the most eminent for rank, birth, and talents, were invited. It was agreed that the portrait should be exhibited at one of his parties, which happened to take place soon after it was finished. A suitable frame being provided, the painting was hung up in one of the rooms. The first guests who arrived, were Amateurs and Artists; and as it was known among them that Robinson was sitting to Mengs for his portrait, it was at once thought to be that picture, and they agreed that they had never seen any painting of the Artist so well coloured. As the guests assembled, the portrait became more and more the subject of attention, and Mr. West sat behind on a sofa equally agitated and delighted by their strictures, which Mr. Robinson reported to him from time to time. In the course of the evening Mr. Dance, an Englishman of great shrewdness, was observed looking with an eye of more than common scrutiny at the portrait, by Mr. Jenkins, another of the guests, who, congratulating Robinson in getting so good a portrait from Mengs, turned to Dance, and said, "The he must now acknowledge that Mengs could colour as well as he could draw." Dance confessed that he thought the picture much better coloured than those usually painted by Mengs, but added that he did not think the drawing either so firm or good as the usual style of that Artist. This remark occasioned some debate, in which Jenkins, attributing the strictures of Dance to some prejudice which he had early conceived against Mengs, drew the company around to take a part in the discussion. Mr. Crespigne seizing the proper moment in their conversation to produce the effect intended, said to Jenkins that he was mistaken, and that Dance was in the right, for, in truth, the picture was not painted by Mengs.

By whom then, vociferated every one, "for there is no other painted now in Rome capable of executing any thing so?" "By that young gentleman there," said Mr. Crespigne, turning to West. At once all eyes were bent towards him, and the Italians, in their way, ran and embraced him. Thus did the best judges at once, by this picture, acknowledge him as only second in the executive department of the art to the first painter then in Rome. Mengs himself, on seeing the picture, expressed his opinion in terms that did great honour to his liberality, and gave the Artist an advice which he never forgot, nor remembered without gratitude. He told him that the portrait showed that he had no occasion to learn to paint at Rome. "You have already, sir," said he, "the mechanical part of your art: what I would, therefore, recommend to you, is to see and examine every thing deserving of your attention here, and after making a few drawings of about half a dozen of the best statues, go to Florence, and observe what has been done for Art in the collections there. Then proceed to Bologna, and study the works of the Caracci; afterwards visit Parma, and examine, attentively, the pictures of Corregio; and then go to Venice and view the productions of Tintoretti, Titian, and Paul Veronese. When you have made this tour, come back to Rome, and paint an historical composition to be exhibited to the Roman public; and the opinion which will then be formed of your talents should determine the line of our profession which you ought to follow." This judicious advice, so different from those absurd academical dogmas which would confine genius to the looking only to the works of art, for that perfection which they but dimly reflect from nature, West found accord so well with his own reflections and principles, that he resolved to follow it with care and attention. But the thought of being in Rome, and the constant excitement arising from extraordinary and interesting objects, so affected his mind, accustomed to the sober and uniform habits of the Quakers, that sleep deserted his pillow, and he became ill and constantly feverish. The public took an interest in his situation. A consultation of the best Physicians in Rome was held on his case, the result of which was a formal communication to Mr. Robinson, that his friend must immediately quit the capital, and seek relief from the irritated state of his sensibility in quiet and retirement. Accordingly, on the 20th of August he returned to Leghorn.

Messrs. Jackson and Rutherford, by whose most friendly recommendation he had obtained so much flattering distinction at Rome, received him into their own house, and treated him with a degree of hospitality that merits for them the honour of being considered among the number of his early patrons. Mr. (afterwards Sir John) Dick, then the British Consul at Leghorn, and his lady, also treated him with great partiality, and procured for him the use of the Imperial baths. His mind being thus relieved from the restless ecstasy which he had suffered in Rome, and the intensity of interest being diminished by the circumscribed nature of the society of Leghorn, together with the bracing effects of sea-bathing, he was soon again in a condition to resume his study in the capital. But the same overpowering attacks on his feelings and imagination soon produced a relapse of his former indisposition, and compelled him to return to Leghorn, where he was again speedily cured of his fever, but it left in its dregs a painful affection in the ancle, that threatened the loss of the limb. The well-known Nanoni, an eminent surgeon, who had introduced many improvements in the treatment of diseased joints, was at this period resident in Florence, and Messrs. Jackson and Rutherford wrote to Sir Horace Mann, then the British Minister at the Ducal Court, to consult him relative to the case of Mr. West: his answer induced them to advise the Artist to go to Florence. After a painful period of eleven months confinement to his couch and chamber, he was perfectly and radically cured.

A state of pain and disease is adverse to mental improvement; but there were intervals in which Mr. West felt his anguish abate, and in which he could not only participate in the conversation of the gentlemen to whose kindness he had been recommended, but was able, occasionally, to exercise his pencil. The testimonies of friendship which he received at this perdiod from Sir Horace Mann, the Marquesses of Creni and Riccardi, the late Lord Cooper, and many others of the British nobility then travelling in Italy, made an indelible impression on his mind, and became a stimulating motive to his wishes to excel in his art, in order to demonstrate by his proficiency that he was not unworthy of their solicitude. He had a table constructed so as to enable him to draw while he lay in bed; and in that situation he amused and improved himself in delineating the picturesque conceptions which were constantly presenting themselves to his fancy.

When he was so far recovered as to be able to take exercise, and to endure the fatigue of travelling, a circumstance happened which may be numbered among the many fortunate accidents of his professional career. Mr. Matthews, the manager of the important commercial concerns of Messrs. Jackson and Rutherford, was one of those singular men who are but rarely met with in mercantile life, combining the highest degree of literary and elegant accomplishments with the best talents for active business. He was not only confessedly one of the finest classical scholars in all Italy, but, out of all comparison, the best practical antiquary, perhaps, then in that country, uniting, along with the minutest accuracy of criticism, a delicacy of taste in the perception of the beauty and judgment of the antients, seldom found blended with an equal degree of classical erudition. Affairs connected with the business of the house, and a wish to see the principal cities of Italy, led Mr. Matthews, about the period of Mr. West's recovery, to visit Florence, and it was agreed between them that they should together make the tour recommended by Mengs.

In the mean time, the good fortune of West was working to happy effects in another part of the world. The story of Mr. Robinson's portrait had made so great a noise among the travellers in Italy, that Messrs. Jackson and Rutherford, in sending back the ship to Philadelphia, in which the Artist had come passenger, mentioned it in their letters to Mr. Allen. It is seldom that commercial affairs are mingled with those of art, and it was only from the Italian shore that a mercantile house could introduce such a topic into their correspondence. It happened that on the very day this letter reached Mr. Allen, Mr. Hamilton, then Governor of Pennsylvania, and the principal members of the government, along with the most considerable citizens of Philadelphia, were dining with him. After dinner, Mr. Allen read the letter to the company, and mentioned the amount of the sum of money which West had paid into his hands at the period of his departure from America, adding that it must be pretty far reduced. But, said he with warmth, "I regard this young man as an honour to the country, and as he is the first that America has sent to cultivate the fine arts, he shall not be frustrated in his studies, for I have resolved to write to my correspondents at Leghorn, to give him, from myself, whatever money he may require." Mr. Hamilton felt the force of this generous declaration, and said, with equal animation, "I think exactly as you do, Sir, but you shall not have all the honour of it to yourself, and, therefore, I beg that you will consider me as joining you in the responsibility of the credit." The consequence of this was, that upon West going, previously to leaving Florence, to take a small sum of about ten pounds from the bankers to whom he had been recommended by Messrs. Jackson and Rutherford, a letter was brought in, while he was waiting for his money, and the gentleman who opened it said to him, "that the contents of the letter would probably afford him unexpected pleasure, as it instructed them to give him unlimited credit." A more splendid instance of liberality is not to be found even in the records of Florence. The munificence of the Medici was excelled by that of the magistracy of Philadelphia.

CHAPTER VIII

The result of the Artist's experiment to discover the methods by which Titian produced his splendid colouring —He returns to Rome —Reflections suggested by inspecting the Egyptian Obelisk —Considerations of the Author on the same subject; an anecdote of a Mohawk Indian who became an Actor at New York —Anecdote of a Scottish Fanatic who arrived in Rome, to convert the Pope —Sequel of the Adventure —The Artist prepares to visit England —Having completed his St Jerome, after Corregio's famous picture, he is elected an Honorary Member of the Academy of Parma, and invited to Court —He proceeds by the way of Genoa towards France — Reflections on the State of Italy —Adventure on reaching the French frontiers —State of Taste in France

FROM Florence the Artist proceeded to Bologna, and having staid some time there, carefully inspecting every work of celebrity to which he could obtain access, he went on to Venice, visiting in his route all the objects which Mengs had recommended to his attention. The style of Titian, which in breadth and clearness of colouring so much excels that of almost every other painter, was the peculiar characteristic of the Venetian school which interested him the most, and seemed to him, at first, involved in inexplicable mystery. He was never satisfied with the explanations which the Italian amateurs attempted to give him of what they called the internal light of that master's productions. Repeated experiments, however, enabled him, at last, to make the discovery himself. Indeed, he was from the first persuaded that it was chiefly owing to the peculiar genius of the Artist himself,—to an exquisite delicacy of sight which enabled him to perceive the most approximate tints,—and not to any particular dexterity of pencilling, nor to any superiority in the materials of his colours. This notion led Mr. West to try the effect of painting in the first place with the pure primary colours, and softening them afterwards with the semi tints; and the result confirmed him in the notion that such was probably the peculiar method of Titian. But although this idea was suggested by his visits to the collections of Venice, he was not perfectly satisfied with its soundness as a rule, till many years after his arrival in London, and many unsuccessful experiments.

Having completed his tour to the most celebrated repositories of art in Italy, and enriched his mind, and improved his taste, by the perusal rather than the imitation of their best pieces, he returned to Rome, and applied himself to a minute and assiduous study of the great ornaments of that capital, directing his principal attention to the works of Raphael, and improving his knowledge of the antient costume by the study of Cameos, in which he was assisted by Mr. Wilcox, the author of the Roman Conversations,—to whom he had been introduced by Mr. Robinson, at Mr. Crespigne's, on the occasion of the exhibition of the Portrait,—a man of singular attainments in learning, and of a serene and composed dignity of mind and manners that rendered him more remarkable to strangers than even his great classical knowledge.

Of all the monuments of antient art in Rome, the Obelisk brought from Egypt, in the reign of Augustus, interested his curiosity the most, and even for a time affected him as much as those which so agitated him by their beauty. The hieroglyphics appeared to resemble so exactly the figures in the Wampum belts of the Indians, that it occurred to him, if ever the mysteries of Egypt were to be interpreted, it might be by the aborigines of America. This singular notion was not, however, the mere suggestion of fancy, but the effect of an opinion which his early friend and tutor Provost Smith conceived, in consequence of attending the grand meeting of the Indian chiefs, with the Governors of the British colonies, held at East town, in Pennsylvania, in the year following the disastrous fate of Bradock's army. The chiefs had requested this interview, in order to state to the officers the wrongs and injuries of which they complained; and at the meeting they evidently read the reports and circumstances of their grievances from the hieroglyphical chronicle of the Wampum belts, which they held in their hands, and by which, from the date of their grand alliance with William Penn, the man from the ocean, as they called him, they minutely related all the circumstances in which they conceived the terms and spirit of the treaty had been infringed by the British, defying the officers to show any one point in which the Indians had swerved from their engagements. It seemed to Dr. Smith that such a minute traditionary detail of facts could not have been preserved without some contemporary record; and he, therefore, imagined, that the constant reference made to the figures on the belts was a proof that they were chronicles. This notion was countenanced by another circumstance which Mr. West had himself often noticed. The course of some of the high roads through Pennsylvania lies along what were formerly the war tracks of the Indians; and he had frequently seen hieroglyphics engraved on the trees and rocks. He was told that they were inscriptions left by some of the tribes who had passed that way in order to apprize their friends of the route which they had taken, and of any other matter which it concerned them to know. He had also noticed among the Indians who annually visited Philadelphia, that there were certain old chiefs who occasionally instructed the young warriors to draw red and black figures, similar to those which are made on the belts, and who explained their signification with great emphasis, while the students listened to the recital with profound silence and attention. It was not, therefore, extraordinary, that, on seeing similar figures on the Egyptian trophy, he should have thought that they were intended to transmit the record of transactions like the Wampum belts.—A language of signs derived from natural objects, must have something universal in its very nature; for the qualities represented by the emblematic figure, would, doubtless, be those for which the original of the figure was most remarkable: and, therefore, if there be any resemblance between the Egyptian hieroglyphics and those used by the American Indians, the probability is, that there is also some similar intrinsic meaning in their signification. But the Wampum belts are probably not all chronicles; there is reason to believe that some of them partake of the nature of calendars, by which the Indians are regulated in proceedings dependant on the seasons; and that, in this respect, they answer to the household Gods of the patriarchal times, which are supposed to have been calendars, and the figure of each an emblem of some portion of the year, or sign of the

Zodiac. It would be foreign to the nature of this work to investigate the evidence which may be adduced on this subject, or to collect those various and scattered hints which have given rise to the opinion, and with a faint, but not fallacious ray, have penetrated that obscure region of antient history, between the period when the devotion of mankind, withdrawn from the worship of the Deity, was transferred to the adoration of the stars, and prior to the still greater degradation of the human faculties when altars were raised to idols.

The idea of the Indians being in possession of hieroglyphical writings, is calculated to lead us to form a very different opinion of them to that which is usually entertained by the world. Except in the mere enjoyments of sense, they do not appear to be inferior to the rest of mankind; and their notions of moral dignity are exactly those which are recommended to our imitation by the literature of all antiquity. But they have a systematic contempt for whatever either tends to increase their troubles, to encumber the freedom of their motions, or to fix them to settled habitations. In their unsheltered nakedness, they have a prouder consciousness of their importance in the scale of beings, than the philosophers of Europe, with all their multiplicity of sensual and intellectual gratifications, to supply which so many of the human race are degraded from their natural equality. The Indian, however, is not deficient in mental enjoyments, or a stranger to the exercise of the dignified faculties of our common nature. He delivers himself on suitable occasions with a majesty of eloquence that would beggar the oratory of the parliaments, and the pulpits of Christendom; and his poetry unfolds the loftiest imagery and sentiment of the epic and the hymn. He considers himself as the lord of the creation, and regards the starry heaven as his canopy, and the everlasting mountain as his throne. It would be absurd, however, to assert with Rousseau, that he is, therefore, better or happier than civilized man; but it would be equally so to deny him the same sense of dignity, the same feeling of dishonour, the same love of renown, or ascribe to his actions in war, and his recreations in peace, baser motives than to the luxurious warriors and statesmen of Europe. Before Mr. West left America, an attempt was made to educate three young Indians at New York; and their progress, notwithstanding that they still retained something of their original wildness of character, exceeded the utmost expectations of those who were interested in the experiment. Two of them, however, in the end, returned to their tribe, but they were rendered miserable by the contempt with which they were received; and the brother of the one who remained behind, was so affected with their degradation, that he came to the city determined to redeem his brother from the thraldom of civilization. On his arrival he found he had become an actor, and was fast rising into celebrity on the stage. On learning this circumstance, the resolute Indian went to the theatre, and seated himself in the pit. The moment that his brother appeared, he leapt upon the stage, and drawing his knife, threatened to sacrifice him on the spot unless he would immediately strip himself naked, and return with him to their home in the woods. He upbraided him with the meanness of his disposition, in consenting to make himself a slave. He demanded if he had forgotten that the Great Spirit had planted the Indian corn for their use, and filled the forests with game, the air with birds, and the waters with fish, that they might be free. He represented the institutions of civilized society as calculated to make him dependant on the labour of others, and subject to every chance that might interrupt their disposition to supply his wants. The actor obeyed his brother, and returning to the woods, was never seen again in the town.[2]

It may, perhaps, not be an impertinent digression to contrast this singular occurrence in the theatre of New York with another truly European, to which Mr. West was a witness, in the Cathedral of St. Peter. Among other intelligent acquaintances which he formed in Rome was the Abate Grant, one of the adherents of that unfortunate family, whom the baseness of their confidential servants, and the factions of ambitious demagogues, deprived, collectively, of their birthright. This priest, though a firm Jacobite in principle, was, like many others of the same political sentiments, liberal and enlightened, refuting, by his conduct, the false and fraudulent calumnies which have been so long alleged against the gallant men who supported the cause of the ill-fated Stuarts. On St. Peter's day, when the Pope in person performs high mass in the cathedral, the Abate offered to take Mr. West to the church, as he could place him among the ecclesiastics, in an advantageous situation to witness the ceremony. Glad of such an offer, Mr. West willingly accompa-

---

2 The following Extract from the Journal of a Friend, who has lately travelled through the principal parts of the United States, will probably be found interesting, as it tends to throw some degree of light on the sentiments of the Indians; of which the little that is known has hitherto never been well elucidated.

nied him. The vast edifice; the immense multitude of spectators; the sublimity of the music; and the effect of the pomp addressed to the sight, produced on the mind of the Painter feelings scarcely less enthusiastic than those which the devoutest of the worshippers experienced, or the craftiest inhabitant of the Vatican affected to feel. At the elevation of the host, and as he was kneeling beside the Abate, to their equal astonishment he heard a voice, exclaiming behind them in a broad Scottish accent, "O Lord, cast not the church down on them for this abomination!" The surrounding Italian priests, not understanding what the enthusiast was saying, listened with great comfort to such a lively manifestation of a zeal, which they attributed to the blessed effects of the performance. The Abate, however, with genuine Scottish partiality, was alarmed for his countryman, and endeavoured to persuade him to hold his tongue during the ceremony, as he ran the risk of being torn to pieces by the mob.

It appeared that this zealous Presbyterian, without understanding a word of any civilized language, but only a dialect of his own, had come to Rome for the express purpose of attempting to convert the Pope, as the shortest way, in his opinion, of putting an end to the reign of Antichrist. When mass was over, the Abate, anxious to avert from him the consequences which his extravagance would undoubtedly entail, if he continued to persevere in it, entered into conversation with him. It appeared he had only that morning arrived in Babylon, and being unable to rest until he had seen a glimpse of the gorgeous harlot, he had not then provided himself with lodgings. The Abate conducted him to a house where he knew he would be carefully attended; and he also endeavoured to reason with him on the absurdity of his self-assumed mission, assuring him that unless he desisted, and behaved with circumspection, he would inevitably be seized by the Inquisition. But the prospect of Martyrdom augmented his zeal; and the representations of the benevolent Catholic only stimulated his enterprise; so that in the course of a few days, much to his own exceeding great joy, and with many comfortable salutations of the spirit, he was seized by the Inquisition, and lodged in a dungeon, On hearing this, the Abate applied to King James in his behalf, and by his Majesty's influence he was released, and sent to the British Consul at Leghorn, on condition of being immediately conveyed to his friends in Scotland. It happened, however, that no vessel was then ready to sail, and the taste of persecution partaking more of the relish of adventure than the pungency of suffering, the missionary was not to be so easily frustrated in his meritorious design; and, therefore, he took the first opportunity of stealing silently back to Rome, where he was again arrested and confined. By this time the affair had made some noise, and it was universally thought by all the English travellers, that the best way of treating the ridiculous madman was to allow him to remain some time in solitary confinement in the dungeons of the Inquisition. When he had been imprisoned about three months, he was again liberated, sent to Leghorn, and embarked for England, radically cured of his inclination to convert the Pope, but still believing that the punishment which he had suffered for his folly would be recorded as a trial which he had endured in the service of the faith.

In the mean time West was carefully furnishing his mind by an attentive study of the costume of antiquity, and the beauties of the great works of modern genius. In doing this, he regarded Rome only as an university, in which he should graduate; and, as a thesis preparatory to taking his degree among the students, he painted a picture of Cimon and Iphigenia, and, subsequently, another of Angelica and Madoro. The applause which they received justified the opinion which Mengs had so early expressed of his talent, and certainly answered every object for which they were composed. He was honoured, in consequence, with the marks of academical approbation, usually bestowed on fortunate Artists. He then proposed to return to America, with a view to cultivate in his native country that profession in which he had already acquired so much celebrity. At this juncture he received a letter from his father, advising him, as peace had been concluded between France and England, to go home for a short time before coming to America; for the mother country was at that period still regarded as the home of her American offspring. The advice of his father was in unison with his own wishes, and he mentioned his intention to Mr. Wilcox. That gentleman, conceiving that he spoke of America as his home, expressed himself with grief and surprise at a determination so different from what he had expected; but, upon being informed of the ambiguity in the phrase, he exclaimed that he could hardly have resolved, on quitting Italy, more opportunely, for Dr. Patoune, a Scotish gentleman, of considerable learning, and some taste in painting, was then returning homeward, and waiting at that time in Rome, until he should be able to meet with a companion. It was therefore agreed that West should be introduced to him; and it was soon after arranged that the Doctor should proceed to Florence, while the Artist went to take leave of his friends at Leghorn, to express to them his gratitude for the advantages he had derived from their constant and extraordinary kindness, which he estimated so highly, that he could not think of leaving Italy without performing this pleasing and honourable pilgrimage. It was also agreed between him and his companion, that the Doctor should stop a short time at Parma, until West should have completed a copy of the St. Jerome of Corregio, which he had begun during his visit to that city with Mr. Matthews.

During their stay at Parma, the Academy elected Mr. West a member, an honour which the Academies of Florence and Bologna had previously conferred on him; and it was mentioned to the Prince that a young American had made a copy of the St. Jerome of Corregio in a style of excellence such as the oldest Academicians had not witnessed. The Prince expressed a wish to see this extraordinary Artist, particularly when be heard that he was from Pennsylvania, and a Quaker. Mr. West was, in consequence, informed that a visit from him would be acceptable at Court: and it was arranged that he should be introduced to His Highness by the chief Minister. Mr. West thought that, in a matter of this kind, he should regulate his behaviour by what he understood to be the practice in the court of London; and, accordingly, to the astonishment of the whole of the courtiers, he kept his hat on during the audience. This, however, instead of offending the Prince, was observed with evident pleasure, and made his reception more particular and distinguished; for His Highness had heard of the peculiar simplicity of the Quakers, and of the singularly Christian conduct of William Penn.

From Parma he proceeded to Genoa, and thence to Turin. Considering this City as the last stage of his professional observations in Italy, his mind unconsciously took a retrospective view of the different objects he had seen, and the knowledge which he had acquired since his departure from America. Although his art was always uppermost in his thoughts, and although he could not reflect on the course of his observations without pleasure and hope, he was often led to advert to the lamentable state into which every thing, as well as Art, had fallen in Italy, in consequence of the general theocratical despotism which over-spread the whole country, like an unwholesome vapour, and of those minute subdivisions of territory, in which political tyranny exercised its baleful influence even where the ecclesiastical oppression seemed disposed to spare. He saw, in the infamous establishment of the cicisbeo, the settled effect of that general disposition to palliate vice, which is the first symptom of decay in nations; and he was convinced that, before vice could be thus exalted into custom, there must exist in the community which would tolerate such an institution, a disregard of all those obligations which it is the pride of virtue to incur, and the object of law to preserve. It seemed to him that every thing in Italy was in a state of disease; and that the moral energy was subsiding, as the vital flame diminishes with the progress of old age. For although the forms and graces of the human character were often seen in all their genuine dignity among the common people, still even the general population seemed to be defective in that detestation of vice found in all countries in a healthful state of morals, and which is often strongest among the lowest of the vulgar, especially in what respects the conduct of the great. He thought that the commonalty of Italy had lost the tact by which the good and evil of actions are discriminated; and that, whatever was good in their disposition, was constitutional, and unconnected with any principle of religion, or sense of right. In the Papal states, this appeared to be particularly the case. All the creative powers of the mind seemed there to be extinct. The country was covered with ruins, and the human character was in ashes. Sometimes, indeed, a few embers of intellect were seen among the clergy; but the brightness of their scintillation was owing to the blackness of death with which they were contrasted. The splendour of the nobility struck him only as a more conspicuous poverty than the beggary of the common people; and the perfect contempt with which they treated the feelings of their dependants, seemed to him scarcely less despicable than the apathy with which it was endured. The innumerable examples of the effects of this moral paralysis to which he was a witness on his arrival in Rome, filled him for some time with indescribable anxiety, and all his veneration for the Roman majesty was lost in reflections on the offences which mankind may be brought to commit on one another. But at Genoa, Leghorn, and Venice, the Italians were seen to less disadvantage. Commerce, by diffusring opulence, and interweaving the interests of all classes, preserved in those cities some community of feeling, which was manifested in an interchange of respect and consideration between the higher and the lower orders; and Lucca he thought afforded a perfect exception to the general degeneracy of the country. The inhabitants of that little republic presented the finest view of human nature that he had ever witnessed. With the manliness of the British character they appeared to blend the suavity of the Italian manners; and their private morals were not inferior to the celebrity of their public virtues. So true it is, that man, under the police and vigilance of despotism, becomes more and more vicious; while, in proportion to the extension of his freedom, is the vigour of his private virtue. When deprived of the right of exercising his own judgment, he feels, as it were, his moral responsibility at an end, and naturally blames the system by which he is oppressed, for the crimes which his own unresisted passions instigate him to commit. To an Englishman the remembrance of a journey in Italy is however often more delightful than that of any other country, for no where else is his arrogance more patiently endured, his eccentricities more humourously indulged, nor the generosity of his character more publicly acknowledged.

In coming from Italy into France, Mr. West was particularly struck with the picturesque difference in the character of the peasantry of the two countries; and while he thought, as an Artist, that to give appropriate effect to a national landscape it would not only be necessary to introduce figures in the costume of the country, but in employments and recreations no less national, he was sensible of the truth of a remark which occurs to almost every traveller, that there are different races of the human species, and that the nature of the dog and horse do not vary more in different climates than man himself. In making the observation, he was not, however, disposed to agree with the continental philosophers, that this difference, arising from climate, at all narrowed the powers of the mind, though it influenced the choice of objects of taste. For whatever tends to make the mind more familiar with one class of agreeable sensations than another, will, undoubtedly, contribute to form the cause of that preference for particular qualities in objects by which the characteristics of the taste of different nations is discriminated. Although, of all the general circumstances which modify the opinions of mankind, climate is, perhaps, the most permanent, it does not, therefore, follow that, because the climate of France or Italy induces the inhabitants to prefer, in works of art, certain qualities of the excellence of which the people of England are not so sensible, the climate of Great Britain does not, in like manner, lead the inhabitants to discover other qualities equally valuable as sources of enjoyment. Thus, in sculpture for example, it would seem that in naked figures the inhabitants of a cold climate can never hope to attain that degree of eminence which we see exemplified in the productions of the Grecian and Italian sculptors; not that the Artists may not execute as well, but because they will not so readily find models; or, what is perhaps more to the point, they will not find a taste so capable of appreciating the merits of their performances. In Italy the eye is familiar with the human form in a state of almost complete nudity; and the beauty of muscular expression, and of the osteological proportions of man, is there as well known as that of the features and complexion of his countenance; but the same degree of nakedness could not be endured in the climate of England, for it is associated with sentiments of modesty and shame, which render even the accidental innocent exposure of so much of the body offensive to the feelings of decorum. It is not, therefore, just to allege, that, because the Italians are a calm, persuasive, and pensive people, and the French all stir, talk, and inconstancy, they are respectively actuated by different moral causes. It will not be asserted that, though the sources of their taste in art spring from different qualities in the same common objects, any innate incapacity for excellence in the fine arts is induced by the English climate, merely because that climate has the effect of producing a different moral temperament among the inhabitants.

On the morning after arriving at the first frontier town, in coming from Savoy into France, and while breakfast was preparing, Mr. West and his companion heard the noise of a crowd assembled in the yard of the inn. The Doctor rose and went to the window to inquire the occasion: immediately on his appearance the mob became turbulent, and seemed to menace him with some outrage.—The Peace of 1763 had been but lately concluded, and without having any other cause for the thought, it occurred to the travellers that the turbulence must have originated in some political occurrence, and they hastily summoned the landlord, who informed them, "That the people had, indeed, assembled in a tumultuous manner round the inn on hearing that two Englishmen were in the house, but that they might make themselves easy, as he had sent to inform the magistrates of the riot." Soon after, one of the magistrates arrived, and on being introduced by the landlord to the travellers, expressed himself to the following effect: "I am sorry that this occurrence should have happened, because had I known in time, I should, on hearing that you were Englishmen, have come with the other magistrates to express to you the sentiments of respect which we feel towards your illustrious nation; but, since it has not been in our power to give you that testimony of our esteem; on the contrary, since we are necessitated by our duty to protect you, I assure you that I feel exceedingly mortified. I trust, however, that you will suffer no inconvenience, for the people are dispersing, and you will be able to leave the town in safety!" "This place," he continued, "is a manufacturing town, which has been almost ruined by the war. Our goods went to the ocean from Marseilles and Toulon; but the vigilance of your fleets ruined our trade, and these poor people, who have felt the consequence, consider not the real cause of their distress. However, although the populace do not look beyond the effects which immediately press upon themselves, there are many among us well acquainted with the fountain-head of the misfortunes which afflict France, and who know that it is less to you than to ourselves that we ought to ascribe the disgraces of the late war. You had a man at the head of your government (alluding to the first Lord Chatham), and your counsellors are men. But it is the curse of France that she is ruled by one who is, in fact, but the agent and organ of valets and strumpets. The Court of France is no longer the focus of the great men of the country, but a band of profligates that have driven away the great. This state of things, however, cannot last long, the reign of the Pompadours must draw to an end, and Frenchmen will one day take a terrible revenge for the insults which they suffer in being regarded only as the materials of those who pander to the prodigality of the Court." This singular address, made in the year 1763, requires no comment; but it is a curious historical instance of the commencement of that, moral re-action to oppression which subsequently has so fully realized the prediction of the magistrate, and which, in its violence, has done so much mischief, and occasioned so many misfortunes to Europe.

The travellers remained no longer in Paris than was necessary to inspect the principal works of the French Artists, and the royal collections. Mr. West, however, continued long enough to be satisfied that the true feeling for the fine arts did not exist among the French to that degree which he had observed in Italy. On the contrary, it seemed to him that there was an inherent affectation in the general style of art among them, which demonstrated, not only a deficiency of native sensibility, but an anxious endeavour to conceal that defect. The characteristics of the French School, and they have not yet been redeemed by the introduction of any better manner, might, to a cursory observer, appear to have arisen from a corrupted taste, while, in fact, they are the consequences only of that inordinate national vanity which in so many different ways has retarded the prosperity of the world. In the opinion of a Frenchman, there is a quality of excellence in every thing belonging to France, merely because it is French, which gives at all times a certain degree of superiority to the actions and productions of his countrymen; and this delusive notion has infested not only the literature and the politicks of the nation, but also the principles of Art, to such a deep and inveterate extent, that the morality of painting is not yet either felt or understood in that country. In the mechanical execution, in drawing, and in the arrangement of parts, the great French painters are probably equal to the Italians; but in producing any other sentiment in the spectator than that of admiration at their mechanical skill, they are greatly behind the English. Painting has much of a common character with dramatic literature, and the very best pictures of the French Artists have the same kind of resemblance to the probability of Nature, that the tragedies of their great dramatic authors have to the characters and actions of men. But in rejecting the pretensions of the French to superiority either in the one species of art or in the other, the rejection ought not to be extended too far. They are wrong in their theory; but their practice so admirably accords with it, that it must be allowed, were it possible for a people so enchanted by self-conceit to discover that the true subjects of Art exist only in Nature, they evince a capacity sufficient to enable them to acquire the pre-eminence which they unfortunately believe they have already attained. But these opinions, with respect to the peculiarities of the French taste, though deduced from incidental remarks in conversations with Mr. West, must not be considered as his. The respect which he has always entertained towards the different members of his own profession never allows him to express himself in any terms that might possibly be construed by malice or by ignorance to imply any thing derogatory to a class which he naturally considers among the teachers of mankind. He may think, indeed he has expressed as much, that the style of the French Artists is not the most perspicuous; and that it is, if the expression may be allowed, more rhetorical than eloquent; but still he regards them as having done honour to their country, and, in furnishing objects of innocent interest to the minds of mankind, as having withdrawn so far the inclinations of the heart from mere sensual objects. The true use of painting, he early thought, must reside in assisting the reason to arrive at correct moral inferences, by furnishing a probable view of the effects of motives and of passions; and to the enforcement of this great argument his long life has been devoted, whether with complete success it would be presumptuous in any contemporary to determine, and injudicious in the author of these memoirs to assert.

* * * * *

"One of my fellow-passengers was a settler in the new state of Tenessee, who had come to Charleston with Horses for sale, and was going to Baltimore and Philadelphia for the purpose of investing his money in an assortment of goods suited to the western country. The ideas of civilized and savage life were so curiously blended in this man, that his conversation afforded me considerable amusement. Under the garb and appearance of a methodist preacher, I found him a hunter and a warrior; with no small portion of the adventurous spirit proper to both those characters. He had served as a militia-man or volunteer under General Jackson, in his memorable campaign against the Creek Indians in 1813; and he related to me some interesting particulars of the principal and final action which decided the fate of the war. The Indians had posted themselves at a place called, in their language, *Talapoosie*, and by the Americans, the Horse-shoe; a position of great natural strength, the advantages of which they had improved to the best of their skill, by a breast-work seven feet high, extending across the neck of land which formed the only approach to their encampment. This seems to have been viewed by the Creeks themselves as the last stand of their nation: for, contrary to the usual practice of the Indians, they made every preparation for defence, but none for retreat. Their resistance was proportionably desperate and bloody. For several hours they supported a continued fire of musketry and cannon without shrinking; till at length the American General, finding that he had lost a great number of men, and that he could not otherwise dislodge the enemy, gave orders for a general assault. The breast-work was carried by storm; and the Indians, broken at all points, and surrounded by superior numbers, were nearly all put to the sword. Out of one thousand warriors who composed the Creek Army, scarcely twenty made their escape. A body of Choctaw Indians, who attended the American Army as auxiliaries, were the chief actors in this massacre, and displayed their usual barbarous ferocity. It affords a remarkable illustration of the savage character, that the whole of this bloody scene passed in the most perfect silence on the part of the Indians: there was no outcry, no supplication for mercy: each man met his fate without uttering a word, singly defending himself to the last. The lives of the women and children were spared, but many of the boys were killed in the action, fighting bravely in the ranks with their fathers and elder brothers. My Tennessee friend received four arrows from the bows of these juvenile warriors, while in the act of mounting the breast-work.

"In hearing such a story, it is impossible not to be touched with a feeling of sympathy for a high-minded but expiring people, thus gallantly but vainly contending, against an overwhelming force, for their native woods, and their name as a Nation; or to refrain from lamenting that the settlement of the New World cannot be accomplished at a less price than the destruction of the original and rightful proprietors of the soil."

END OF PART I

Part II

To Simon M'Gillivray, Esq. This Work is inscribed,
with every sentiment of esteem, by the Author.

PREFACE

Nearly the whole of this work was printed during the last illness of Mr. West. The manuscript had long previously been read to him. My custom was, to note down those points which seemed, in our conversations, to bear on his biography, and, from time to time, to submit an entire chapter to his perusal; afterwards, when the whole narrative was formed, it was again carefully read over to him. Still, however, I am apprehensive that some mistakes in the orthography of names may have been committed; for although the same custom was strictly observed in preparing the manuscript of the first part of his Memoirs for the press, yet, in perusing the proofs, he found several errors of that kind. It was intended that he should have read the proofs of this part also, but the progress of his disease unfortunately rendered it impracticable.

30th March, 1820.   J.G.

INTRODUCTION

Although Mr. West was, strictly speaking, a self-taught artist, yet it must be allowed that in his education he enjoyed great and singular advantages. A strong presentiment was cherished in his family, that he would prove an extraordinary man, and his first rude sketch in childhood was hailed as an assurance of the fulfilment of the prediction of Peckover. The very endeavours of his boyish years were applauded as successful attainments; no domestic prejudices were opposed to the cultivation of his genius; even the religious principles of the community in which he lived were bent in his favour, from a persuasion that he was endowed by Heaven with a peculiar gift; and whatever the defects of his early essays may have been, it was not one of the least advantageous circumstances of his youth, that they were seen only by persons, who, without being competent judges of them, as works of art, were yet possessed of such a decided superiority of intellect, that their approbation in any case would have been esteemed great praise.

The incidents attending his voyage to Italy, and his introduction to the artists, virtuosi, and travellers at Rome, were still more auspicious. Taken in connection with his previous history, they form one of the most remarkable illustrations of the doctrine of fortune, or destiny, that is to be found in authentic biography. Without any knowledge of his abilities or acquirements, his arrival in the capital of Christendom, the seat of the arts, was regarded as an interesting event: his person was contemplated as an object of curiosity; and a strong disposition to applaud his productions, was excited by the mere accident of his having come from America to study the fine arts. A prepossession so extraordinary has no parallel. It would almost seem, as if there had been some arrangement in the order of things that would have placed Mr. West in the first class of artists, although he had himself mistaken the workings of ambition for the consciousness of talent. Many men of no inconsiderable fame have set out in their career with high expectations in their favour; but few, of whom such hopes were entertained, have, by a succession of works, in which the powers of the mind were seemingly unfolded with more and more energy, so long continued to justify the presentiments of his early friends. It is not, however, the object of this undertaking to form any estimate of the genius of Mr. West, or of the merits of his works; another opportunity, distinct from his memoirs, will be taken for that purpose; but only to resume the narrative of his progress, in his profession, by which it will appear that a series of circumstances no less curious than those which tended to make him an artist, facilitated his success, and placed him in that precise station in society, where, in this country, at the time, there was the only chance of profitable employment as an historical painter.

CHAPTER I

Mr. West arrives in England —Relative Condition of Artists in Society —Mr. West's American Friends in this Country —Of Governor Hamilton and Mr. Allen —- Circumstances favourable to their Reception in the Circles of Fashion —Mr. West's Visit to Bath, and Excursions to see some of the Collections of Art in England —He settles as a Portrait Painter —Introduction to Burke and Dr Johnson —Anecdote of a Monk, the Brother of Mr. Burke —Introduction to Archbishop Drummond —- Mr West's Marriage

MR. West arrived in England on the 20th of August, 1763. The sentiments with which he approached the shores of this island, were those of a stranger visiting interesting scenes, mingled with something of the solicitude and affections of a traveller returning home. He had no intention of remaining in London: he was only desirous to see the country of his ancestors, and his mind, in consequence, was more disengaged from professional feelings than at any period from that in which his genius was first awakened. He considered his visit to England as devoted to social leisure, the best kind of repose after mental exertion; but the good fortune which had hitherto attended him in so remarkable a manner, still followed him, and frustrated the intentions with which he was at that time actuated.

Those who have at all attended to what was then the state of the arts in this country, and more particularly to the relative condition of artists in society, and who can compare them with the state of both at the present period, will not hesitate to regard the arrival of Mr. West as an important event. In the sequel of this work, it may be necessary to allude to the moral and political causes which affect the progress of the fine arts, and opportunities will, in consequence, arise to show how meanly they were considered, how justly, indeed, it may be said, they were rejected, not only by the British public in general, but even by the nobility. A few eminent literary characters were sensible of their importance, and lamented the neglect to which they were consigned; but the great body of the intelligent part of the nation neither felt their influence, nor were aware of their importance to the commerce and renown of the kingdom. Artists stood, if possible, lower in the scale of society than actors; for Garrick had redeemed the profession of the latter from the degradation to which it had been consigned from the time of the Commonwealth; but Reynolds, although in high repute as a portrait-painter, and affecting a gentlemanly liberality in the style of his living, was not so eminently before the public eye as to induce any change of the same consequence towards his profession.

Mr. West found, on his arrival in London, several American families who had come across the Atlantic after the peace to visit their relations, and he had the unexpected pleasure of hearing that Mr. William Allen, Governor Hamilton, and Dr. Smith, his earliest friends and patrons, were in this country.

Mr. Allen, like many others in the colonies at that time, was both a professional man and a merchant. He held indeed the dignified office of chief justice in Pennsylvania, and was a person of powerful and extensive connections in the mother-country. Hamilton, who had been many years governor, was chiefly indebted to him for the rank which he enjoyed, in consequence of having married his sister.

The naval and military officers who had occasion, during the war, to visit Philadelphia, found in the houses of the governor and Mr. Allen a cordial hospitality which they never forgot. Many of these officers were related to persons of distinction in London, and being anxious to testify to the Americans their grateful sense of the kindness which they had experienced, rendered the strangers objects of hospitable solicitude and marked respect in the first circles of the metropolis. Mr. West, accordingly, on his arrival, participated in the advantages of their favourable reception, and before he was known as an artist, frequented the parties of several of the highest characters in the state.

His first excursion from London was to Hampton Court to see the Cartoons of

Raphael. Soon after, he visited Oxford, Blenheim, and Corsham; whence he proceeded to Bath, where Mr. Allen was at that time residing. Here he remained about a month; and in returning to town made a short tour, in the course of which he inspected the collections of art at Storehead, Fonthill, Wilton House, the Cathedral of Salisbury, and the Earl of Radnor's seat at Longford. At Reading he staid some time with his half-brother, Mr. Thomas West, the eldest son of his father. When he returned to London he was introduced by Mr. Patoune, his travelling companion from Rome, to Reynolds, and a friendship commenced between them which was only broken by death. He also, much about the same time, formed an acquaintance with Mr. Richard Wilson, the landscape painter, to whom indeed he had brought very warm letters of introduction, from some of that great artist's friends and admirers in Italy.

The first lodgings which Mr. West occupied, in his professional capacity, were in Bedford-Street, Covent-Garden, where, when it was understood that he intended to practise, he was visited by all the artists of eminence then in London, and welcomed among them with a cordiality that reflected great honour on the generosity of their dispositions. In this house the first picture which he painted in England was executed. The subject was Angelica and Medora, which, with the Cymon and Iphiginia, painted at Rome, and a portrait of General Moncton, (who acquired so much celebrity by his heroic conduct as second in command under General Wolfe at Quebec,) by the advice of Reynolds and Wilson, he sent to the exhibition in Spring Gardens in 1764.

While he was engaged on the picture of Angelica and Medora, Dr. Markham, then Master of Westminster-School, paid him a visit and invited him to a dinner, at which he introduced him to Dr. Johnson, Mr. Burke; Mr. Chracheroide, and Mr. Dyer. On being introduced to Burke he was so much surprised by the resemblance which that gentleman bore to the chief of the Benedictine monks at Parma, that when he spoke he could scarcely persuade himself he was not the same person. This resemblance was not accidental; the Protestant orator was, indeed, the brother of the monk.

It always appeared to Mr. West that there was about Mr. Burke a degree of mystery, connected with his early life, which their long intercourse, subsequent to the introduction at Dr. Markham's, never tended to explain. He never spoke of any companions of his boyhood, nor seemed to have any of those pleasing recollections of the heedless and harmless days of youth, which afford to most men of genius some of the finest lights and breaks of their fancy; and his writings corroborate the observation. For, although no prose writer ever wrote more like a poet than this celebrated man, his imagery is principally drawn from general nature or from art, and but rarely from any thing local or particular.

The conversation after dinner chiefly turned, on American subjects, in which Mr. Burke, as may well be supposed, took a distinguished part, and not more delighted the Artist with the rich variety and affluence of his mind, than surprised him by the correct circumstantiality of his descriptions; so much so, that he was never able to divest himself of an impression received on this occasion, that Mr. Burke had actually been in America, and visited the scenes, and been familiar with many of the places which he so minutely seemed to recollect. Upon a circumstance so singular, and so much at variance with all that has hitherto been said respecting the early history of this eminent person, it is needless to dilate. The wonder which it may excite I have no means of allaying; but I should not omit to mention here, when Mr. Burke was informed that Mr. West was a Quaker, that he observed, he had always regarded it among the most fortunate circumstances of his life, that his first preceptor was a member of the Society of Friends.

Dr. Markham in 1765 introduced Mr. West to Dr. Newton, Bishop of Bristol, Dr. Johnson, Bishop of Worcester, and Dr. Drummond, Archbishop of York. Dr. Newton engaged him to paint the Parting of Hector and Andromache, and afterwards sat to him for his portrait, in the back ground of which a sketch of this picture was introduced: and for the Bishop of Worcester he painted the Return of the Prodigal Son. The encouragement which he thus received from these eminent divines was highly creditable to their taste and liberality, and is in honourable contrast to the negligence with which all that concerned the fine arts were treated by the nobility and opulent gentry. It is, however, necessary to mention one illustrious exception. Lord Rockingham offered Mr. West a regular, permanent engagement of L700 per annum to paint historical subjects for his mansion in Yorkshire: but the Artist on consulting his friends found them unanimously of opinion, that although the prospect of encouragement which had opened to him ought to make him resolve to remain in England, he should not confine himself to the service of one patron, but trust to the public. The result of this conversation was a communication to Dr. Smith and Mr. Allen, of the attachment he had formed for the lady whom he afterwards married, and that it was his intention to return to America in order to be united to her. In consequence of this, an arrangement took place, by which the father of Mr. West came over to this country with the bride, and the marriage was solemnised on the 2d of September, 1765, in the church of St. Martin in the Fields.

CHAPTER II

Some Notice of Archbishop Drummond —Mr. West paints a Picture for His Grace —His Grace's Plan to procure Engagements for Mr. West as an Historical Painter —Project for ornamenting St Paul's Cathedral with Pictures —Anecdote of Dr Terrick, Bishop of London —The Altarpiece of St Stephens, Walbrook —State of public Taste with respect to the Arts —Anecdotes of Hogarth and Garrick

IN Archbishop Drummond Mr. West found one of the most active and efficient patrons that he had yet met with. This eminent prelate was esteemed, by all who enjoyed the pleasure of his acquaintance, for a peculiar dignity of mind, and a liberality of sentiment that reflected lustre on his exalted rank. He had in his youth travelled on the Continent, and possessing an innate sensibility to the moral influence of the fine arts, had improved his natural taste by a careful inspection of every celebrated work to which he could obtain access. He lamented that in this great, flourishing, and triumphant nation, no just notion of the value of the fine arts was entertained; and on all occasions, when a suitable opportunity presented itself, he never failed to state this opinion, and to endeavour to impress it on others. He frequently invited Mr. West to his table; and the Artist remarked that he seemed to turn the conversation on the celebrity which the patronage of the arts had in all ages reflected on the most illustrious persons and families, addressing himself with particular emphasis to his sons. In the course of one of these conversations, he engaged Mr. West to paint for him the story of Agrippina landing with the ashes of Germanicus, and sent one of the young gentlemen to the library for the volume in which Tacitus describes the circumstances. Having read the passage, he commented on it at some length, in order to convey to Mr. West an idea of the manner in which he was desirous the subject should be treated.

The painter, on returning home, felt his imagination so much excited by the historian's description, and the remarks of the Archbishop, that he immediately began to compose a sketch for the picture, and finished it before going to bed. Next morning he carried it to His Grace, who, equally surprised and delighted to find his own conception so soon embodied in a visible form, requested the Artist to proceed without delay in the execution of the picture.

In the interim, the Archbishop endeavoured, by all the means in his power, to procure encouragement for Mr. West to devote himself exclusively to historical composition; and with this view he set on foot a scheme to raise three thousand guineas to constitute a fund, which would be a sufficient inducement for the Artist, in the first instance, to forego, at least for a time, the drudgery of portrait painting. But the attempt failed: so little was the public disposed to patronise historical subjects from the pencil of a living artist, that after fifteen hundred pounds were subscribed, it was agreed to relinquish the undertaking. As this fact is important to the history of the progress of the arts in this country, I present my readers with a copy of the subscription-paper, with the names and amount of the sums attached to them, by the respective subscribers,

In 1766 Mr. West made a proposal to his friend Bishop Newton, who was then Dean of St. Paul's, to present a gratuitous offering to the Cathedral, by painting a religious subject to fill one of the large spaces which the architect of the building had allotted for the reception of pictures; and speaking on the design one day after dinner at the Bishop's when Reynolds was present, he said that the giving of the Law on Mount Sinai would make an appropriate subject. Reynolds was delighted with the idea of decorating St. Paul's by the voluntary offerings of artists, and offered to paint a Nativity as his contribution. A formal proposal was in consequence made to the Dean and Chapter, who embraced it with much satisfaction. But Dr. Terrick, the Bishop, felt some degree of jealousy at the design being adopted, without consulting him, and set himself so decidedly against it that it was necessarily abandoned. Dr. Newtorn had, in his capacity of Dean, obtained (without reflecting that Terrick had a veto over all) the consent of the other curators of the Cathedral, namely, of the Lord Mayor, the Archbishop of Canterbury, and the King. "But," exclaimed Dr. Terrick, with the energy of an ancient martyr, "I have heard of the proposition, and as I am head of the Cathedral of the metropolis, I will not suffer the doors to be opened to introduce popery." It is to be hoped that the declaration proceeded from the fear implied, and not because Dr. Newton omitted to ask his consent before applying to the King and the Archbishop.

Mr. West was, however, too deeply impressed with the advantage which would accrue to the arts by inducing the guardians of the Church to allow the introduction of pictures, to be discouraged by the illiberality of the Bishop of London. He therefore made a proposal to paint an Altar-piece for the beautiful church of St. Stephen's, Walbrook, and it was accepted. In the same year his friend, Mr. Wilcox, gave him a commission to execute another sacred subject, which he presented to the Cathedral of Rochester, and it is placed over the communion-table. In these biographical sketches it cannot be expected that a history of all Mr. West's numerous works should be related. It is the history of the Artist, not of his works, that is here written; and, therefore, except where the incidents connected with them are illustrative of the state of public feeling towards the arts, it is unnecessary to be more particular. I have, however, prepared a complete catalogue of his designs, with such remarks concerning them as must satisfy any want that may be felt by this systematic omission in the narrative. I should, however, mention that, in this stage of his career, the two of his earliest pictures, which attracted the greatest share of public attention, were *the Orestes and Pylades*, and *the Continence of Scipio*. He had undertaken them on speculation, and the applause which they obtained, when finished, were an assurance of his success and reward. His house was daily thronged with the opulent and the curious to see them; statesmen sent for them to their offices; princes to their bedchambers, and all loudly expressed their approbation, but not one ever enquired the price; and his imagination, which had been elevated in Italy to emulate the conceptions of those celebrated men who have given a second existence to the great events of religion, history, and poetry, was allowed in England to languish over the unmeaning faces of portrait-customers. It seemed to be thought that the genius of the Artist could in no other way be encouraged, than by his friends sitting for their own likenesses, and paying liberally for them. The moral influence of the art was unfelt and unknown; nor can a more impressive instance of this historical truth be adduced, than the following anecdote of Hogarth, which Garrick himself related to Mr. West.

When that artist had published the plates of the Election, he wished to dispose of the paintings, and proposed to do so by a raffle of two hundred chances, at two guineas the stake; to be determined on an appointed day. Among a small number of subscribers, not half what Hogarth expected, Garrick had put down his name; and when the day arrived he went to the artist's house to throw for his chance. After waiting a considerable time no other person appeared, and Hogarth felt this neglect not only as derogatory to his profession, but implying that the subscription had something in it of a mendicant character. Vexed by such a mortifying result of a plan which he had sanguinely hoped would prove, at least, a morning's amusement to the fashionable subscribers, he insisted that, as they had not attended, nor even sent any request to him to throw for them, that Garrick should go through the formality of throwing the dice; but only for himself. The actor for some time opposed the irritated artist; but at last consented. Instead, however, of allowing Hogarth to send them home, he begged that they might be carefully packed up, until his servant should call for them; and on returning to his house, he dispatched a note to the painter, stating that he could not persuade himself to remove works so valuable and admired, without acquitting his conscience of an obligation due to the author and to his own good fortune in obtaining them. And knowing the humour of the person he addressed, and that if he had sent a cheque for the money it would in all probability be returned, he informed him that he had transferred two hundred guineas at his bankers, which would remain at the disposal of Hogarth or his heirs, whether it was or was not then accepted. The charge of habitual parsimony against Garrick was not well founded; and this incident shows that he knew when to be properly munificent. In the acquisition and management of his affluent fortune, it would have been more correct to have praised him for a judicious system of economy, than to have censured him for meanness. It ought to have been considered, that he was professionally required to deal with a class of persons not famed for prudence in pecuniary concerns, and to whom the methodical disbursements of most private gentlemen would probably have appeared penurious.

CHAPTER III

Archbishop Drummond's Address in procuring for Mr. West the Patronage of the King —Singular Court Anecdote of a Lady of Fashion —Character of the King in his Youth —Anecdotes of the King and Queen —The King employs Mr. est to paint the Departure of Regulus —Mr. West's Celebrity as a Skater,—Anecdote of Lord Howe —His Fame as a Skater of great Service in his professional Success

THE coldness with which Archbishop Drummond's scheme for raising three thousand guineas had been received by the persons to whom he had applied, and the prejudice which he found almost universally entertained against the efforts of living genius, chagrined him exceedingly. He regarded the failure as a stigma on the age, and on his country; and, as a public man, he thought it affected himself personally. With this feeling, he declared to the gentlemen who had exerted themselves in the business, that he saw no way of engrafting a taste for the fine arts on the British public, unless the King could be so far engaged in the attempt, as to make it fashionable to employ living artists, according to the bent of their respective talents. But, about this period, the affair of Wilkes agitated the nation; and the Duke of Portland and Lord Rockingham, who were among the most strenuous of Mr. West's friends, being both of the Whig party, undervalued the importance attached to His Majesty's influence and countenance. The Archbishop was not, however, discouraged by their political prejudices; on the contrary, he thought that His Majesty was one of those characters who require to be personally interested in what it is desired they should undertake; and he resolved to make the attempt. The address with which His Grace managed the business, evinced great knowledge of human nature, and affords a pleasing view of the ingenuousness of the King's disposition.

When the picture of Agrippina was finished, the Archbishop invited the most distinguished artists and amateurs to give him their opinion of the work; and satisfied by the approbation which they all expressed, he went to court, and took an opportunity of speaking on the subject to the King, informing His Majesty, at the same time, of all the circumstances connected with the history of the composition; and on what principle he had always turned his conversations with Mr. West to excite an interest for the promotion of the arts in the minds of his family. The dexterity with which he recapitulated these details produced the desired effect. The curiosity of the King was roused, and he told the Archbishop that he would certainly send for the Artist and the picture.

This conversation probably lasted longer than the usual little reciprocities of the drawing-room; for it occasioned a very amusing instance of female officiousness. A lady of distinguished rank, having overheard what passed, could not resist the delightful temptation of being the first to communicate to Mr. West the intelligence of the honour that awaited him. On quitting the palace, instead of returning home, she went directly to his house, and, without disclosing her name, informed him of the whole particulars of the conversation which had passed between the Archbishop and the King. In the evening, Barnard, who had been an attendant on the King from the cradle, and who was not more attached to His Majesty, than he was himself in return affectionately beloved, came to Mr. West, and requested him to be in attendance next morning at the Queen's house, with the picture of Agrippina. In delivering the message, this faithful servant was prompted by his own feelings to give the Artist some idea of His Majesty's real character, which at that time was very much misrepresented to the public; and Mr. West during the long term of forty years of free and confidential intercourse with the King, found the account of Barnard to be in every essential and particular point correct.

The King was described to him as a young man of great simplicity and candour of disposition, sedate in his affections, and deeply impressed with the sanctity of principle; scrupulous in forming private friendships; but, when he had taken any attachment, not easily swayed from it, without being convinced of the necessity and propriety of so doing.

At the time appointed, Mr. West was in attendance with the picture; and His Majesty came into the room where he was waiting. After looking at it some time with much apparent satisfaction, he enquired if it was in a proper light; and, on being told that the situation was certainly not the most advantageous, he conducted the Artist through several apartments himself, till a more satisfactory place was found. He then called several of the domestics into the room, and, indeed, assisted them himself to remove the picture. When the servants had retired, and he had satisfied himself with looking at it, he went out of the apartment and brought in the Queen, to whom he introduced the Artist with so much warmth, that Mr. West felt it at the moment as something that might be described as friendliness.

The Queen, though at this period very young, possessed a natural graciousness of manner, which her good sense and the consciousness of her dignity rendered peculiarly pleasing; so that our Artist was not only highly gratified by the unexpected honour of this distinguished introduction, but delighted with the affability and sweetness of her disposition.

When Their Majesties had examined the picture, the King observed that he understood the same subject had seldom been properly treated. Mr. West answered, that it was, indeed, surprising it should have been neglected by Poussin, who was so well qualified to have done it justice, and to whose genius it was in so many respects so well adapted. His Majesty then told the Queen the history of the picture before them, dwelling with some expressions of admiration on the circumstance of the sketch having been made in the course of one evening after the artist had taken coffee with the Archbishop of York, and shown to His Grace the next morning. Turning briskly round to Mr. West, he said, "There is another noble Roman subject which corresponds to this one, and I believe it also has never been well painted; I mean the final departure of Regulus from Rome. Don't you think it would make a fine picture?" The Artist replied, that it was undoubtedly a magnificent subject. "Then," said His Majesty, "you shall paint it for me;" and, ringing the bell in the same moment, ordered the attendant who answered to bring the volume of Livy in which the event is related, observing to the Queen, in a sprightly manner, that the Archbishop had made one of his sons read to Mr. West; but "I will read to him myself the subject of my picture;" which, on the return of the servant with the book, he did accordingly. And the Artist was commanded to come with the sketch as soon as possible.

The Archbishop was highly delighted at the successful result of his scheme, and augured from the event the happiest influence to the progress of the arts; nor has his patriotic anticipations been unrewarded; for, without question, so great and so eminent a taste for the fine arts as that which has been diffused throughout the nation, during the reign of George the Third, was never before produced in the lifetime of one monarch, in any age or country.

But in relating the different incidents which contributed to bring Mr. West into favourable notice, there is one of a peculiar nature, which should not be omitted. During winter, at Philadelphia, skating was one of the favourite amusements of the youth of that city, and many of them excelled in that elegant exercise. Mr. West, when a boy, had, along with his companions, acquired considerable facility in the art; and having become exceedingly fond of it, made himself, as he grew up to manhood, one of the most accomplished skaters in America. Some of the officers at that time quartered there, also practised the amusement; and, among others, Colonel Howe, who afterwards succeeded to the title of his elder brother, and who, under the name of General Howe, is so well known in the disastrous transactions of the subsequent civil war, which ended in establishing the independence of the United States. In the course of the winter preceding Mr. West's departure for Italy, they had become acquainted on the ice.

In Italy Mr. West had no opportunity of skating; but when he reached Lombardy, where he saw so much beautiful frozen water, he regretted that he had not brought his skates with him from America. The winter, however, which succeeded his arrival in England, proved unusually severe; and one morning, when he happened to take a walk in St. James's park, he was surprised to see a great concourse of the populace assembled on the canal. He stopped to look at them, and seeing a person who lent skates on hire, he made choice of a pair, and went on the ice. A gentleman who had observed his movements, came up to him as he retired to unbuckle the skates, and said, "I perceive, Sir, you are a stranger, and do not perhaps know that there are much better places than this for the exercise of skating. The Serpentine River, in Hyde Park, is far superior, and the basin in Kensington Gardens still more preferable. Here, only the populace assemble; on the Serpentine, the company, although better, is also promiscuous; but the persons who frequent the basin in the Gardens are generally of the rank of gentlemen, and you will be less annoyed among them than at either of the other two places."

In consequence of this information, on the day following, Mr. West resolved to visit the Gardens; and, in going along Piccadilly with that intention, bought a pair of skates, which, on reaching the margin of the ice, he put on, After a few trial-movements on the skirts of the basin, like a musician tuning his violin before attempting a regular piece of composition, he dashed off into the middle of the company, and performed several rounds in the same style which he had often practised in America. While engaged in this manner, a gentleman called to him by name; and, on stopping, he found it was his old acquaintance Colonel Howe.

The Colonel immediately came up, and exclaimed, "Mr. West, I am truly glad to see you in this country, and at this time. I have not heard of you since we parted on the wharf at Philadelphia, when you sailed for Italy; but I have often since had occasion to recollect you. I am, therefore, particularly glad to see you here, and on the ice; for you must know that, in speaking of the American skaters, it has been alleged, that I have learnt to draw the long bow among them; but you are come in a lucky moment to vindicate my veracity."

He then called to him Lord Spencer Hamilton, and some of the Cavendishes, who were also on the ice, and introduced Mr. West to them as one of the American skaters, of whom they had heard him so often speak, and would not credit what he had said of their performance; and he requested Mr. West to show them what, in Philadelphia, was called the Salute. Mr. West had been so long out of practice, that he was at first diffident of attempting this difficult and graceful movement: but, after a few trials, and feeling confidence in himself, he at last performed it with complete success. Out of this trivial incident, an acquaintance arose between him and the young noblemen present. They spoke of his talents as a skater; and their praise, in all their usual haunts, had such an effect, that, in the course of a few days, prodigious crowds of the fashionable world, and of all descriptions of people, assembled to see the American skater. When it was afterwards known to the public that he was an artist, many of the spectators called at his rooms; and he, perhaps, received more encouragement as a portrait-painter on account of his accomplishment as a skater, than he could have hoped for by any ordinary means to obtain.

CHAPTER IV

The King's personal Friendship for Mr. West —Circumstances which led to the Establishment of the Royal Academy —First Exhibition of the Works of British Artists —The Departure of Regulus finished, and taken to Buckingham House —Anecdote of Kirby —The Formation of the Royal Academy —Anecdote of Reynolds —The Academy instituted

THE King, at the period when he was pleased to take Mr. West under his own particular patronage, possessed great conversational powers, and a considerable tincture of humour. He had read much, and his memory was singularly exact and tenacious: his education had, indeed, been conducted with great prudence, and, independent of a much larger stock of literary information than is commonly acquired by princes, he was fairly entitled to be regarded as an accomplished gentleman. For the fine arts he had not, perhaps, any natural taste; he had, however, been carefully instructed in the principles of architecture by Chambers, of delineation by Moser, and of perspective by Kirby; and he was fully aware of the lustre which the arts have, in all ages, reflected on the different countries in which the cultivation of them has been encouraged to perpetuate the memory of great events. His employment of Mr. West, although altogether in his private capacity, was therefore not wholly without a view to the public advantage, and it is the more deserving of applause, as it was rather the result of principle than of personal predilection.

When Mr. West had made a sketch for the Regulus, and submitted it to His Majesty, after some conversation, as to the dimensions, the King fixed on an advantageous part of the walls in one of the principal apartments, and directed that the picture should be painted of a size sufficient to fill the whole space. During the time that the work was going on, the Artist was frequently invited to spend the evening at Buckingham-house, where he was often detained by the King as late as eleven o'clock, on topics connected with the best means of promoting the study of the fine arts in the kingdom. It was in these conversations that the plan of the Royal Academy was digested; but it is necessary to state more particularly the different circumstances which co-operated at this period to the formation of that valuable institution.

At the annual exhibitions of the paintings and drawings, which obtained the premiums of the Society for the Encouragement of Arts, Agriculture, and Commerce, it was then customary with artists to send occasionally their works to be exhibited with those of the competitors, as a convenient method of making themselves known to the public. But the visitors hearing from the newspapers only of the pictures which had gained the prizes, concluded that they were the best in the exhibition; and the works of the matured artists were overlooked in the attention paid to the efforts of juvenile emulation. This neglect mortified the artists, and induced them to form themselves into an association for the exhibition of their own productions. The novelty of this plan attracted much attention, and answered the expectations of those with whom it originated. Such was the state of things with the artists when Mr. West came to England; and to the first exhibition, after his arrival, he sent, as I have already mentioned, three pictures. The approbation which these works obtained, induced the association to elect him one of the directors, and he held this situation till, the society beginning to grow rich by the receipts of the exhibitions, the management of its concerns became an object of ambition. This association was incorporated in 1765, under the designation of the Incorporated Artists.

Chambers and Payne, who were leading members in the Society, being both architects, were equally desirous that the funds should be laid out in the decoration of some edifice adapted to the objects of the institution. This occasioned so much debate, division, and rivalry, among their respective partisans, that Mr. West was induced to resign the office of director, and to withdraw along with Mr. Reynolds (afterwards Sir Joshua) and others, disgusted with the bickering animosities which disgraced the proceedings at their meetings. This transaction made some noise at the time, and it happened on the very day when Mr. West waited on the King, with his sketch of the Departure of Regulus, that the newspapers contained some account of the matter. His Majesty enquired the cause and particulars of the schism, and Mr. West, in stating what they were, mentioned that the principles of his religion made him regard such proceedings as exceedingly derogatory to the professors of the arts of peace.

This led the King to say that he would gladly patronise any association which might be formed more immediately calculated to improve the arts. Mr. West, after retiring from the palace, communicated this to Chambers and Moser, and, upon conferring on the subject with Mr. Coats, it was agreed that the four should constitute themselves a committee of the dissenting artists, to draw up the plan of an academy. When this was mentioned to His Majesty, he not only approved of their determination, but took a great personal interest in the scheme, and even drew up several of the laws himself with his own hand. Nor should one remarkable circumstance be omitted; he was particularly anxious that the whole design should be kept a profound secret, being apprehensive that it might be converted into some vehicle of political influence.

In the mean time the picture of the Departure of Regulus was going forward, and it was finished about the time that the code of rules for the academy was completed. The incorporated artists were also busy, and had elected as their president Mr. Kirby, who had been preceptor in perspective to the King, and who had deservedly gained great celebrity by his treatise on the principles of that branch of art. Kirby, having free access to the royal presence, and never hearing from His Majesty any thing respecting the academy, was so satisfied in his own mind that the rumours, respecting such an institution being intended, were untrue, that, in his inaugural address from the chair, he assured the incorporated artists there was not the slightest intention entertained of establishing a Royal Academy of Art.

When the Departure of Regulus was finished, the King appointed a time for Mr. West to bring the picture to Buckingham-house. The Artist having carried it there, His Majesty, after looking at it some time, went and brought in the Queen by the hand, and seated her in a chair, which Mr. West placed in the best situation for seeing the picture to advantage. While they were conversing on the subject, one of the pages announced Mr. Kirby; and the King consulted Her Majesty in German about the propriety of admitting him at that moment. Mr. West, by his residence among the German inhabitants of Lancaster in America, knew enough of the language to understand what they said, and the opinion of the Queen was that Kirby might certainly be admitted, but for His Majesty to take his own pleasure. The attendant was in consequence ordered to show him in, and Mr. West was the more pleased at this incident, as it afforded him an advantageous opportunity of becoming personally known to Kirby, with whom, on account of his excellent treatise, he had for some time been desirous to become acquainted.

When Kirby looked at the picture he expressed himself with great warmth in its praise, enquiring by whom it had been painted; upon which the King introduced Mr. West to him. It would perhaps be doing injustice to say that the surprise with which he appeared to be affected on finding it the production of so young a man, had in it any mixture of sinister feeling; but it nevertheless betrayed him into a fatal indiscretion. As a preceptor to the King, he had been accustomed to take liberties which ought to have terminated with the duties of that office; he, however, inadvertently said, "Your Majesty never mentioned any thing of this work to me." The tone in which this was uttered evidently displeased the King, but the discretion of the unfortunate man was gone, and he enquired in a still more disagreeable manner, "Who made this frame?" Mr. West, anxious to turn the conversation, mentioned the maker's name; but this only served to precipitate Mr. Kirby into still greater imprudence, and he answered somewhat sharply, "That person is not Your Majesty's workman;" and naming the King's carver and gilder said, "It ought to have been made by him." The King appeared a good deal surprised at all this, but replied in an easy good-humoured way, "Kirby, whenever you are able to paint me a picture like this, your friend shall make the frame." The unhappy man, however, could not be restrained, and he turned round to Mr. West, and in a tone which greatly lessened the compliment the words would otherwise have conveyed, said, "I hope you intend to exhibit this picture." The Artist answered, that as it was painted for His Majesty, the exhibition must depend on his pleasure; but that, before retiring, it was his intention to ask permission for that purpose. The King immediately said, "Assuredly I shall be very happy to let the work be shown to the public."—"Then, Mr. West," added Kirby, "you will send it to my exhibition," (meaning to the exhibition of the Incorporated Artists). "No," interposed the King, firmly, "it must go to my exhibition,—to the Royal Academy." Poor Kirby was thunderstruck; but only two nights before, in the confidence of his intercourse with the King, he had declared that even the design of forming such an institution was not contemplated. His colour forsook him, and his countenance became yellow with mortification. He bowed with profound humility, and instantly retired, nor did he long survive the shock.

* * * * *

On the day following, a meeting of the artists who had separated themselves from the incorporated association, was to be holden in the evening at the house of Wilton the sculptor, in order to receive the code of laws, and to nominate the office-bearers of the Academy. In the course of the morning, Mr. Penny, who was intended to be appointed professor of painting, called on Mr. West and mentioned that he had been with Reynolds, and that he thought, for some unfathomable reason or another, that distinguished artist would not attend the meeting. Soon after, Moser likewise called, and stated the same thing. Mr. West was much perplexed at this information; for it had been arranged with the King that Reynolds, although not in the secret, nor at all consulted in the formation of the Academy, should be the president. He therefore went immediately to his house, and finding him disengaged, mentioned, without alluding to what he had heard, the arrangements formed for instituting an academy, and that a meeting of thirty artists named by the King, of the forty members of which it was intended the Academy should consist, was that evening to take place at Wilton's. Reynolds was much surprised to hear matters were so far advanced, and explained to Mr. West that Kirby had assured him in the most decided manner, that there was no truth whatever in the rumour of any such design being in agitation, and that he thought it would be derogatory to attend a meeting, constituted, as Kirby represented it, by persons who had no sanction or authority for doing what they had undertaken. To this Mr. West answered, "As you have been told by Mr. Kirby that there is no intention to form any institution of the kind, and by me that there is, that even the rules are framed, and the officers condescended on, yourself to be president, I must insist on your going with me to the meeting, where you will be satisfied which of us deserves to be credited in this business."

In the evening, at the usual hour, Mr. West went to take tea with Reynolds, before going to the meeting, and it so fell out, either from design or accident, that it was not served till a full hour later than common, not indeed till the hour fixed for the artists to assemble at Wilton's, so that, by the time they arrived there, the meeting was on the point of breaking up, conceiving that as neither Reynolds nor West had come, something unexpected and extraordinary must have happened. But on their appearing, a burst of satisfaction manifested the anxiety that had been felt, and without any farther delay the company proceeded to carry into effect the wishes of the King. The code of laws was read, and the gentlemen recommended by the King to fill the different offices being declared the officers, the code of laws was accepted. Reynolds was declared president, Chambers treasurer, Newton secretary, Moser keeper, Penny professor of painting, Wale professor of perspective, and Dr. William Hunter professor of anatomy. A report of the proceedings was made to His Majesty next morning, who gave his sanction to the election, and the Academy was thus constituted. The academicians afterwards met and chose a council to assist the president, and visitors to superintend the schools in three branches of art, painting, sculpture, and architecture. Thus, on the 10th December, 1768, under the title of the Royal Academy of the Arts in London, that Institution, which has done more to excite a taste for the fine arts in this country, than any similar institution ever did in any other, was finally formed and established.

CHAPTER V

The opening of the Royal Academy —The Death of General
Wolfe —Anecdote of Sir Joshua Reynolds —New Pictures ordered by the
King —Origin of the Series of Historical Pictures painted for Windsor
Castle —Design for a grand Chapel in Windsor Castle, to illustrate
the History of revealed Religion —His Majesty's Scruples on the
Subject —His confidential Consultation with several eminent
Divines —The Design undertaken

WHEN the Academy was opened, the approbation which *the Regulus* received at the exhibition gratified the King, and he resolved to give Mr. West still farther encouragement. Accordingly, he soon after sent for him, and mentioned that he wished him to paint another picture, and that the subject he had chosen was Hamilcar making his son Hannibal swear implacable enmity against the Romans. The painting being finished it was earned to Buckingham-house, and His Majesty, after looking at it with visible satisfaction, said, that he thought Mr. West could not do better than provide him with suitable subjects to fill the unoccupied pannels of the room in which the two pictures were then placed.

* * * * *

About this period, Mr. West had finished his Death of Wolfe, which excited a great sensation, both on account of its general merits as a work of art, and for representing the characters in the modern military costume. The King mentioned that he heard much of the picture, but he was informed that the dignity of the subject had been impaired by the latter circumstance; observing that it was thought very ridiculous to exhibit heroes in coats, breeches, and cock'd hats. The Artist replied, that he was quite aware of the objection, but that it was founded in prejudice, adding, with His Majesty's permission, he would relate an anecdote connected with that particular point.

* * * * *

"When it was understood that I intended to paint the characters as they had actually appeared in the scene, the Archbishop of York called on Reynolds and asked his opinion, the result of which was that they came together to my house. For His Grace was apprehensive that, by persevering in my intention, I might lose some portion of the reputation which he was pleased to think I had acquired by his picture of Agrippina, and Your Majesty's of Regulus; and he was anxious to avert the misfortune by his friendly interposition. He informed me of the object of their visit, and that Reynolds wished to dissuade me from running so great a risk. I could not but feel highly gratified by so much solicitude, and acknowledged myself ready to attend to whatever Reynolds had to say, and even to adopt his advice, if it appeared to me founded on any proper principles. Reynolds then began a very ingenious and elegant dissertation on the state of the public taste in this country, and the danger which every attempt at innovation necessarily incurred of repulse or ridicule; and he concluded with urging me earnestly to adopt the classic costume of antiquity, as much more becoming the inherent greatness of my subject than the modern garb of war. I listened to him with the utmost attention in my power to give, but could perceive no principle in what he had delivered; only a strain of persuasion to induce me to comply with an existing prejudice,—a prejudice which I thought could not be too soon removed. When he had finished his discourse, I begged him to hear what I had to state in reply, and I began by remarking that the event intended to be commemorated took place on the 13th of September, 1758, in a region of the world unknown to the Greeks and Romans, and at a period of time when no such nations, nor heroes in their costume, any longer existed. The subject I have to represent is the conquest of a great province of America by the British troops. It is a topic that history will proudly record, and the same truth that guides the pen of the historian should govern the pencil of the artist. I consider myself as undertaking to tell this great event to the eye of the world; but if, instead of the facts of the transaction, I represent classical fictions, how shall I be understood by posterity! The only reason for adopting the Greek and Roman dresses, is the picturesque forms of which their drapery is susceptible; but is this an advantage for which all the truth and propriety of the subject should be sacrificed? I want to mark the date, the place, and the parties engaged in the event; and if I am not able to dispose of the circumstances in a picturesque manner, no academical distribution of Greek or Roman costume will enable me to do justice to the subject. However, without insisting upon principles to which I intend to adhere, I feel myself so profoundly impressed with the friendship of this interference, that when the picture is finished, if you do not approve of it, I will consign it to the closet, whatever may be my own opinion of the execution. They soon after took their leave, and in due time I called on the Archbishop, and fixed a day with him to come with Reynolds to see the painting. They came accordingly, and the latter without speaking, after his first cursory glance, seated himself before the picture, and examined it with deep and minute attention for about half an hour. He then rose, and said to His Grace, Mr. West has conquered. He has treated his subject as it ought to be treated. I retract my objections against the introduction of any other circumstances into historical pictures than those which are requisite and appropriate; and I foresee that this picture will not only become one of the most popular, but occasion a revolution in the art."

* * * * *

On Mr. West pausing, the King said, "I wish that I had known all this before, for the objection has been the means of Lord Grosvenor getting the picture; but you shall make a copy for me." His Majesty then entered into some further conversation respecting subjects for paintings to adorn the apartment; and Mr. West suggested that the Death of Epaminondas would, as a classic subject, and with Grecian circumstances, make a suitable contrast with the Death of Wolfe. The King received this idea with avidity; and the conversation being pursued further on the same topic, the Artist also proposed the Death of the Chevalier Bayard for another picture, which would serve to illustrate the heroism and peculiarities of the middle ages. Two pannels were still unprovided; and Mr. West, with submission to His Majesty, begged that he might be allowed to take the incident of Cyrus liberating the Family of the King of Armenia for the one, and of Segestus, and his daughter, brought before Germanicus, for the other. The King was much pleased with the latter idea; a notion being entertained by some antiquaries that the Hanoverian family are the descendants of the daughter.

During the time that our Artist was engaged in these works, he was frequently at the palace with the King; and His Majesty always turned the conversation on the means of promoting the fine arts, and upon the principles which should govern artists in the cultivation of their genius. In one of these conversations, Mr. West happened to remark, that he had been much disgusted in Italy at seeing the base use to which the talents of the painters in that country had been too often employed; many of their noblest efforts being devoted to illustrate monkish legends, in which no one took any interest, while the great events in the history of their country were but seldom touched. This led to some further reflections; and the King, recollecting that Windsor-Castle had, in its present form, been erected by Edward the Third, said, that he thought the achievements of his splendid reign were well calculated for pictures, and would prove very suitable ornaments to the halls and chambers of that venerable edifice. To this incident, the arts are indebted for the series of pictures which bring the victories of Cressy and Poictiers, with the other triumphal incidents of that time, again, as it were, into form and being, with a veracity of historical fact and circumstance which render the masquerades by Vario even a greater disgrace to St. George's Hall than they are to the taste of the age in which they were painted.

* * * * *

In the execution of these different historical subjects, the King took a great personal interests, and one piece became the cause of another, until he actually acquired a feeling like enthusiasm for the arts. When he had resolved to adorn Windsor-Castle with the achievements and great events of the reign of Edward the

Third, he began to think that the tolerant temper of the age was favourable to the introduction of pictures into the churches: at the same time, his scrupulous respect for what was understood to be the usage, if not the law, relative to the case, prevented him for some time from taking any decisive step. In the course of different conversations with Mr. West, on this subject, he formed the design of erecting a magnificent oratory, or private chapel, in the Horns' Court of Windsor-Castle, for the purpose of displaying a pictorial illustration of the history of revealed religion. But, before engaging in this superb project, he thought it necessary to consult some eminent members of the Church, who enjoyed his confidence, as to the propriety of the design. Accordingly, he desired Mr. West to draw up a list of subjects from the Bible, susceptible of pictorial representation, which Christians, of all denominations, might contemplate without offence to their tenets; and he invited Dr. Hurd, afterwards Bishop of Worcester, Dr. Douglas, Bishop of Salisbury, the Dean of Windsor, and several other dignitaries, along with the Artist, to consider the business. He explained to the meeting his scruples, declaring that he did not, in a matter of this kind, owing to his high station in the state, feel himself a free agent; that he was certainly desirous of seeing the churches adorned with the endeavours of art, and would deem it the greatest glory of his reign to be distinguished, above all others in the annals of the kingdom, for the progress and successful cultivation of the arts of peace. "But, when I reflect," said His Majesty, "how the ornaments of art in the churches were condemned at the Reformation, and still more recently in the unhappy times of Charles the First, I am anxious to govern my own wishes not only by what is right, but by what is prudent, in this matter. If it is conceived that I am tacitly bound, as Head of the Church of England, to prevent any such ornaments from being introduced into places of worship; or if it be considered as at all savouring in any degree of a popish practice, however decidedly I may myself think it innocent, I will proceed no farther in the business. But, if the church may be adorned with pictures, illustrative of great events in the history of religion, as the Bible itself often is with engravings, I will gladly proceed with the execution of this design." Little else passed at this interview; but he requested the churchmen to examine the matter thoroughly; and appointed a particular day for them to report to him the result of their investigation: presenting to them, at the same time, a paper, containing a list of thirty-five subjects which he had formed with the Artist, for the decorations of the intended chapel.

On the day appointed, Mr. West again met those eminent members of the hierarchy in the royal presence: when Dr. Hurd reported to His Majesty, that they had very seriously considered the important business which had been confided to them; that, having bestowed on it their gravest attention, they were unanimously of opinion, that the introduction of paintings into the chapel, which His Majesty intended to erect, would, in no respect whatever, violate the laws or usages of the Church of England; and that, having examined the list of subjects, which he proposed should constitute the decorations, there was not one of them, but, which properly treated, even a Quaker might contemplate with edification. This inadvertent observation attracted the King's attention; and he said, that the Quakers were a body of Christians for whom he entertained the very highest respect, and that he thought, but for the obligations of his birth, he should himself have been a Quaker; and he particularly enlarged on their peaceful demeanour and benevolence towards one another.

* * * * *

The result of this conference was, that Mr. West immediately received instructions to make designs from the list of subjects; and afterwards with the King himself, he assisted to form an architectural plan of the chapel, which it was proposed should be ninety feet in length by fifty in breadth. When some progress had been made in the paintings, Mr. Wyat, who had succeeded Sir William Chambers as the royal architect, received orders to carry this plan into execution; and the grand flight of steps in the great staircase, executed by that architect, was designed to lead immediately to a door which should open into the royal closet, in the new chapel of REVEALED RELIGION.

CHAPTER VI

Singular Anecdote respecting the Author of the Letters of Junius —Of Lachlan M'Lean —Anecdote of the Duke of Grafton —Of the Marquis of Lansdowne —Of Sir Philip Francis; Critique on the Transfiguration of Raphael by Sir Philip Francis, and Objections to his opinion

BY the eminent station which Mr. West has so long held among the artists, and admirers of the fine arts, in this country, he became personally acquainted with almost every literary man of celebrity; and being for many years a general visitor at the literary club, immortalised as the haunt of Johnson, Burke, Garrick, Goldsmith, and Reynolds, he acquired, without particularly attending to the literature of the day, an extensive acquaintance with the principal topics which, from time to time, engaged the attention of men of letters. An incident, however, of a curious nature, has brought him to be a party, in some degree, with the singular question respecting the mysterious author of the celebrated letters of Junius. On the morning that the first of these famous invectives appeared, his friend Governor Hamilton happened to call, and enquiring the news, Mr. West informed him of that bold and daring epistle: ringing for his servant at the same time, he desired the newspaper to be brought in. Hamilton read it over with great attention, and when he had done, laid it on his knees, in a manner that particularly attracted the notice of the painter, who was standing at his easel. "This letter," said Hamilton, in a tone of vehement feeling, "is by that damned scoundrel M'Lean."—"What M'Lean?" enquired Mr. West.—"The surgeon of Otway's regiment: the fellow who attacked me so virulently in the Philadelphian newspaper, on account of the part I felt it my duty to take, against one of the officers, a captain, for a scandalous breach of the privileges of hospitality, in seducing the wife of a very respectable man. This letter is by him. I know these very words: I may well remember them," and he read over several phrases and sentences which M'Lean had employed against him. Mr. West then informed the Governor, that M'Lean was in this country, and that he was personally acquainted with him. "He came over," said Mr. West, "with Colonel Barry, by whom he was introduced to Lord Shelburn, (afterwards Marquis of Lansdowne,) and is at present private secretary to His Lordship."

Throughout the progress of the controversy with Junius, Hamilton remained firm in his opinion, that the author was no other than the same Lachlan M'Lean, but at the literary club the general opinion ascribed the letters for some time to Samuel Dyer. The sequel of this anecdote is curious. M'Lean, owing to a great impediment in his utterance, never made any figure in conversation; and passed with most people as a person of no particular attainments. But when Lord Shelburn came into office, he was appointed Under Secretary of State, and subsequently nominated to a Governorship in India: a rapidity of promotion to a man without family or parliamentary interest, that can only be explained by a profound conviction, on the part of his patron, of his superior talents, and perhaps, also, from a strong sense of some peculiar obligation. M'Lean sailed for India in the Aurora frigate, and was lost, in the wreck of that ship, on the coast of Africa. That the letters of Junius were not ascribed to him by any party is not surprising, for his literary talents were unknown to the public; but the general opinion of all men at the time was that they were the production of some person in connection with Lord Shelburn.

Upon this subject, I hold no particular opinion of my own; nor, indeed, should I have perhaps noticed the circumstance at all, but for a recent most ingenious publication which has ascribed these celebrated letters to the late Sir Philip Francis. One thing, however, merits attention in this curious controversy. In the Monthly Magazine for July, 1813, there is an interesting account of a conversation between Sir Richard Phillips and the Marquis of Lansdowne on this subject; in which His Lordship speaks of the obligation to secrecy imposed on himself in the question as having been removed by death; an incidental expression that at once intimated a knowledge of the author, and that he was dead at the time when this conversation took place. The importance of the matter, as an object of literary curiosity, will excuse the introduction, in an abbreviated form, of what passed at that interview, as well as of some minor circumstances connected with the question.

During the printing of Almon's edition of Junius, in which he endeavoured to show that the letters were written by a Mr. Walter Boyd, Sir Richard Phillips, the publisher of that work, sought opinions among the characters then surviving, whose names had been mixed with the writings of Junius; and he addressed himself particularly to the Duke of Grafton, the Marquis of Lansdowne, Mr. Horne Tooke, and Mr. Grattan. Through two friends of the Duke of Grafton he was informed, "that His Grace had endeavoured to live down the calumnies of Junius, and to forget the name of the author; and that, at the period of the publication, offers were made to him of legal evidence on which to convict the author of a libel; but that, as he had then treated the man with contempt, he should decline to disturb him after so great a lapse of time." From this communication it would seem, that the Duke believed that he knew the author, and also that he was still alive.

Sir Richard, on calling upon the Marquis of Lansdowne, to whom he was personally known, found him in his sick chamber, suffering under a general breaking up of the constitution, but in his usual flow of spirits, anecdote, and conversation. On mentioning Almon's new edition of Junius, and that the editor had fixed on Boyd as the author, the Marquis exclaimed, "I thought Almon had known better: I gave him credit for more discernment: the world will, however, not be deceived by him; for there is higher evidence than his opinion. Look at Boyd's other writings: he never did write like Junius; and never could write like Junius. Internal evidence destroys the hypothesis of Almon." Sir Richard then said, that many persons had ascribed these letters to His Lordship; and that the world at large conceived that, at least, he was not unacquainted with the author. The Marquis smiled, and said, "No, no: I am not equal to Junius: I could not be the author; but the grounds of secrecy are now so far removed by death, and changes of circumstances, that it is unnecessary the author of Junius should much longer be unknown. The world are curious about him; and I could make a very interesting publication on the subject. I knew Junius; and I knew all about the writing and production of those letters. But look at my own condition now: I don't think I can live another week: my legs, my strength, tell me so; but the doctors, who always flatter sick men, assure me I am in no immediate danger. They order me into the country, and I am going there. If I live over the summer, which, however, I do not expect, I promise you a very interesting pamphlet about Junius. I will put my name to it: I will set that question at rest for ever."

Sir Richard looked at the swollen limbs and other symptoms threatening the dissolution of this distinguished nobleman; and, convinced that he was, in truth, never likely to see him again, and that the secret of Junius might be lost with him, turned the conversation to the various persons who had, at different times, been named as the Junius; and, after mentioning five or six whose respective pretensions the Marquis treated as ridiculous, His Lordship said, "It is of no use to pursue the matter further at this time. I will, however, tell you this for your guide, Junius has never yet been publicly named. None of the parties ever guessed at as Junius were the true Junius. Nobody has ever suspected him. I knew him, and knew all about it; and I pledge myself, if these legs will permit me, to give you a pamphlet on the subject, as soon as I feel myself equal to the labour." Sir Richard soon after took his leave; and about a week after the Marquis expired.

From Horne Tooke no information could be obtained: whenever Junius was mentioned, he lost the balance of his mind, and indulged himself in so much vanity, conceit, and ingenuity, that it was almost useless to speak with him on the subject.

Mr. Grattan wrote a very candid denial of any knowledge of the matter, in a letter which was printed in the preface to Almon's edition.

Of the pretension afterwards set forward for Dr. Wilmot, I believe it was never entertained or supported by any good evidence: Dr. Francis, the father of Sir Philip, had been long before mentioned, but for what reason I have never been able to ascertain. The answer of Sir Philip himself on the subject is, however, curiously equivocal, at least it so strikes me; although it is generally considered as a decided denial. It is as follows: "The great civility of your letter induces me to answer it, which, with reference merely to its subject-matter, I should have declined. Whether you will assist in giving currency to a silly, malignant falsehood, is a question for your own discretion: to me it is a matter of perfect indifference." But notwithstanding all this, an amusingly mysterious circumstance has, I am informed, transpired since the death of Sir Philip. In a box, it is said, which he carefully deposited with his banker's, and which was not to be opened till after his death, a copy of the publication, "Junius identified," with a common copy of the letters of Junius, were found. I shall offer no comment on this occurrence, for even granting that it was true, it might have been but a playful trick—if Sir Philip Francis was, in any respect, a humorist. But I have already digressed too far from the immediate object of my work; and I cannot make a better amends to my readers than by inserting here a short paper, written by that eminent person, and addressed to Mr. West. It is a critique on the Transfiguration by Raphael, in which Sir Philip evinces considerable ingenuity, by attempting not only to explain a defect in the composition, felt by every man of taste, in the midst of the delight which, in other respects, it never fails to produce, but to show that, so far from being any defect, it is in fact a great beauty.

* * * * *

Transfiguration by Raphael

The title of this picture is a misnomer. The picture itself tells you it is *the Ascension*. The Transfiguration is another incident, which happened long before the Ascension, and is recited in the ninth chapter of St. Luke:—"When the countenance of Jesus was changed, and he became [Greek: etethon] and his clothing was *white*, and lightened." The robe of the ascending Christ is BLUE.

The painter brings different incidents together to constitute one plot. The picture consists of three separate groupes, combined and united in one scheme or action.

I. Jesus ascending perpendicularly into the air, clothed in blue raiment, and attended by two other figures.

II. Some of his disciples on the Mount, who see the ascent, and lie dazzled and confounded by the sight.

III. A number of persons at the bottom of the Mount, who appear to look intently on a young man possessed by a devil, and convulsed. None of them see the Ascension but the young man, or rather the devil, who was in him, does see it. On all similar occasions, those fallen angels know the Christ, and acknowledge him. The other figures are agitated with astonishment and terror, variously and distinctly expressed in every one of them, at sight of the effect which they see is made upon him by some object which *they* do not see.

This is the sublime imagination, by which the lower part of the picture is connected with the upper.

13th July, 1816.   P. FRANCIS.

But although it must be confessed that this comment is exceedingly ingenious, in so far as it explains the painter's design in representing the demoniac boy, as the connecting link between the action on the Mount, and the groupe at the foot of it; yet, upon an examination of the picture, it will be found that it does not exhibit the Ascension, but the Transfiguration; and I beg leave to refer to a letter, from my friend Mr. M'Gillivray, in the Appendix which seems to me as perfectly satisfactory on the subject as any thing of the kind I ever met with. Mr. West was of the same opinion as Mr. M'Gillivray; but in conversing with him on the subject, he did not enter into so distinct an explanation of his reasons for dissenting from the speculation of Sir Philip Francis. In criticism, however, whether the matter in question be works of art, or of literature, the best opinion is exactly that which is the most reasonable; and the point at issue here, is not one in which an artist's judgment can be allowed greater weight than that of any other man.

CHAPTER VII

Observations on Mr. West's Intercourse with the King —Anecdote of the American War —Studies for the Historical Pictures at Windsor Castle —Anecdote of the late Marquis of Buckingham —Anecdote of Sir Joshua Reynolds; and of the Athenian Marbles —Election of Mr. West to the Presidency of the Royal Academy —His Speech to the Academicians on that occasion

WHILE Mr. West was engaged on the series of religious and historical works for the King, he had frequent opportunities of becoming acquainted with political incidents, that a man less intent on his art, and more ambitious of fortune, might have turned to great advantage. This was particularly the case during the American War, for His Majesty knowing the Artist's connections with that country, and acquaintance with some of the most distinguished of the rebels, often conversed with him on the subject; and on different occasions Mr. West was enabled to supply the King with more circumstantial information respecting some important events than was furnished by the official channels. I do not consider myself at liberty, nor this a fit place, to enter upon subjects so little in unison with the arts of peace, or the noiseless tenour of an artist's life; but, among other curious matters that may be thrown out for the investigation of the future historian, is an opinion which prevailed among some of the best informed in America, that when General Washington was appointed to the supreme command of the army, it was with the view and intention of effecting a reconciliation between the two countries. A communication to this purpose is said to have been made by that illustrious man, which communication was never answered, nor ever laid formally before the Privy Council, at least not until more than six weeks after it had been received, and then it was too late. America was lost; and millions spent, and thousands sacrificed afterwards in vain. Whether, indeed, the King ever did know the whole affair, may be doubted.

The mind of Mr. West, however, had no enjoyment in political cabals, in the petty enmities of partizans, or the factious intrigues of party leaders. He was by his art wholly enchanted, and saw in the prospect before him an adequate recompense in fame for all his exertions, his days of labour, and his nights of study. The historical pictures for Windsor Castle cost him many a patient hour of midnight research; for the means to assist his composition, especially in architecture, and the costume of the time, were then far from being so easy of access as they are at present. A long period of preference for classic literature, and the illustration of the Greek and Roman story, had withdrawn the public taste from the no less glorious events of our own annals. To mark, therefore, the epoch, and manners of the age of Poictiers and Cressy, of the Institution of the Garter, and the other heroic and magnificent incidents of the reign of Edward the Third, with that historical truth which the artist thought essential to historical painting, required the inspection of many an ancient volume, and much antiquarian research. In the composition for the Institution of the Garter, the late Marquis of Buckingham offered several suggestions, which were adopted; and on His Lordship mentioning to the King, that Mr. West was descended of the Delawarre family, the head of which bore a distinguished part in the great events of that time, His Majesty ordered Mr. West to insert his own portrait among the spectators represented in the gallery, and immediately over the shield bearing the arms of the Earl of Delawarre. Mr. West himself was not, at that period, acquainted with the descent of his pedigree; but it happened in a conversation one day with Lord Buckingham, that His Lordship enquired from what part of England his family had been originally, and upon Mr. West telling him, His Lordship said, that the land which his ancestors had formerly possessed was become his by purchase; and that the Wests of Long Crandon were sprung from the ancient Earls of Delawarre.

But, except the historical information required for his pictures, in which he was indefatigable, until master of all that could be obtained, Mr. West, following the early and wise advice of Dr. Smith of Philadelphia, wasted none of his time in other literary pursuits. Among his learned and ingenious cotemporaries, however, he acquired a general knowledge of the passing literature of the day, and in consequence, there are few authors of any celebrity, especially the cotemporaries of Johnson, of whom he does not possess interesting anecdotes, as well as an acquaintance with the merit which they were severally allowed to possess.

One day at Sir Joshua Reynolds, after dinner when Dr. Johnson, Goldsmith, and Burke were present, the conversation turned on the degree of excellence which sculpture attained among the Greeks. It was observed incidentally, that there was something in the opinion of the ancients, on this subject, quite inexplicable; for, in the time of Alexander the Great, although painting was allowed to have been progressive, sculpture was said to have declined, and yet the finest examples of the art, the Apollo and Venus, were considered as the works of that period. Different theories were sported on this occasion, to explain this seeming contradiction; none of them, however, were satisfactory. But, on the arrival of the Athenian marbles, which Lord Elgin brought to this country, Mr. West was convinced, at the first sight of them, of the justness of ancient criticism, and remembered the conversation alluded to.

Perhaps I may be allowed to mention here, without impropriety, that I was at Athens when the second cargo of these celebrated sculptures was dispatched; that I took some interest in getting the vessel away; and that I went with her myself to the island of Idra. Two circumstances occasioned this interference on my part;—an Italian artist, the agent of Lord Elgin, had quarrelled about the marbles with Monsieur Fauvelle, the French Consul, a man of research and taste, to whom every traveller that visited Athens, even during the revolutionary war, might have felt himself obliged. Fauvelle was, no doubt, ambitious to obtain these precious fragments for the Napoleon Museum at Paris; and, certainly, exerted all his influence to get the removal of them interdicted. On the eve of the departure of the vessel, he sent in a strong representation on the subject to the governor of the city, stating, what I believe was very true, that Lord Elgin had never any sufficient firman or authority for the dilapidations that he had committed on the temples. Luseri, the Italian alluded to, was alarmed, and called on me at the monastery of the Roman propaganda, where I then resided; and it was agreed between us, that if any detention was attempted, I should remonstrate with the governor, and represent to him that such an arrest of British property would be considered as an act of hostility. But our fears were happily removed. No notice was taken by the governor of Monsieur Fauvelle's remonstrance. In the evening I embarked on board the vessel at the Pireus, and next morning was safely landed on the island of Idra, where the vessel, after remaining a day or two, sailed for Malta.

But to return to the biographical narrative. On the death of Sir Joshua Reynolds, in 1791, Mr. West was unanimously elected President of the Royal Academy. The choice was not more a debt of gratitude on the part of the Institution, to one who had essentially contributed to its formation, than a testimony of respect deservedly merited by the conduct and genius of the Artist who, when the compass, number, and variety of his pictures are considered, was, at that period, decidedly the greatest historical painter then living, who had been born a British subject. This event, at once so honourable to his associates and himself, was confirmed by the sanction of His Majesty on the 24th of March, 1792; on which occasion, on taking the chair, Mr. West addressed the Academicians to the following effect:—

* * * * *

"GENTLEMEN,

"The free and unsolicited choice with which you have called me to fill this chair, vacated by the death of that great character, Sir JOSHUA REYNOLDS, is so marked an instance of your friendship and good opinion, that it demands the immediate acknowledgment of my thanks, which I beg you to accept.

"I feel more sensibly the dignity to which you have raised me, as I am placed in succession after so eminent a character, whose exalted professional abilities, and very excellent discourses delivered under this roof, have secured a lasting honor to this Institution and to the country; while his amiable dispositions, as a man, will make his loss to be long regretted by all who had the happiness to know him.

"HIS MAJESTY having been graciously pleased to approve and confirm the choice which you have made of me as your President, it becomes my duty, as far as my humble abilities will permit, to study and pursue whatever may be the true interest, the prosperity, and the glory of this ACADEMY. In the prosecution of this duty, I can make no doubt of success, when I reflect that all the departments and classes of this Institution are filled with men of established professional reputation, selected from professors of the three great branches of art, which constitute the objects of your studies and, when I see this union of abilities strengthened by many ingenious productions of other able artists, who, although they have not as yet the honour of belonging to this body, will, nevertheless, enable us to maintain the accustomed brilliancy of our Exhibitions, and, consequently, to secure to us the approbation of a liberal and judicious public.

"The Exhibitions are of the greatest importance to this Institution; and the Institution is become of great importance to the country. Here ingenious youth are instructed in the art of design; and the instruction acquired in this place, has spread itself through the various manufactures of this country, to which it has given a taste that is able to convert the most common and simple materials into rare and valuable articles of commerce. Those articles the British merchant sends forth into all the quarters of the world, where they stand preeminent over the productions of other nations.

"But important as this is, there is another consequence of a more exalted kind; I mean, the cultivating of those higher excellences in refined art, which have never failed to secure to nations and to the individuals who have nourished them, an immortality of fame, which no other circumstances have been equally able to perpetuate. For it is by those higher and more refined excellences of painting, sculpture, and architecture, that Grecian and Roman greatness are transmitted down to the age in which we live, as if it was still in existence. Many centuries have elapsed since Greeks and Romans have been overthrown and dissolved as a people; but other nations, by whom similar refinements were not cultivated, are erased from the face of the earth, without leaving any monument or vestige to give the demonstration that they were ever great.

"It may, therefore, be fairly assumed, that an ACADEMY, whose objects and effects are so enlightened and extensive as those which are prosecuted here, is highly worthy of the protection of a patriot-king, of a dignified nobility, and of a wise people.

"Another circumstance, permit me, gentlemen, to mention, because I can speak of it with peculiar satisfaction, as important to the best interests of this Institution, and with the fullest assurance of its truth, from the personal knowledge I have had of you all, and the intimacy in which I have stood with most of you; it is this, that I have ever found you steadily determined to support the regulations under which this ACADEMY has been governed, and brought to its present conspicuous situation, and by an attention to which, we shall always be sure to go on with the greatest prudence and advantage.

"It is a matter of no less satisfaction to me, when I say, that I have always observed your bosoms to glow with gratitude and loyal affection to our August Founder, Patron, and Benefactor. I am convinced, it is your wish to retain His friendship, and the friendship of every branch of His Illustrious Family. I know these to be your sentiments, and they are sentiments in which I participate with you. In every situation of my life it shall be my invariable study to demonstrate my duty to my sovereign, my love for this Institution, and my zeal for the cultivation of genius, and the growth of universal virtue."

Mr. West having thus been raised to the head of an institution, embracing within itself the most distinguished artists at that time in the world, it might be proper to pause here to review the merits of the works and exertions by which he acquired this eminent honour, had he not, since that time, attained still more distinction in his profession. I shall, however, for the present, suspend the consideration of his progress, as an artist, to trace his efforts, in the situation of President of the Royal Academy, to promote the improvement of the pupils, by those occasional discourses, which, in imitation of the excellent example of Sir Joshua Reynolds, he deemed it an essential part of his duty to deliver.

CHAPTER VIII

The first Discourse of Mr. West to the Students of the
Academy —Progress of the Arts —Of the Advantages of Schools of
Art —On the Natural Origin of the Arts —Of the Patronage which
honoured the Patrons and the Artists —Professional Advice —
Promising State of the Arts in Britain

MR. West's first discourse to the students of the Royal Academy was delivered on the 10th of December, 1792, on the occasion of the distribution of the prizes. Without ostensibly differing in his views from Sir Joshua Reynolds, who by his lectures acquired, as an author, a degree of celebrity equal to his fame as an artist, the new President confined himself more strictly to professional topics. He recalled to the remembrance of his auditors the circumstances in which the Academy originated, and reminded them of the encouragement which the efforts of artists had received from the countenance which the King had given to the arts. "Let those," said he, "who have traced the progress of the fine arts, say among what people did the arts rise, from such a state as that in which they were in this country about forty years ago, to the height which they have attained here in so short a period. In ancient Greece, from the retreat of Xerxes, when they were in their infancy, to the age of Alexander the Great, when they reached their maturity, we find a period of no less than one hundred and fifty years elapsed. In Rome we can make no calculation directly applicable; for among the Romans the habit of employing Greek artists, and the rage of collecting, suffered no distinct traces to be left of the progress of the arts among them. Even in architecture, to which their claims were most obviously decided, we see not sufficiently the gradations of their own peculiar taste and genius. But in modern Italy, leaving out of view the age of Cimabue, and even that of Giotto, and dating from the institution of the Academy of St. Luke at Florence, it required a hundred and fifty years to produce a Michael Angelo, a Raphael, and a Bramante."

Mr. West, after a few general observations on the necessary union between moral conduct and good taste, adverts to the alleged influence which such institutions as the Royal Academy have in producing mannerism in the students, than which nothing can be more obnoxious to the progress of refined art. "But," said he, "while I am urging the advantage of freedom and nature in study to genius, let me not be misunderstood. There is no untruth in the idea that great wits are allied to great eccentricity. Genius is apt to run wild if not brought under some regulation. It is a flood whose current will be dangerous if it is not kept within proper banks. But it is one thing to regulate its impetuosity, and another very different to direct its natural courses. In every branch of art there are certain laws by which genius may be chastened; but the corrections gained by attention to these laws amputate nothing that is legitimate, pure, and elegant. Leaving these graces untouched, the schools of art have dominion enough in curbing what is wild, irregular, and absurd.

"A college of art founded in this part of the world cannot be expected, like a college of literature, to lay before its young members all that may be necessary to complete their knowledge and taste. What is to be had from books may be obtained almost every where; but the books of instruction by which the artist alone can be perfected, are those great works which still remain immoveable in that part of the world, where the fine arts in modern times have been carried to their highest degree of perfection. I trust a period will come, when this Academy will be able to send the young artist, not from one spot or one seminary to another, but to gather improvement from every celebrated work of art wherever situated. But the progress and all future success of the artist must depend upon himself. He must be in love with his art or he will never excel in it.

"That the arts of design were among the first suggestions vouchsafed by Heaven to mankind, is not a proposition at which any man needs to start. This truth is indeed manifested by every little child, whose first essay is to make for itself the resemblance of some object to which it has been accustomed in the nursery.

"In the arts of design were conveyed the original means of communicating ideas, which the discoverers of countries show us to have been seized upon, as it were involuntarily, by all the first stages of society. Although the people were rude in knowledge and in manners, yet they were possessed of the means by which they could draw figures of things, and they could make those figures speak their purposes to others as well as to themselves. The Mexicans conversed in that way when Cortes came among them; and the savages of North America still employ the same means of communicating intelligence.

"When, therefore, you have taken up the arts of design as your profession, you have embraced that which has not only been sanctioned by the cultivation of the earliest antiquity, but to which their is no antiquity prior, except that of the visible creation.

"Religion itself in the earlier days of the world, would probably have failed in its progress without the arts of design, for religion was then emblematic; and what could an emblematic theology do without the aid of the fine arts, and especially the art of sculpture? Religion and the arts, in fact, sprung up together, were introduced by the same people, and went hand in hand, first through the continent of Asia, then through Egypt, next through Greece and her colonies, and in process of time through every part of Italy, and even to the north of Europe. In the pagodas of India, in some caverns of Media, and among various ruins in Persia, are still to be seen the early monuments of emblematic art, and wrought in all the possible difficulties of skill.

"When in the space of two thousand years, after the erection of some of those monuments, the fine arts came to be established in Greece in a better spirit as to taste, a higher estimation could not be annexed to any circumstance in society, than was given to the arts by the wise and elegant inhabitants of that country. They regarded them as their public records, as the means of perpetuating all public fame, all private honour, and all valuable instruction. The professors of them were considered as public characters who watched over the events that were passing, and who had in their hands the power of embodying them for ever. And is not this still the case with the artists of every country, how varied soever may be its maxims, or its system of action, from those of Greece? Is the artist indeed not that watchman who observes the great incidents of his time, and rescues them from oblivion?

"When he turns from these views to contemplate the patronage which has been given to the fine arts, will he have less reason to esteem his profession,—a profession so richly cherished by all the greatest characters of the earth? and which in return has immortalised its patrons. Posterity has never ceased to venerate the names of the Cosmos and Lorenzos who sought art, and fostered to their full maturity the various talents of their countrymen. The palace of the Medici, still existing in Florence, exhibits not only in its treasures the proofs of their munificence, but also within its walls those apartments and offices for artists, in every branch which those great men considered requisite to the decoration of their residence. And history has immortalised the solicitude with which the vast fortune of the family, acquired originally in honourable commerce, and rising gloriously to sovereign power, was made contributory to the nourishing of the arts and literature; of every thing that was intellectual, liberal, and great."

Mr. West then continued to enumerate the honour which the successive illustrious patrons of the fine arts have acquired, deducing from it motives of emulation to the young students to strive for similar distinction, that their names may be mingled with those illustrious races and families to whom Heaven is pleased to give superior eminence and influence in human affairs. In doing this he took occasion to animadvert on the base adulation of the artists of France in the age of Louis XIV.; or rather of the dishonour which the patronage of that monarch has drawn upon himself, by the unworthy manner in which he required the artists to gratify his personal vanity. He then proceeded to give some professional advice. "I wish," said he, "to leave this impression on the minds of all who hear me, that the great alphabet of our art is the human figure. By a competent knowledge of that figure the painter will be enabled to give a more just character and motion to that which he intends to delineate. When that motion is actuated by passion, and combined with other figures, groups are formed. These groups make words, and these words make sentences; by which the painter's tablet speaks a universal language;" and he concluded with saying, "Gentlemen, It is a great treasure and a great trust which is put into our hands. The fine arts were late before they crossed the British Channel, but now we may fairly pronounce that they have made their special abode with us. There is nothing in this climate unpropitious to their growth; and if the idea has been conceived in the world, enough has been done by the artists of Great Britain to disprove it. I know that I am speaking to the first professional characters in Europe in every branch of elegant art, as well as those who are most distinguished in taste and judgment. If there be diffused through this country a spirit of encouragement equal to the abilities which are ripe to meet it, I may venture to predict that the sun of our arts will have a long and glorious career."

CHAPTER IX

Discourse to the Royal Academy in 1794. —Observations on the Advantage of drawing the Human Figure correctly —On the Propriety of cultivating the Eye, in order to enlarge the Variety of our Pleasures derived from Objects of Sight —On characteristic Distinctions in Art —Illustrations drawn from the Apollo Belvidere, and from the Venus de Medici; comprehending critical Remarks on those Statues

THE prizes in the Royal Academy being distributed every second year, on the 10th of December, 1794, Mr. West delivered another Discourse, in which he took a more scientific view of the principles of the fine arts, than in the desultory observations which constituted the substance of his first lecture. As it contained much valuable information, mixed up with remarks incidental to the occasion, I have taken the liberty of abstracting the professional instruction from the less important matter, in order to give what deserves to be preserved and generally known in a concise and an unbroken form.

"It may be assumed," said Mr. West, "as an unquestionable principle, that the artist who has made himself master of the drawing of the human figure, in its moral and physical expression, will succeed not only in portrait-painting, but in the delineation of animals, and even of still life, much better than if he had directed his attention to inferior objects. For the human figure in that point of consideration, in which it becomes a model to art, is more beautiful than any other in nature; and is distinguished, above every other, by the variety of the phenomena which it exhibits, arising from the different modifications of feeling and passion. In my opinion, it would, therefore, be of incalculable advantage to the public, if the drawing of the human figure were taught as an elementary essential in education. It would do more than any other species of oral or written instruction, to implant among the youth of the noble and opulent classes that correctness of taste which is so ornamental to their rank in society; while it would guide the artizan in the improvement of his productions in such a manner, as greatly to enrich the stock of manufactures, and to increase the articles of commerce; and, as the sight is perhaps the most delightful of all our senses, this education of the eye would multiply the sources of enjoyment.

"The value of the cultivated ear is well understood; and the time bestowed on the acquisition of the universal language of music, is abundantly repaid by the gratification which it affords, although not employed in the communication of knowledge, but merely as a source of agreeable sensation. Were the same attention paid to the improvement of the eye, which is given to that of the ear, should we not be rewarded with as great an increase of the blameless pleasures of life,—from the power of discriminating hues and forms,—as we derive from the knowledge of musical proportions and sounds? The cultivation of the sense of sight would have such an effect in improving even the faculty of executing those productions of mechanical labour which constitute so large a portion of the riches of a commercial and refined people, that it ought to be regarded among the mere operative classes of society as a primary object in the education of their apprentices. Indeed, it may be confidently asserted, that an artizan, accustomed to an accurate discrimination of outline, will, more readily than another not educated with equal care in that particular, perceive the fitness or defects of every species of mechanical contrivance; and, in consequence, be enabled to suggest expedients which would tend to enlarge the field of invention. We can form no idea to ourselves how many of the imperfections in the most ingenious of our machines and engines would have been obviated, had the inventors been accustomed to draw with accuracy.

"But, to the student of the fine arts, this important branch of education will yield but few of the advantages which it is calculated to afford, unless his studies are directed by a philosophical spirit, and the observation of physical expression rendered conducive to some moral purpose. Without the guidance of such a spirit, painting and sculpture are but ornamental manufactures; and the works of Raphael and Michael Angelo, considered without reference to the manifestations which they exhibit of moral influence, possess no merit beyond the productions of the ordinary paper-hanger.

"The first operation of this philosophical spirit will lead the student to contemplate the general form of the figure as an object of beauty; and thence instruct him to analyse the use and form of every separate part; the relation and mutual aid of the parts to each other; and the necessary effect of the whole in unison.

"By an investigation of this kind, he will arrive at what constitutes character in art; and, in pursuing his analysis, he will discover that the general construction of the human figure in the male indicates strength and activity; and that the form of the individual man, in proportion to the power of being active, is more or less perfect. In the male, the degree of beauty depends on the degree of activity with which all the parts of the body are capable of performing their respective and mutual functions; but the characteristics of perfection of form in the female are very different; delicacy of frame and modesty of demeanour, with less capability to be active, constitute the peculiar graces of woman.

"When the student has settled in his own mind the general and primary characteristics, in either sex, of the human figure, the next step will enable him to reduce the particular character of his subject into its proper class, whether it rank under the sublime or the beautiful, the heroic or the graceful, the masculine or the feminine, or in any of its other softer or more spirited distinctions. For the course of his studies will have made him acquainted with the moral operations of character, as they are expressed upon the external form; and the habit of discrimination, thus acquired, will have taught him the action or attitude by which all moral movements of character are usually accompanied. By this knowledge of the general figure, this habitual aptitude to perceive the beauty and fitness of its parts, and of the correspondence between the emotions of the mind and the actions of the body, he will find himself in possession of all that Zeuxis sought for in the graces of the different beautiful women whom he collected together, that he might be enabled to paint a proper picture of Helen; and it is the happy result of this knowledge which we see in the Apollo Belvidere and the Venus de Medici, that renders them so valuable as objects of study.

"But the student must be always careful to distinguish between objects of study and objects of imitation; for the works which will best improve his taste and exalt his imagination, are precisely those which he should least endeavour to imitate; because, in proportion to their appropriate excellences, their beauties are limited in their application.

"The Apollo is represented by the mythologists as a perfect man, in the vigour of life; tall, handsome and animated; his locks rising and floating on the wind; accomplished in mind and body; skilled in the benevolent art of alleviating pain; music his delight, and poetry and song his continual recreation. His activity was shown in dancing, running, and the manly exercises of the quoit, the sling, and the bow. He was swift in his pursuits, and terrible in his anger.—Such was the Pythian Apollo; and were a sculptor to think of forming the statue of such a character, would he not determine that his body, strong and vigorous from constant exercise, should be nobly erect; that, as his lungs were expanded by habits of swiftness in the chase, his chest should be large and full; that his thighs, as the source of movement in his legs, should have the appearance of enlarged vigour and solidity; and that his legs, in a similar manner, should also possess uncommon strength to induce and propagate the action of the feet? The nostrils ought to be elevated, because the quick respirations of running and dancing would naturally produce that effect; and, for the same reason, the mouth should appear to be habitually a little open. While his arms, firm and nervous by the exercise of the quoit, the sling, and the bow, should participate in the general vigour and agility of the other members;—and would not this be the Apollo Belvidere?

"Were the young artist, in like manner, to propose to himself a subject in which he would endeavour to represent the peculiar excellences of woman, would he not say, that these excellences consist in a virtuous mind, a modest mien, a tranquil deportment, and a gracefulness in motion? And, in embodying the combined beauty of these qualities, would he not bestow on the figure a general, smooth, and round fulness of form, to indicate the softness of character; bend the head gently forward, in the common attitude of modesty; and awaken our ideas of the slow and graceful movements peculiar to the sex, by limbs free from that masculine and sinewy expression which is the consequence of active exercise?—and such is the Venus de Medici. It would be utterly impossible to place a person so formed in the attitude of the Apollo, without destroying all those amiable and gentle associations of the mind which are inspired by contemplating 'the statue which enchants the world.'

"Art affords no finer specimens of the successful application of the principles which I have laid down than in those two noble productions."

CHAPTER X

Discourse to the Academy in 1797. —On the Principles of Painting and Sculpture —Of Embellishments in Architecture —Of the Taste of the Ancients —Errors of the Moderns —Of the good Taste of the Greeks in Appropriations of Character to their Statues —On Drawing —Of Light and Shade —Principles of Colouring in Painting —Illustration —Of the Warm and Cold Colours —Of Copying fine Pictures —Of Composition —On the Benefits to be derived from Sketching;—and of the Advantage of being familiar with the Characteristics of Objects in Nature

IN the discourse which Mr. West delivered from the chair of the Academy in 1797, he resumed the subject which he had but slightly opened, in that of which the foregoing chapter contains the substance. I shall therefore endeavour in the same manner, and as correctly as I can, to present a view of the mode in which he treated his argument, and as nearly as possible in his own language.

"As the foundation of those philosophical principles," said Mr. West, "on which the whole power of art must rest, I wish to direct the attention of the student, especially in painting and sculpture, to an early study of the human figure, with reference to proportion, expression, and character.

"When I speak of painting and sculpture, it is not my intention to pass over architecture, as if it were less dependent on philosophical principles, although what

I have chiefly to observe with respect to it relates to embellishment;—a branch of art which artists are too apt to regard as not under the control of any principle, but subject only to their own taste and fancy. If the young architect commences his career with this erroneous notion, he will be undone, if there is any just notions of his art in the country.

"It is, therefore, necessary, as he derives his models from the ancients, that he should enquire into the origin of those embellishments with which the architects of antiquity decorated their various edifices. In the prosecution of his enquiries, he will find that the ornaments of temples and mausolea, may be traced back to the periods of emblematic art, and become convinced that the spoils of victims, and instruments of sacrifice, were appropriate ornaments of the temple; while urns, containing the ashes of the dead, and the tears of the surviving friends, were the invariable decorations of the mausoleum. The good taste of the classic ancients prevented them from ever intermixing the respective emblems of different buildings, or rather, in their minds custom preserved them from falling into such an incongruous error, as to place the ornaments belonging to the depositaries of the dead on triumphal arches, palaces, and public offices. They considered in the ornaments the character and purpose of the edifice; and they would have been ashamed to have thought it possible that their palaces might be mistaken for mausolea, or their tombs for the mansions of festivity.

"Is the country in which we live free from the absurdities which confound these necessary distinctions? Have we never beheld on the porticoes of palaces, public halls, or places of amusement, the skins of animals devoted to the rites of the pagan religion, or vases consecrated to the ashes of the dead, or the tears of the living? Violations of sense and character, in this respect, are daily committed. We might, with as much propriety, adorn the friezes of our palaces and theatres with the skulls and cross thigh-bones of the human figure, which are the emblems of death in every country throughout modern Europe!

"I do not here allude to any particular work, nor do I speak of this want of principle as general. It is indeed impossible that I can be supposed to mean the latter; for we have among us men distinguished in the profession of architecture, who would do honour to the most refined periods of antiquity. But all are not equally chaste; and in addressing myself to the young, it is my duty to guard them against those deviations from good taste, which, without such a caution, they might conceive to be sanctioned by some degree of example. It is my wish to preserve them from the innovations of caprice and fashion, to which the public is always prone; and to assure the youth of genius, that while he continues to found the merit of his works on true principles, he will always find, notwithstanding the apparent generality of any fashion, that there is no surer way, either to fame or fortune, than by acting in art, as well as life, on those principles which have received the sanction of experience, and the approbation of the wise of all ages.

"I shall now return to the consideration of painting and sculpture.

"The Greeks, above all others, afford us the best and most decided proofs of the beauty arising from the philosophical consideration of the subject intended to be represented. To all their deities a fixed and appropriate character was given, from which it would have perhaps been profanity to depart. This character was the result of a careful consideration of the ideal beauty suitable to the respective attributes of the different deities. Thus in their Jupiter, Neptune, Hercules, Vulcan, Mars, and Pluto; the Apollo, Mercury, Hymen, and Cupid, and also in the goddesses Juno, Minerva, Venus, Hebe, the Nymphs and Graces; appeared a vast discrimination of character, at the same time as true an individuality as if the different forms had been the works of Nature herself.

"In your progress through that mechanical part of your professional education, which is directed to the acquisition of a perfect knowledge of the human figure, I recommend to you a scrupulous exactness in imitating what is immediately before you, in order that you may acquire the habit of observing with precision every object that presents itself to your sight. Accustom yourselves to draw all the deviations of the figure, till you are as much acquainted with them as with the alphabet of your own language, and can make them with as much facility as your letters; for they are indeed the letters and alphabet of your profession, whether it be painting or sculpture.

"These divisions consist of the head, with its features taken in three points of view, front, back, and profile; the neck in like manner, also the thorax, abdomen, and pelvis; thigh, knee, leg, ankle, the carpus, metacarpus, and toes; the clavicula, arm, fore-arm, wrist, carpus, metacarpus, and fingers. While you are employed on these, it would be highly proper to have before you the osteology of the part on which you are engaged, as in that consists the foundation of your pursuit. And, in this period of your studies, I recommend that your drawings be geometrical, as when you draw and study a column with its base and capital. At the same time you should not neglect to gain a few points in perspective, particularly so far as to give effect to the square and cylinder, in order to know what constitutes the vanishing point, and point of distance, in the subject you are going to draw.

"After you have perfected yourselves in the parts of the figure, begin to draw the Greek figures entire, with the same attention to correctness as when you drew the divisions in your earlier lessons. Attend to the perspective according to the vanishing point opposite to your eye. You will naturally seek to possess your mind with the special character of the figure before you;—and of all the Grecian figures, I would advise you to make from the Apollo and Venus a general measurement or standard for man and woman, taking the head and its features, as the part by which you measure the divisions of those figures.

"Light and shade must not be neglected; for what you effect in drawing by the contour of the figure, light and shade must effect with the projections of those parts which front you in the figure. Light and shade there produce what becomes outline to another drawing of the same object in a right angle to the place where you sit.

"It seems not impossible to reduce to the simplicity of rule or principle, what may have appeared difficult in this branch of art to young students, and may have been too often pursued at random by others. All forms in nature, both animate and inanimate, partake of the round form more than of any other shape; and when lighted, whether by the sun or flame, or by apertures admitting light, must have two relative extremes of light and shadow, two balancing tints, the illuminated and the reflected, divided by a middle tint or the aerial. The effect of illumination by flame or aperture, differs from that of the sun in this respect; the sun illuminates with parallel rays, which fall over all parts of the enlightened side of the subject, while the light of a flame or an aperture only strikes directly on the nearest point of the object, producing an effect which more or less resembles the illumination of the sun in proportion to the distance and dimensions of the object.

"Let us then suppose a ball to be the object on which the light falls, in a direction of forty-five degrees or the diagonal of a square, and at a right angle from the ball to the place where you stand. One half of the ball will appear illuminated, and the other dark. This state of the two hemispheres constitutes the two masses of light and shadow. In the centre of the mass of light falls the focus of the illumination in the ball; between the centre of the illumination and the circle of the ball, where the illumination, reaches its extremity, lies what may be called the transparent tint; and between it and the dark side of the ball lies the serial or middle tint. The point of darkness, the extreme of shade, is diametrically opposite to the focus of illumination, between which and the aerial tint lies the tint of reflection. If the ball rests on a plain, it will throw a shadow equal in length to one diameter and a quarter of the ball. That shadow will be darker than the shade on the ball, and the darkest part will be where the plain and ball come in contact with each other.

"This simple experiment, whether performed in the open sun-shine, or with artificial illumination, will lead you to the true principles of light and shade over all objects in nature, whether mountains, clouds, rocks, trees, single figures, or groups of figures. It would therefore be of great use, when you are going to give light and shade to any object, first to make the experiment of the ball, and in giving that light and shade, follow the lessons with which it will furnish you.

"You will find that this experiment will instruct you, not only in the principles of light and shade, but also of colours; for that there is a corresponding hue with respect to colours is not to be disputed. In order to demonstrate this, place in the ball which you have illuminated, the prismatic colours, suiting their hues to those of the tints. Yellow will answer to the focus of illumination, and the other secondary and primary hues will fall into their proper places. Hence, on the enlightened side of a group or figure, you may lay yellow, orange, red, and then violet, but never on the side where the light recedes. On that side must come the other prismatic colours in their natural order. Yellow must pass to green, the green to blue, and the blue to purple. The primary colours of yellow, orange, and red, are the warm colours, and belong to the illuminated side of objects; the violet is the intermediate, and green, blue, and purple are the cold colours, and belong to the retiring parts of your composition.

"On the same principle, and in the same order, must be placed the tints which compose the fleshy bodies of men and women, but so blended with each other, as to give the softness appropriate to the luminous quality and texture of flesh; paying attention, at the same time, to reflections on its surface from other objects, and to its participation of their colours. The latter is a distinct circumstance arising from accident.

"When the sun illuminates a human body, in the same manner as the ball, the focus of the illumination in that body will partake of the yellow; and the luminous or transparent tint, will have the orange and the red. These produce, what is called, the carnation. The pure red, occasioned by the blood, lies in the lips, cheeks, joints, and extremities of the figure, and no where else. On the receding side of the focus is the local colour of the flesh, and on the receding side of that is the greenish tint; in the shade will fall the cold or bluish, and in the reflection will fall the tint of purple. The most perfect tint of ground, from which to relieve this arrangement of colours, is either blue, grey, or purple, for those colours partake of the complexion of the watery sky in which the rainbow appears, or the ground which best exhibits the prismatic colours.

"In acquiring a practical knowledge of the happiest manner of distributing your colours according to nature, it will assist you, if you will copy with attention some pieces of Titian, Correggio, Reubens, and Vandyke; the masters in whose works you will most eminently find the system pursued, which I have endeavoured to illustrate by the simple image of the ball.

"Having passed from the antique school, to that in which you draw after the living figure, still adhere to that scrupulous exactness of drawing with which you first set out; marking with precision the divisions of the figure. After you have made yourselves acquainted with the drawing of the living figure, you must then begin to enlarge your lines, and to give softness and breadth, to direct your attention to what constitutes style and character, and to discriminate these from what constitutes manner.

"To assist you in this nice discrimination, consult the prints and works of Michael Angelo, Raphael, and Hannibal Carracci. In them you will find the strongest and purest evidence of style and character, yet all differing from each other, and all equally brought out of nature. I do not recommend them with a view that you should adopt the style and character of any of them; but to show from those great examples, that style and character, although ever founded in nature, are as various as the individual genius of every artist; that they are as free to you as they were to those masters; that if you will consult your own mind, you will draw forth a style and character of your own, and therefore no man can ever be excused for sinking into a mannerist.

"And I cannot omit to observe here, that in the order of your studies, your mental powers should be cherished and brought into action by reading and reflection, but not until you have acquired practical facility in your art. Too often it happens, and I have seen it with concern, that the presumption of youth, or the errors of instruction, have reversed this order, and have carried many to attempt essays of research and learning, before they were well grounded in the principles of professional practice. What other consequences can follow from such a course, but that the student will turn in discontent from his own productions, because they fall short of the ideas in his mind; and induce him, perhaps, to abandon, with disgust, a profession in which he might have shone with distinction, had he taken a right method of cultivating his own powers!

"The great masters were all at an early age great in the mechanical department of their art, before they established any name by their philosophical style and character. Michael Angelo, when a mere youth, modelled and drew in a manner which astonished his own master. Raphael, at not more than nineteen years of age, rivalled his instructor, Pietro Perugino, in his executive talent; and, owing to this, he was enabled, at the age of only twenty-five, to send forth his two great works, *the Dispute on the Sacrament*, and *the School of Athens*. Guido, Bernini, and many others of the first class, pursued the same course of study, and were in the full possession of their powers very young. Vandyke, before he was twenty years old, assisted Reubens in his greatest works; and on a certain occasion, when the pupils of Reubens were amusing themselves in the absence of their master, one of them happened to fall against 'the Mother,' in the Descent from the Cross, which Vandyke repaired in a manner so admirable, that when the painter came next to the picture, he expressed himself surprised at the excellence of his own work, and said, that he thought he had not done that arm so well. In a word, wherever we find the executive power high at an early age, whether in painting or sculpture, we have an assurance of future excellence, which nothing but indolence can prevent. And, to give that early facility correctness of execution, remember and pursue the great maxim of Apelles:—

"'*Nulla dies, sine linea.*'

"The young artist may, indeed, draw lines every day and every hour with advantage, whether it be to amuse himself in society or in the fields. He should accustom himself to sketch every thing, especially what is rare and singular in nature. Let nothing of the animate creation on the earth, or in the air, or in the water, pass you unnoticed; especially those which are distinguished for their picturesque beauty, or remarkable for dignity of form or elegance of colour. Fix them distinctly in your sketch-book and in your memory. Observe, with the same contemplative eye, the landscape, the appearance of trees, figures dispersed around, and their aerial distance, as well as lineal forms. In this class of observations, omit not to observe the light and shade, in consequence of the sun's rays being intercepted by clouds or other accidents. Besides this, let your mind be familiar with the characteristics of the ocean; mark its calm dignity when undisturbed by the winds, and all its various states between that and its terrible sublimity when agitated by the tempest. Sketch with attention its foaming and winding coasts with distant land, and that awful line which separates it from the Heavens. Replenished with these stores, your imagination will then come forth as a river, collected from little springs, spreads into might and majesty. The hand will then readily execute what it has been so practised in acquiring; while the mind will embrace its subjects with confidence, by being so well accustomed to observe their picturesque effect."

CHAPTER XI

Discourse —Introduction —On the Philosophy of Character in Art—
Of Phidias —Of Apelles —Of the Progress of the Arts among the
Moderns —Of Leonardo da Vinci —Of Michael Angelo, Raphael,
and Bartolomeo —Of Titian —Of the Effects of Patronage

IT is not my intention to give all the discourses which Mr. West addressed to the students of the Academy, but only those which contain, what may be called, illustrations of the principles of his art. The following, however, is so interesting and so various in its matter, that it would be improper in me to make any attempt to garble or abridge it, beyond omitting the mere incidental notice of temporary circumstances.

"The discourse which I am about to deliver, according to usual custom on the return of this day, must be considered as addressed more immediately to those among the students, who have made so much progress in art, as to be masters of the human figure, of perspective, and of those other parts of study, which I have heretofore recommended as the elements of painting and sculpture; and who are therefore about to enter on the higher paths of professional excellence. It will consequently be my object, now, to show how that excellence is to be attained; and this will best be done, as I conceive, by showing how it has been attained by others, in whom that excellence has been most distinguished in the ancient and modern world. By pursuing the principles on which they moved, you have the best encouragement in their illustrious example, while, by neglecting those principles, you can have no more reason to hope for such success as they met with, than you can think of reaching a distant land, without road or compass to direct your steps.

"The ground which I shall propose for your attention is this—to investigate those philosophical principles on which all truth of character is founded, and by which that sublime attainment, the highest refinement in art, and without which every thing else is merely mechanical, may be brought to a decided point, in all the variety by which it is distinguished through the animated world.

"On this ground, and on this alone, rose Phidias and Apelles to the celebrity which they held among the Greeks; and among the Italians, Leonardo da Vinci, Michael Angelo, Raphael, Titian, Correggio, and some others, who became the completest models in sculpture and painting. Their predecessors, indeed, in both countries, had for a considerable time been preparing the way, but not having equally studied the best means, or those means not having been equally before them, it was reserved of course for the great characters I have mentioned, to unite philosophical with professional truth, and to exhibit to the world in their works the standards of style. From the same source arose another consequence, ever worthy and pleasing to be mentioned;—the exhibition of those perfections was always accompanied by that ardent patronage, which not only cheered their minds, and invigorated their powers, but has left a glory on their country, which no subsequent events have been able to obliterate, and which never will be obliterated in any country where the sublimity of art, involving the most refined embellishments of civilized life, is cherished by those who are in a capacity to cherish it.

"In a very early period of the arts in Greece, we meet with a circumstance which shows the advantages derived from consulting with philosophy, if it does not also show the origin and outset of those advantages. The circumstance to which I allude is, that in the period when the sculptors contented themselves with the stationary forms and appearance of figures, in imitation of their predecessors, the Egyptians; at that time they began to submit their works to the judgment of philosophers, one of whom, being called in to survey a statue, which a sculptor, then eminent, was going to expose to public view, remarked, that the human figure before him wanted motion, or that expression of intellect and will, from which motion and character too must arise; for man had a soul and mind, which put him at the head of the animal creation, and, therefore, without that soul and mind, the form of man was degraded.

"This observation touched the point, then, necessary to be obviated, in order to overcome the primitive rudeness which still attached to sculpture; and without the application of the principle contained in the observation, sculpture and painting too might have stood still for ages. And from what other source than the principles of philosophic study, or, in other words, from reflection on the moral powers or passions of man, their several effects, as produced in their workings on the human figure, could that improvement be obtained? It was the constant employment of the philosophic mind, to study those causes and effects, and to reduce them to a more distinct display for the truth and utility of their own writings. The philosophers were, therefore, the most likely to assist the artist in those displays of character which tended to illustrate the truth of his own works. Nor on this account is it any disparagement to the artists of those days, when philosophic studies were confined to particular classes of men, that this moral view of art was not sufficiently taken up by the more mechanical part of the profession.

"Thus, however, the opening was made to the important expression of character. And the lesson suggested by the philosopher alluded to, is not confined to the Greeks alone. I wish, young gentlemen, to leave it in all its force upon your minds. For if the figures you design, whether singly or in groups, have not their actions correspondent to what their minds appear to be pursuing, they will suit any other subject as well as that in which they are placed. This remark is the more worthy of attention, as it does not apply to any of the figures of the Grecian masters whom I have mentioned. The figure by Phidias on Monte Cavallo at Rome, the Apollo, the Laocoon, the Venus, the Hercules, and the fighting gladiator, are all perfect on the just principles I have mentioned. There is no room for amendment; their propriety is unquestionable; their truth eternal. And so in the works of modern art, we see the same truth and perfection in the Capella Sestina by Michael Angelo, in the Supper by Leonardo da Vinci at Milan, in the Cartoons by Raphael, the St. Peter Martyr by Titian, and the Note by Correggio.

"Having mentioned the figure on Monte Cavallo, representing, as you all know, a young man curbing a horse, I cannot help stopping to remark, that if any work of sculpture ever demonstrated more strongly the value of uniting philosophic science with that of art, for the production of character, it is that work by Phidias. Never did the power of art express more evidently than is done in the head of the young man, that every feature is moved by an internal mental power, and corresponds in the most perfect truth with what we see to be the labouring passion. When we view it in front we are astonished that the mouth does not speak. No observer ever thinks that the head is a block of stone. But the whole group is masterly on the most refined principles of science. It was intended to be seen at an elevated point, as well as at a distant one. All its forms, therefore, are grand without the minutiae of parts; its effects are striking and momentary; and in every circumstance considered, it is plainly the work of consummate genius and science united.

"Was it possible that in an age which gave a Phidias to the Greeks, there should not have been a Pericles to reward, by his patronage, merit so exalted?

"We may carry the same reflections into the progress of the pencil. As the Greeks became refined in their minds, they gained an Apelles to paint, and an Alexander to patronise. We are not enabled now to speak of the works of that great master. His figure of Alexander, in the character of young Ammon, is described as his master-piece. Such was the expression with which the hand grasped the thunder-bolt, that it seemed actually to start from the pannel. The expression and force of character given to the whole, was equally marvellous. And when we consider the refinement to which the human mind had then arrived among the Greeks, the immense value which they put upon the works of that artist, and that they were too wise to devote their applause to things which fell short of consummate excellence, we cannot doubt but it was by the cultivation of the public mind that the arts reached such attainments among them. What must have been their exquisite state when the simple line drawn by Protogenes,—in the consciousness of his acknowledged perfection, and which was intended to announce the man who drew it, as much as if he had told his name,—was so far excelled by another simple line over it by Apelles, that the former at once confessed himself outdone? Those two lines, simple as they were, were by no means trifling in their instruction. They gave us, as it were, an epitome of the progress which the arts had long been making in Greece. For if the drawing of a simple line, of such a master as Protogenes, who was conceived by many to hold the first pencil in the world, was surpassed, to his great surprise, by another, how high must refinement have been raised by the exertions of the artists in a period so emulous of perfection!

"The stages in the progress of modern art, have been frequently distinguished by ages similar to those which succeed one another in the human growth. We may safely assert, that in the infantine and youthful period of modern art, literature and science were only seen in their infancy and growth. The opening of nature displayed in the works of Massaccio; the graces exhibited in those of Lorenzo Ghiberti; and the advancement in perspective made by one or two others, kept pace nearly with that progress in philosophy which appeared in the best writings of those days. As the one took a larger step in the next stage or period, the other stepped forth in a like degree at the same time; so that in Leonardo da Vinci we see the great painter and the great philosopher: his painting most clearly refined in its principles, and enlarged in its powers by his philosophical studies. As a philosopher, and especially in those parts of knowledge which were most interesting to his profession, he laid that foundation of science which has ever since been adopted and admired. As a painter, he not only went far beyond his predecessors, but laid down those principles of science in the expression of individual character, and of a soul and figure specifically and completely appropriated to each other, which opened the way to the greatness acquired by those who followed him in his studies. In that point of excellence, Leonardo da Vinci was original; and it was the natural result of a mind like his, formed to philosophical investigation, and deeply attentive to all the variety of appearances by which the passions are marked in the human countenance and frame. These he traced to their sources: he found them in their radical principles, and by his knowledge of these principles, his expression of character became perfected.

"The *nature* exhibited by Massaccio had not gone to that extent of expression. It however spoke a soul: he drew forth an inward mind on the outward countenance: he gave a character; but that character was not so discriminated as to become the index of one particular passion more than another; or to decide, for instance, the head of Jupiter from that of a Minerva: so at with the aid, of different types, it should not befit a Saviour or a Magdalene.

"We must take along with us in this review, that the splendid patronage of the house of Medici came forward, to meet, and to cherish the happy advancements made by the masters of those days; so that Florence, which was then the greatest seat of the arts, was no less brilliant and illustrious in the generosity which strove to perpetuate them, than in the genius by which they had been cultivated.

"Leonardo da Vinci, by the principles which he so effectually realised, has always been considered as having established the manly as well as the graceful age of modern art. But manhood is never so fixed as to be incapable of progress. The manhood then attained in art was capable of farther advancement beyond the growth which the powers of Da Vinci had given it. This was eminently illustrated by the sublimity of style which was attained by the genius of Michael Angelo and of Raphael;—quality equally original in both, although issuing from different principles. In the former, it was founded on that force and grandeur, allied to poetic spirit, which rises above all that is common, and leaves behind it all that is tame and simply correct; which, not content with engaging the senses, seizes on the imagination, while it never departs from truth. In the latter, it was made up of the beautiful and graceful, which attracts by the assemblage of whatever is most perfect and elevated in the character or subject.

"Raphael coming somewhat later than Michael Angelo on the theatre of art, had the advantage of many of that master's works, as well as of all the improvements which had been made before. His life was a short one, and the first studies of it were almost lost in the dry school of Pietro Perugino. But he soon found his way to the philosophy of Leonardo da Vinci, and to the profound principles on which his admirable expression of character is founded. The dignity of drapery, and of light and shade, opened by Bartolomeo, invited his studies; and the sublimity of the human figure in the sculptures of his cotemporary, Michael Angelo, fastened on his contemplation. Thus he entered at once, as it were, into the inheritance of whatever excellencies had been produced before him. With these advantages he was called to adorn the apartments of the Vatican. And can we wonder that his first works there, at the age of seven-and-twenty, were the Dispute on the Sacrament, and the School of Athens?

"But what was it that contributed very much to the production of those works? It was not the profound studies of Raphael's mind, but the spirit of the age which warmed those studies.—It was a great age, in which learning and science were become diffused, at least throughout Europe:—a great age replete with characters studious of philosophy; and, therefore, fond of the instruction conveyed by the arts;—fond of those high and more profound compositions which entered into the spirit of superior character, and made some study and research necessary to develope their beauties. To meet the taste of such an age, the two first public works of

Raphael, above mentioned, were well suited, inasmuch as they were intended to convey the comparative views of theology and human science, or, in other words, the improvement of the human mind arising from the two great sources of national wisdom and revealed light. It must not also be forgotten, that while the spirit of the age was warming his mind to the peculiar dignity of theme and style which marks his works, the generous and noble patronage of the papal court was exerting its utmost power to immortalise him, and every other great master that arose within the circle of its influence. Their merit and their fame found as animated a protector in Leo X. as Phidias experienced in Pericles, or Apelles in Alexander the Great.

"As the Florentine and Roman schools were thus gradually refined in the excellence of design and character, by the aid of philosophical studies; so the Venetian masters were equally indebted to the like studies, without which, they would never have reached their admirable system of colouring. If any have conceived otherwise, they have taken a very superficial view of their system. Where is there greater science concerned than in the whole theory of colours? It employed the investigation of Newton; and shall that pass for a common or easy attainment which took up so much of his profound studies? The Venetian masters had been long working their way to the radical principles of this science, not only for a just and perfect arrangement of their colouring, but for that clear and transparent system in the use of it, which have equally marked that school in the days of its maturity under Titian. He it was who established, on unerring principles, founded on nature and truth, that accomplished system which John Bellini had first laboured to discover, and in which Giorgioni had made further advancements. Besides his zeal in his profession, Titian was born in that higher rank of life which might be supposed to give him an easier access to the elegant studies of philosophic science; and he had prosecuted, with great ardour, the science of chemisty, the better to understand the properties of colour, their homogeneous blendings, purity, and duration; as well as the properties of oils, gums, and other fluids, which might form the fittest vehicles to convey his colours upon canvass.

"The elegant Charles V. was to Titian in liberal pratronage what Leo X. was to Raphael. That munificent prince carried him into Spain, where his works laid the foundation of the Spanish school in painting, and gave a relish for that art to all the succeeding monarchs.

"What has been remarked respecting Titian and the Venetian school, is equally true of that of Correggio among the Lombard painters. The mind of Correggio appears evidently, by his works, to have been profoundly enlightened; and especially in the philosophical arrangement and general doctrine of colours. What has been said by some concerning the low circumstances of his fortune, (which is not true,) neither proves the obscurity of his birth, nor that philosophical researches were out of his reach, or beside his emulation. The truth is, that he was born of a very honourable family, and was accomplished in the elegancies of life; not that it is necessary for any man to have the advantages of birth, in order to become enlightened by science in any way whatever. The patronage which attended him was of the most elevated kind, being dispensed by the illustrious houses of Mantua and Modena, as well as by the institution of the Doma of Parma. But what is by no means less worthy of our notice is, that of all the masters who have risen up in any of the schools of Italy, not one has been the means of giving success and reputation to those who have followed any of their respective styles equally with Correggio. The ineffable softness, sweetness, and grace in his paintings, have never varied in their effects with the course of time. And they who have since partaken of these powers in his style, have very generally become great masters, (distinguished by none of the excesses which have sometimes attended the imitation of other models,) and successful in gainng the approbation and favour of the world.

"The paths pursued by those great examples must become yours, young gentlemen, or you can neither be eminent in colouring, nor sure in the execution of your art. It is possible, that by habits of practice, handed over from one to another, or by little managements in laying colours on the canvass, where little or nothing of the general science has been studied and attained, many may so far succeed as to avoid glaring errors, and a violation of those first principles which have their foundation in nature. But that success is at all times extremely hazardous and dependent on chance. More frequently it has introduced invincible conflicts between the primary and secondary colours, to the ruin of harmony and aerial perspective, and to the overthrow of the artist, whenever the picture is glanced upon by the eye of scientific discernment. Contemptible are the best of such managements, ever in the hands of those that know them best, compared with a full and masterly possession of the philosophy by which this part of your art must be guided. If the ordonnance of colour, on each figure and on the whole, is not disposed according to the immutable laws of the science, no fine effect, or accordant tones of colours, can possibly be produced. There is, therefore, but one way to make sure of success, and to raise your characters in this point, and that is by making yourselves masters of the whole philosophy of colours, as Titian and Correggio did, and some others, in whose works, from first to last, the minutest scrutiny will never find a colour misplaced or prejudiced by its disposition with others.

"To be perfect, is the emulation which belongs to those arts in which you are engaged, and the anxious hope of the country in which you live. To animate you to that perfection, is the object of what I have now addressed to you. I am persuaded it is your ambition to be perfect. This Academy looks with pleasure on the progress of your studies, as it may look with pride on the high and cultivated state to which the arts have been raised among us ever since they have had the establishment of a regular school. It is no flattery to the present aera in Britain to say, that in no age of the world have the arts been carried in any country to such a summit as they now hold among us, in so short a period as half a century at most. Among the Greeks some centuries had elapsed, amidst no little emulation in the arts, before they obtained an Apelles. In modern Italy, without going as far back as we might, it took up a century from the appearance of Massaccio to the perfection of a Raphael. If, then, the British school has risen so much more speedily to that celebrity in art, which it is too well known and established to need any illustration here, what should hinder her professors from becoming the most distinguished rivals of the fame acquired by the Greeks and Italians, with a due perseverance in the studies which lead to perfection, and with those encouragements and support of patronage which are due to genius?

"As the source of that patronage, we look up with affectionate gratitude to the benign and flattering attention of our most gracious Sovereign, to whose regard for the elegant arts, and munificent disposition to cherish every enlargement of science, and improvement of the human mind, his people are indebted for this public seminary, his own favoured Institution, and the first which this country has ever been so fortunate as to see established. Under his royal patronage and support, this Academy has risen to its present strength and flourishing condition. His patronage, which would be improperly estimated by mere expenditure, in a country not similar in the latitude of government, or in the controul over revenue, to ancient Greece or modern Italy, but properly by its diffusive influence, has been the source of every other patronage in the country; has inspired that refined taste and ardour for elegant arts, which have given in fact a new character to the people, and has raised within and without this Academy that body of distinguished men, whose works have contributed to immortalise his reign, as his love for the arts has become the means of immortalising them.

"The patronage which has flowed from other quarters, deserves very honourable mention; and is of so much importance, that without it the spirit of art must droop, and the very profession of it be contracted in every situation whatever. It is not by the influence and support of any individual character, how elevated soever, or how warm soever in his attachment to taste and elegance, that the extent of professional talents spread through a country, can be effectually sustained with adequate encouragements. It is the wealthy and the great, who are commonly trained by their situations to the perception of what is elegant and refined, that must come forward in such an illustrious undertaking. It is only they who can meet every where the merit, let it be disseminated as it may, which is entitled, to distinction. Without the patronage of such, the arts could never have obtained their high meridian in Greece and Italy. Had not the communities and rich individuals in Greece taken the arts under their protection, not all the encouragement of Pericles, or of Alexander the Great, could have drawn forth that immense body of painting and sculpture which filled the country. Had the patronage of Italy rested with the popes and princes, unaccompanied by those munificent supports which flowed from the churches and convents, as well as from private individuals of rank and wealth, the galleries of that country could never have been so superbly filled as they were, nor could those collections have been made from thence, which have filled so many galleries and cabinets elsewhere.

"These facts are not to be denied; but they also lead us to another lesson, which is, that the patronage so generally dispensed was for the protection of living genius, and that they by whom it was so dispensed sought no other collections than the works of native and living artists. On any other ground there can be no such thing as patronage. Nothing else is worthy of that name. The true and generous patron of great works selects those which are produced by the talents existing around him.

By collecting from other countries, he may greatly enrich himself, but can never give celebrity to the country in which he lives. The encouragement extended to the genius of a single artist, though it may produce but one original work, adds more to the celebrity of a people, and is a higher proof of true patriotic ardour, and of a generous love for the progress of art, than all the collections that ever were made by the productions of other countries, and all the expenditures that ever were bestowed in making them. Did the habits of our domestic circumstances, like those of Italy, permit the ingenious student to have access to those works of established masters, procured by the spirit of their noble and wealthy possessors, and of many distinguished amateurs on the most liberal terms, and with the honourable purpose of forming the taste, as well as enriching the treasures, of the country, every thing would then be done, which is wanting to complete the public benefit of such collections, and the general gratitude to which they who have made them would be entitled. So abundant are the accomplished examples in art already introduced among us, that there would then be no necessity for students to run to other countries for those improvements which their own can furnish.

"It cannot be improper at any time to make these remarks; while it must also be observed, that the patronage held forth by many great and noble characters needs no spur; and the means projected by other spirited individuals in opulent stations, for extending and perpetuating the works of British masters, fall short in no degree of the most fervid energies and examples, of which any country has been able to boast.

"It is your duty, young gentlemen, to become accomplished in your professions, that you may keep alive those energies and examples of patronage, when you come to draw the attention of the world to your own works. It is by your success that the arts must be carried on and preserved here. Patronage can only be expected to follow what is eminently meritorious, and more especially that general patronage diffused through the more respectable ranks of society, which is to professional merit, what the ocean is to the earth;—the great fund from whence it must ever be refreshed, and without whose abundance, conveyed through innumerable channels, every thing must presently become dry, and all productions cease to exist."

CHAPTER XII

Discourse —Introduction —Of appropriate Character in Historical Composition —Architecture among the Greeks and Romans —Of the Athenian Marbles —Of the Ancient Statues —Of the Moses and Saviour of Michael Angelo —Of the Last Judgment of Michael Angelo —Of Leonardo da Vinci —Of Bartolomeo —Of Raphael —Of Titian, and his St. Peter Martyr —Of the different Italian Schools —Of the Effects of the Royal Academy —Of the Prince Regent's Promise to encourage the Fine Arts

AFTER a careful examination of all the remaining notes of Mr. West, it appeared to me, that the discourse which he delivered on the 10th of December, 1811, was the only one that required particular notice, after those which I have already introduced. In some respects it will, perhaps, be deemed the most interesting of the whole.

"The few points," said the President, "upon which I mean to touch in the present Discourse, are those which more immediately apply to the students, who are generously striving to attain excellence in the first class of refined art,—historical painting.

"Whether their exertions are directed to painting, or the sister arts, architecture and sculpture, the first thing they must impress upon their minds, and engraft upon every shoot of their fancy, is that of the appropriate character, by which the subject they are about to treat, is distinguished from all other subjects. On this foundation, all the points of refined art which are, in the truest sense, intellectual, invariably rest; for without justness of character the works of the pencil can have but little value, and can never entitle the artist to the praise of a well-governed genius, or of possessing that philosophical precision of judgment, which is the source of excellence in the superior walk of his profession. At the same time, let it be indelibly fixed in your minds, that when decided character is to be given, that character must be accompanied by correctness of outline, whether it be in painting or in sculpture. Any representation of the human figure, in the higher department of art, wanting these requisites, is, to the feelings of the educated artist, deficient in that, for the loss of which no other excellency can compensate.

"Architecture.—This department of art received its decided character from the Greeks. They distinctly fixed the embellishments to the several orders; and, by their adaptation of these embellishments and orders, their buildings obtained a distinct and appropriate character, which declared the uses for which they were erected.

"The Romans, in their best era of taste, copied their Grecian instructors in that appropriate character of embellishment which explained, at a glance, the use of their respective buildings; but, in their latter ages, they declined from this original purity; and it is the fragments of that corruption, in which they lost the characteristic precision of the Greeks, that we have seen of late years employed upon many of our buildings. The want of mental reflection in employing the orders of architectures with a rational precision as to character, produces the same sort of deficiency which we find in an historical picture; where, although each figure, in correct proportion, be well drawn, with drapery elegantly folded, yet, not being employed appropriately to the subject, affords no satisfaction to the spectator.

"The Greeks were in architecture what they were in sculpture; and it is to them you must look for the original purity of both. We feel rejoiced, that the exertions recently made by a noble personage to enrich our studies in both of these departments of art are such, that we may say, London has become the Athens for study. It is the mental power displayed in the Elgin marbles that I wish the juvenile artist to notice. Look at the equestrian groups of the young Athenians in this collection, and you will find in them that momentary motion which life gives on the occasion to the riders and their horses. The horse we perceive feels that power which the impulse of life has given to his rider; we see in him the animation of his whole frame; in the fire of his eyes, the distention of his nostrils, and in the rapid motion of his feet, yielding to the guidance of his rider, or in the speeding of his course: they are, therefore, in perfect unison with the life in each. At this moment of their animation, they appear to have been turned into stone by some majestic power, and not created by the human hand. The single head of the horse, in the same collection, seems as if it had, by the same influence, been struck into marble, when he was exerting all the energy of his motion.

"These admirable sculptures, which now adorn our city, are the union of Athenian genius and philosophy, and illustrate my meaning respecting the mental impression which is so essentially to be given to works of refined art. It was this point which the Grecian philosophers wished to impress on the minds of their sculptors, not to follow their predecessors the Egyptians in sculpture, who represented their figures without motion, although nearly perfect in giving to them the external form. 'It is the passions,' said they, 'with which man is endowed, that we wish to see in the movements of your figures.' This advice of the philosophers was felt by the sculptors, and the Athenian marbles are the faithful records of the efficacy of that advice.

"That you may distinctly perceive and invariably distinguish what we mean by appropriate character in art, particularly in sculpture, I would class with these sculptures, the Hercules, the Apollo, the Venus, the Laocoon, and the Gladiator. In these examples you will find what is appropriate in character to subject, united with correctness of outline; and it is this combination of truths which has arrested the attention of an admiring world, ever since they were produced; and which will attract to them the admiration of after ages, so long as the workings of the mind on the external form can be contemplated and understood.

"Now let us see what works there are since the revival of art in the modern world, which rest on the same basis of appropriate character and correctness of outline, with those of the ancient Greeks.

"The Moses which the powers of Michael Angelo's mind has presented to our view, claims our first attention. In this statue the points of character, in every mode of precise, determinate, and elevated expression, have been carried to a pitch of grandeur which modern art has not since excelled. In this figure of Moses, Michael Angelo has fixed the unalterable standard of the Jewish lawgiver,—a character delineated and justified by the text in inspired sculpture. The character of Moses was well suited to the grandeur of the artist's conceptions, and to the dreadful energy of his feelings. Accordingly, in mental character, this figure holds the first station in modern art; and I believe we may venture to say, had no competitor in ancient, except those of the Jupiter and Minerva by Phidias. But the Saviour, all meekness and benevolence, which Michael Angelo made to accompany the Moses, was not in unison with his genius. The figure is mean, but slightly removed from an academical figure, and in no point appropriate to the subject: so are most of the single figures of the artist, in his great work on the Day of Judgment; but his groups in that composition are every where in character, and have not their rivals either in painting or sculpture. His Bacchus claims our admiration, as being appropriate to the subject, by the same excellence in delineation which distinguish the groups in the Day of Judgment. No person can have a higher veneration than I have for that grandeur of character impressed on the figures by Michael Angelo; but it is the fitness of the characters and of the action to the subject, to which I wish to draw your attention, and not to pour out praise on those points, in which he and other eminent masters are deficient. On this occasion, I must therefore be permitted to repeat, that most of the single figures in his great work of the Day of Judgment, are deficient in the fitness of appropriate character, and in the fitness of appropriate action to the subject; although as single figures they demand our admiration. But excellent as they are, they are but the ingenious adaptation of legs, arms, and heads, to the celebrated Torso, which bears his name, and which served as the model to most of his figures. All figures in composition, however excellent they may be in delineation, which have not their actions and expressions springing from the subject in which they are the actors, can only be considered as academical efforts, without the impress of mental power, and without any philosophical attention to the truth of the subject which the artist intended to illustrate.

"Leonardo da Vinci is the first who had a full and right conception of the principle which I wish to inculcate, and he has shown it in his picture of the Last Supper. But it is necessary to distinguish what parts of the picture deserve consideration. It is the decision, the appropriate character of the apostles to the subject; the significance of expression in their several countenances, and the diversity of action in each figure; their actions seemingly in perfect unison with their minds, and their figures individually in unison with their respective situations; some are confused at the words spoken by our Saviour: "There is one amongst you who shall betray me;" others are thrown under impressions of a different feeling. In this respect the picture has left us without an appeal, either to nature or to art. But Da Vinci failed in the head of our Saviour. He has failed in his attempt to combine the almost incompatible qualities of dignity and meekness which are demanded in the countenance of the Saviour. He had exhausted his powers of characteristic discrimination in the heads of the apostles; and in his attempt to give meekness to the countenance of Jesus, he sank into insipience. He had the prudence, therefore, to leave the face unfinished, that the imagination of the beholder might not be disappointed by an imperfect image, but form one in his mind more appropriate to his feelings and to the subject. The ruin of this picture, the report of which I understand is true, has deprived the world and the arts of one of the mental eyes of painting. But pleasing as the works of Leonardo da Vinci are in general, had he not produced this picture of the Last Supper, and the cartoon of the equestrian combatants for the standard of victory, he would scarcely have emerged, as a painter of strong character, above mediocrity. Indeed the back-ground, and general distribution of this picture, sufficiently mark their Gothic origin. But his pictures, generally speaking, are more characterised by their laborious finishing, gentleness, and sweetness of character, than by the energies of a lively imagination.

"Fra. Bartolomeo di St. Marco, of Florence, was one of the first who became enamoured of that superiority which grandeur and decision of character gives to art; and, indeed, of all those higher excellences which the philosophical mind of Da Vinci had accomplished. In the pictures of Bartolomeo we behold, for the first time, that breadth of the clair-obscure—the deep tones of colour, with their philosophical arrangement, united to that noble folding of drapery appropriate to, and significant of, every character it covered; a point of excellence in this master, from which Raphael caught his first conception of that noble simplicity which distinguishes the dignity of his draperies, and which it became his pride through life to imitate.

"Bartolomeo, in his figure of St. Mark, has convinced us how important and indispensable is the union of mental conception with truth of observation, in order to give a decided and appropriate character to an Evangelist of the Gospel. None of the pictures of this artist possess the excellence of his St. Mark except one, which is in the city of Lucca, the capital of the republic of that name; and, as that picture is but little known to travellers, and almost unknown to many artists who have visited Italy, a description of it may not be unacceptable.

"The picture is on pannel, and its dimensions somewhat about twenty feet in height by fourteen in width. The subject is the Assumption of the Virgin Mary. The composition is divided into three groups; the Apostles and the sepulchre form the centre group, from the midst of which the Virgin ascends; her body-drapery is of a deep ruby colour, which is the only decided red in the picture, and her mantle blue, but in depth of tone approaching to black, and extended by angels to nearly each side of the picture. This mantle is relieved by a light, in tone resembling that of the break of day, seen over the summit of a dark mountain, which gives an awful grandeur to the effect of the picture on entering the chapel, in which it is placed over the altar. That awful light of the morning is contrasted with the golden effulgence above; in the midst of which, our Saviour is seen with extended arms, to receive and welcome his mother.

"From the sepulchre, and the Apostles in the centre, to the fore-ground, the third group of figures partly lies in shade, occasioned by the over-shadowing of the Virgin's deep-toned mantle extended by angels. On the other part of the group, on the side where the light enters, the figures are seen in the broad blaze of day; and amongst them is the portrait of the artist.

"When I first saw this picture, my sensations were in unison with its awful character; and I confess that I was touched with the same kind of sensibility as when I heard the inexpressibly harmonious blendings of vocal sounds in the solemn notes of *Non nobis Domine*. I never felt more forcibly the dignity of music and the dignity of painting, than from these two compositions of art.

"When we consider the combination of excellence requisite to produce the sublime in painting; the union of propriety with dignity of character; the graceful grouping; the noble folding of drapery, and the deep sombrous tones of the clair-obscure, with appropriate colours harmoniously blending into one whole;—if there is a picture entitled to the appellation of *sublime*, from the union of all these excellences, It is that which I have described: considered in all its parts, it is, perhaps, superior to any work in painting, which has fallen under my observation.

"When these powerful essays in art by Da Vinci, Bartolomeo di St. Marco, and Michael Angelo became celebrated, Raphael, having attained his adult age, made his appearance at Florence; where the influence of the works of those three great artists pervaded all the avenues to excellence in art.

"The gentle sensibility of Raphael's mind was like the softened wax which makes more visible and distinct the form of the engraving with which it is touched. Blest by Nature with this endowment, he became like the heir to the treasured wealth of many families. Enriched by the accumulated experience which was then in Florence, united to the early tuition of delineating from nature under Pietro Perugino, and the subsequent discoveries of the Grecian relics, Raphael's mind became stored with all that was excellent; and he possessed a practised hand, to make his conceptions visible on his tablets. Possessing these powers, he was invited to Rome, and began his picture of *The Dispute on the Sacrament*. This picture he finished, together with *The School of Athens*, before he had attained his twenty-eighth year. At Rome he found himself amidst the splendour of a refined court, and in the focus of human endowment. He became sensible of the rare advantages of his situation; he had industry and ardour to combine and to embrace them all; and the effect is visible in his works. The theological arrangement of the disputants on the Sacrament, and the scholastic controversies at Athens, convince us of this truth. In the upper part of the Dispute on the Sacrament, something may be observed of that taste of Bartolomeo in drapery, and of the dryness and hardness of his first master Pietro Perugino; but in the parts which make the aggregate of that work, he has blended the result of his own observations. In his School of Athens, this is still more strikingly the case; and in his Heliodorus we see additional dignity and an enlargement of style.

"At this period of his life, such was the desire of his society by the great, and such the ambition of standing forward amongst his patrons by all who were eminent for rank and taste, that he was seduced into courtly habits, and relaxed from that studious industry, with which he had formerly laboured; and there are evident marks in many of his works in the Vatican, of a decline of excellence, and that he was suffering pleasure and indolence to rob him of his fame. Sensible of this decline in his compositions, the powers of his mind re-assumed their energies; and that re-animation stands marked in his unrivalled compositions of the Cartoons which are in this country, and in the picture of the Transfiguration.

"The transcendant excellence in composition, and in appropriate character to subject, in the cartoon of Paul preaching at Athens, has left us to desire or expect nothing farther to be done in telling this incident of history.

"In the composition of the death of Ananias, and in the single figure of Elymas the sorcerer struck blind, we have the same example of excellence. We have indeed in many of the characters and groups in the cartoons, the various modes of reasoning, speaking, and feeling; but so blended with nature and truth, and so precise and determined in character, that criticism has nothing wherewith in that respect to ask for amendment.

"Had the life of this illustrious painter, which closed on his birth-day in his thirty-seventh year, been prolonged to the period of that of Leonardo da Vinci, Michael Angelo, or Titian, when in the space of seventeen years at Rome he has given the world more unrivalled works of art, than has fallen to the lot of any other painter, what an additional excellence might we not have expected in his works for subsequent generations to admire.

"The next distinguished artist who comes under our consideration is Titian. The grandeur which Michael Angelo gave to the human figure, Titian has rivalled in colour, and both were dignified during their lives with the appellation of The Divine.

"I will pass over the many appropriate portraits which he painted of men, and the portraits of women, though not the most distinguished for beauty, in the character of Venus, to meet the fashion of the age in which he lived; and notice only those works of mental power, which have raised him to eminence in the class of refined artists. On this point, you will find that his picture of St. Peter Martyr will justify the claim he has to that rank.

"St. Peter the Martyr was the head of a religious sect: when on his way from the confines of Germany to Milan with a companion, he was attacked by one in opposition to his religious principles while passing through a wood, and murdered. This is the subject of the picture. The prostrate figure of the Saint, just fallen by a blow from the assassin, raises one of his hands towards heaven, with a countenance of confidence in eternal reward for the firmness of his faith; while the assassin grasps with his left hand the mantle of his victim, the better to enable him, by his uplifted sword in the other hand, to give the fatal blow to the fallen saint. The companion is flying off in frantic dismay, and has received a wound in the head from the assassin.

"The ferocious and determined action of the murderer bestriding the body of the fallen saint, completes a group of figures which have not a rival in art. The majestic trees, as well as the sable and rugged furze, form an awful back-ground to this tragical scene, every way appropriate to the subject. The heavenly messengers seen in the glory above, bearing the palm branches as the emblem of reward for martyrdom, form the second light; the first being the sky and cloud, which gives relief to the black drapery of the wounded companion; while the rays of light from the emanation above, sparkling on the dark branches of the trees as so many diamonds, tie together by their light all the others from the top to the bottom of the picture. The terror which the act of the murderer has spread, is denoted by the speed of the horseman passing into the gloomy recesses of a distant part of the forest.

"This picture, taken in the aggregate, is the first work in art in which the human figure and landscape are combined as an historical landscape, and where all the objects are the full size of nature.

"When I saw this picture at Venice in 1761, it was then in the same state of purity as when the Bologna artists saw and studied it; and it is recorded that Caracci declared this picture to be without fault. But we have to lament the fatal effects which the goddess Bellona has ever occasioned to the fine arts when she mounts her iron chariot of destruction. When this picture fell under her rapacious power, on board a French vessel passing down the Adriatic sea from Venice, one of our cruisers chased the vessel into the port of Ancona, and a cannon-shot pierced the pannel on which the picture was painted, and shivered a portion of it into pieces.

"On its arrival at Paris, the committee of the fine arts found it necessary to remove the painting from the pannel, and place it on canvass; but the picture has lost the principal light.

"But to sum up Titian's powers of conception, no one has equalled him in the propriety and fitness of colour. His pictures of St. Peter Martyr; the David and Goliah; and the Last Supper, which is in the Escurial, stand in the very highest rank in art. On the latter of these pictures being finished, Titian in his letter to the King, announcing the circumstance, says that it had been the labour of seven years. But by his original sketch in oil colours, which I have the good fortune to possess, and by which we may form an estimate, although the general effect and composition are unrivalled, the characters of the heads of the apostles are not equal to those of

Leonardo da Vinci on the same subject.

"Antonio Allegri da Correggio is the sixth source, whose emanating powers have illuminated the fine arts in the modern world. A superstitious mind, on seeing his works, would suppose that he had received his tuition in painting from the angels; as his figures seem to belong to another race of being than man, and to have something too celestial for the forms of earth to have presented to his view. Such have been the sayings of many on seeing his works at Parma, but, to my conception, he painted from the nature with which he was surrounded. His pictures of the Note, St. Gierolimo, and the St. George, are evident proofs of the observation. In the first of these pictures his mental conception shines supreme. It is the idea of illuminating the child in the subject of our Saviour's nativity. This splendid thought of giving light to the infant Christ, whose divine mission was to illuminate the human mind from Pagan darkness, no painter has since been so bold as to omit in any composition on the same subject. The two latter pictures have all the beauties seen in the paintings of this master, but they are deficient in appropriate character.

"The inspiring power of Correggio's works illuminated the genius of Parmegiano, the energetic movements of whose graceful figures have never been equalled, nor are they deficient in the moral influence of the art. His Moses breaking the tables in a church at Parma, and his picture of the vision of St. Gierolimo, now in England, are filled with the impress of his intellectual powers, and stand pre-eminent over all his works.

"I have thus taken a survey of the works of art, which stand supreme among the productions of Grecian and Italian genius, and which are the sources from which the subsequent schools have derived most of the principles of their celebrity.

"The papal vortex drew into it nearly all the various powers of human refinement, and the inspiring influence of the first school in art having centered in Rome gave it superiority, till the Constable Bourbon, by sacking that city, obliged the fine arts to fly from their place, like doves from the vultures: they never re-appeared at Rome but with secondary power.

"About a century subsequent to their flight from Rome they were re-animated, and formed the second school of art in Italy at the city of Bologna under the Carracci, at the head of which was Ludovico. He and his two relatives, Hanibal and Augustin Carracci, derived their principles from the Venetian School, from Titian,

Paul Veronese, and Tintoret, and from the Lombard School of Correggio and Parmegiano. But the good sense of Ludovico raised by them and himself a school of their own, which excelled in the power of delineating the human figure, but which power gave to that school more academical taste than mental character.

"Their great work was that in the convent of St. Michael in Boresco, near Bologna; but this work has perished by damp, and the only remains on record of what it was, are in the coarse prints which were done from copies executed when it was in good condition. But grand as it must have been according to the evidence of these prints, it was but an academical composition.

"The picture by Ludovico, however, of our Saviour's Transfiguration on the Mount, consisting of six figures double the size of life, has embraced nearly all the points of art, and has placed the artist high in the first class of painters.

"The masters of the Bolognese school going to Rome and other parts of Italy, their successors at Bologna contented themselves by retailing the several manners of the three Carracci—Guido, Domenichino and Guercino. This system of retailing continued to descend from master to pupil, until the school of Bologna sunk into irrecoverable imbecility.

"The most esteemed work in painting by Augustine Carracci is the Communion of St. Jerom. It possesses grandeur of style, is bold in execution, and the faces are not deficient in the appropriate expression of sensibility towards the object before them. It was on the composition of this picture, that Domenichino formed his on the same subject, so much celebrated as to be considered next in merit to Raphael's Transfiguration. But fine as it is admitted to be, we must say, as a borrowed idea, it lessens the merit of the artist's originality of mind.

"The finest picture by Guido is in a church at Genoa, where he has brought to a focus all the force of his powers in grace and beauty, with an expression and execution of pencil rarely to be met with in art. The subject is the Assumption of the Virgin Mary. The angels, who surround the Virgin, have something in their faces so celestial, that they seem as if they had really descended from Heaven, and sat to the artist while he painted them. The Virgin herself seems to have had the same complacency. The characters of the Apostles' heads are so exquisitely drawn and painted, as to be without competition in the works of any other painter.

"The most esteemed picture by Guercino is is that of Santa Petranella, which he painted for St. Peter's Church, at Rome.

"But, Gentlemen, if you aspire to excellence in your profession, you must not rest your future studies on the excellence of any individual, however exalted his name or genius; but, like the industrious bee, survey the whole face of nature, and sip the sweets from every flower. When thus enriched, lay up your acquisitions for future use; and with that enrichment from Nature's inexhaustible source, examine the great works of art to animate your feelings, and to excite your emulation. When you are thus mentally enriched, and your hand practised to obey the powers of your will, you will then find your pencils, or your chisels, as magic wands, calling into view creations of your own, to adorn your name and your country.

"I cannot, however, close this Discourse, without acknowledging a debt due from this Academy, as well as that which is due to the Academy itself. Soon after His present Majesty had ascended the throne, his benign regard for the prosperity of the fine arts in these realms was manifested by his gracious commands to establish this favoured Institution.

"The heart of every artist, and of the friend of art, glowed with mutual congratulation to see a British King, for the first time, at the head of the fine arts. His Majesty nominated forty members guardians to his infant academy; and that they have been faithful to the trust which he graciously reposed in them, the several apartments under this roof sufficiently testify. The professors are highly endowed with accomplishments and scientific knowledge in the several branches to which they are respectively appointed; and the funds able to render relief to the indigent and decayed artists, their widows and children.

"Who can reflect for a moment on the rare advantages here held out for the instruction of youthful genius, and the aid given to the decayed, their widows and helpless offspring, without feeling the grateful emotions of the heart rise towards a patriot King, for giving to the arts this home within the walls of a stately mansion, and towards the members of this Academy, who, as his faithful guardians, have so ably fulfilled the purposes for which the Institution was formed.

"United to what the Academicians have done, and are doing, another honourable establishment, sanctioned by His Majesty for promoting the fine arts, has been created and composed of noblemen and gentlemen whose known zeal for the success of refined art is so conspicuous and honourable to themselves.

"Such have been the efforts to give splendour to the fine arts in this country, and such are the results which have attended these exertions; that knowing, as we do, the movements of the arts on the Continent, I may confidently say, that our annual exhibitions, both as to number and taste, engrafted on nature and the fruit of mental conception, are such that all the combined efforts in art on the continent of Europe in the same time have not been able to equal. To such attainments, were those in power but to bestow the crumbs from the national table to cherish the fine arts, we might pledge ourselves, that the genius of Britain would, in a few years, dispute the prize with the proudest periods of Grecian or Italian art. But, Gentlemen, let us not despair; we have heard from this place, the promise of patronage from the Prince Regent, the propitious light of a morning that will open into perfect day, invigorating the growth of all around—the assurance of a new era to the elevation of the fine arts, in the United Kingdom."

CHAPTER XIII

Mr. West's Visit to Paris —His distinguished Reception by the Members of the French Government —Anecdote of Mr. Fox —Origin of the British Institution —Anecdotes of Mr. Fox and Mr. Percival —Anecdote of the King —History of the Picture of Christ Healing the Sick —Extraordinary Success attending the Exhibition of the Copy in America

DURING the Peace of Amiens, Mr. West, like every other person who entertained any feeling of admiration for the fine arts, was desirous of seeing that magnificent assemblage of paintings and sculptures, which constituted the glory and the shame of Buonaparte's administration. He accordingly furnished himself with letters from Lord Hawkesbury, then Secretary of State, to Mr. Merry, the British representative at the consular court; and also with introductions from Monsieur Otto, the French minister in London, to the most distinguished members of his government.

On delivering Lord Hawkesbury's letters to Mr. Merry, that gentleman informed him that one of the French ministers had, the preceding evening, mentioned that Monsieur Otto had written in such terms respecting him, that he and his colleagues were resolved to pay him every mark of the most distinguished attention. Mr. Merry, therefore, advised Mr. West to call on the several ministers himself with the letters, and leave them with his card. As the object for which the Artist had procured these introductions was only to obtain, with more facility, access to the different galleries, he was rather embarrassed by this information; and would have declined delivering the letters altogether; but Mr. Merry said, that, as his arrival in Paris was already known to the government, he could not with any propriety avoid paying his respects to the ministers.

After delivering his letters and card accordingly, the hotel where he resided was, in the course of the week, visited by all the most distinguished of the French statesmen; and he had the honour of being invited to dine with them successively. At these parties, the conversation turned very much on the importance of the arts to all nations aspiring to fame and eminence; and he very soon perceived, that the vast collection of trophies which adorned the Louvre, had not been formed so much for ostentatious exhibition, as with a view to furnish models of study for artists; constituting, in fact, but the elementary part of a grand system of national decoration designed by Buonaparte, and by which he expected to leave such memorials to posterity as would convince the world that his magnificence was worthy of his military achievements.

It happened at this particular period, that the galleries of the Louvre were closed to the public for some time, but a deputation from the Central Administration of the Arts, under whose care the collections were particularly placed, waited on Mr. West, and informed him, that orders were given to admit him and his friends at all times. Denon was at the head of this deputation; and in the course of the conversation which then took place, that accomplished enthusiast explained to Mr. West more circumstantially the extensive views entertained by the French government with respect to the arts, mentioning several of the superb schemes which were formed by the First Consul for the decoration of the capital.

This information made a very deep impression on the mind of Mr. West, and he felt extremely sorrowful when he reflected, that hitherto the British government had done nothing decidedly with a view to promote the cultivation of those arts, which may justly be said to constitute the olive wreath on the brows of every great nation. Mr. Fox and Sir Francis Baring, who were at this same time in Paris, happened soon after the departure of Monsieur Denon to call, and they went with Mr. West to the Louvre, where, as they were walking in the gallery, he explained to them what he had heard. An interesting discussion took place in consequence; and Mr. West endeavoured to explain in what manner he considered the cultivation of the fine arts of the utmost importance even in a commercial point of view to England.

Mr. Fox paid great attention to what he said, and observed, in a tone of regret, "I have been rocked in the cradle of politics from my infancy, and never before was so much struck with the advantage, even in a political bearing, of the fine arts to the prosperity, as well as the renown, of a kingdom; and I do assure you, Mr. West, that if ever I have it in my power to influence our government to promote the arts, the conversation that we have had to-day shall not be forgotten." Sir Francis Baring also concurred in opinion, that it was really become an imperious duty, on the part of the British nation, to do something for a class of art that, undoubtedly, tended to improve the beauty, and multiply the variety of manufactures, independent of all monumental considerations.

When Mr. West had returned home, the subject was renewed with Sir Francis Baring; and he endeavoured to set on foot the formation of a society, which should have the encouragement of the line arts for its object, and thought that government might be induced to give it pecuniary assistance. Sir Thomas Barnard took up the idea with great zeal; and several meetings took place at Mr. West's house, at which Mr. Charles Long and Sir Abraham Hume were present, which terminated in the formation of that association that now constitutes the British Institution, in Pall Mall. Mr. Long undertook to confer with Mr. Pitt, who was then again in power, on the subject, and the proposal was received by him with much apparent sincerity. But a disastrous series of public events about the same time commenced: the attention of the Minister was absorbed in the immediate peril of the state; and he fell a victim to his anxieties, without having had it in his power to further the objects of the association.

At the death of his great rival, Mr. Fox came into office; and he soon after called on Mr. West, and, reminding him of the conversation in the gallery of the Louvre, said, "It is my earnest intention, as soon as I am firmly seated on the saddle, to redeem the promise that I then made." But he also was frustrated in his intentions, and fell a sacrifice to disease, without being able to take any step in the business. In the mean time, the Shaksperian Gallery was offered for sale; and the gentlemen interested in this project raised a sum of money, by subscription, and purchased that building with the intention of making it the approach to a proposed national gallery.

From Mr. Percival the scheme met with a far different reception. He listened to the representations which Mr. West made to him with a repressive coldness, it might almost be said with indifference, had it not been marked with a decided feeling; for he seemed to consider the whole objects of the British Institution, and the reasons adduced in support of the claims which the interests of the arts had on government, as the visionary purposes of vain enthusiasts. It was not within the small compass of that respectable individual's capacity to consider any generous maxim as founded in what *he* deemed wisdom, or to comprehend, that the welfare of nations could be promoted by any other means than precedents of office, decisions of courts, and Acts of Parliament. An incident, however, occurred, which induced him to change his opinion of the utility of the fine arts.

At the anniversary dinner, in 1812, before the opening of the Academy, he was present, with other public characters. On the right hand of the President was seated the Lord Chancellor Eldon, on his left Lord Liverpool, and on the right of the Chancellor Mr. Percival. A conversation took place, naturally inspired by the circumstances of the meeting, in which Mr. West recapitulated what he had formerly so often urged; and Mr. Percival, perceiving the impression which his observations made on those to whom they were particularly addressed, requested him to put his ideas on the subject in writing, and he would lay it before the Prince Regent. This took place on Saturday; on Wednesday Mr. West delivered his memorial; on the Friday following Mr. Percival was assassinated; and since that time nothing farther has been done in the business.

It is perhaps necessary to notice here, that when it was first proposed to the King to sanction the establishment of the British Institution with his patronage, he made some objection, conceiving that it was likely to interfere with the Royal Academy, which he justly considered with the partiality of a parent. But on Mr. West explaining to him that the two institutions were very different in their objects, the Academy being formed for the instruction of pupils, and the other for the encouragement of artists arrived at maturity in their profession, His Majesty readily consented to receive the deputation of the association appointed to wait on him in form to solicit his patronage. Except, however, the honour of the King's name, the British Institution, formed expressly for the improvement of the public taste with a view to the encouragement of the arts, has received neither aid nor countenance as yet from the state.

Before concluding this summary account of the origin and establishment of the British Institution, it may be expected of me to take some notice of the circumstances connected with the purchase and exhibition of Mr. West's picture of Christ Healing the Sick in the Temple; an event which formed an era in the history of the arts in Britain, and contributed in no small degree to promote the interests of the Institution. Perhaps the exhibition of no work of art ever attracted so much attention, or was attended with so much pecuniary advantage to the proprietors; independent of which, the history of the picture is itself interesting.

Some years before, a number of gentlemen, of the society of Quakers in Philadelphia, set on foot a subscription for the purpose of erecting an hospital for the sick poor in that city. Among others to whom they applied for contributions in this country, they addressed themselves to Mr. West. He informed them, however, that his circumstances did not permit him to give so liberal a sum as he could wish, but that if they would provide a proper place in the building, he would paint a picture for it as his subscription, which perhaps would prove of more advantage than all the money he could afford to bestow, and with this intention he began the *Christ Healing the Sick*. While the work was going forward, it attracted a great deal of notice in his rooms, and finally had the effect of inducing the association of the British Institution to make him an offer of three thousand guineas for the picture. Mr. West accepted the offer, but on condition that he should be at liberty to make a copy for the hospital at Philadelphia, and to introduce into the copy such alterations and improvements as he might think fit. This copy he also executed, and the success which attended the exhibition of it in America was so extraordinary, that the proceeds have enabled the committee of the hospital to enlarge the building for the reception of no less than thirty additional patients.

CHAPTER XIV

Reflections —Offer of Knighthood —Mr. Wyatt chosen President of the Academy —Restoration of Mr. West to the Chair —Proceedings respecting the Pictures for Windsor Castle —Mr. West's Letter to the King —Orders to proceed with the Pictures —The King's Illness —Mr. West's Allowance cut off, and the Pictures countermanded —Death of Mrs. West —Death of the Artist

HITHERTO it has been my pleasant task to record the series of prosperous incidents by which Mr. West was raised to the highest honours of his profession; and had he survived the publication of this volume, I should have closed the narrative with the last chapter. But his death, which took place after the proof was sent to me for his inspection, has removed an obligation which I had promised to respect during his life, while it was understood between us that the circumstances to which it related were to be carefully preserved for a posthumous publication. The topics are painful, and calculated to afford a far different view of human nature from that which I have ever desired to contemplate: I do not allude to those things, connected with political matters, in which Mr. West was only by accident a witness, but of transactions which personally affected himself.

During the time that he was engaged in the series of great pictures for Windsor Castle, he enjoyed, as I have already mentioned, an easy and confidential intercourse with the King, and I ought, perhaps, to have stated earlier, that when he was chosen President of the Royal Academy, the late Duke of Gloucester called on him, and mentioned that His Majesty was desirous to know if the honour of knighthood would be acceptable. Mr. West immediately replied, that no man had a greater respect for political honours and distinctions than himself, but that he really thought he had already earned by his pencil more eminence than could be conferred on him by that rank. "The chief value," said he, "of titles are, that they serve to preserve in families a respect for those principles by which such distinctions were originally obtained. But simple knighthood, to a man who is at least already as well known as he could ever hope to be from that honour, is not a legitimate object of ambition. To myself, then, Your Royal Highness must perceive the title could add no dignity, and as it would perish with myself, it could add none to my family. But were I possessed of a fortune, independent of my profession, sufficient to enable my posterity to maintain the rank, I think that with my hereditary descent, and the station I occupy among artists, a more permanent title than that of knighthood might become a desirable object. As it is, however, that cannot be, and I have been thus explicit with Your Royal Highness that no misconception may exist on the subject." The Duke was not only pleased with the answer, but took Mr. West cordially by both the hands, and said, "You have justified the opinion which the King has of you, and His Majesty will be delighted with your answer;" and when Mr. West next saw the King his reception was unusually warm and friendly.

But notwithstanding all these enviable circumstances, Mr. West was doomed to share some of the consequences which naturally attach to all persons in immediate connection with the great. After his return from Paris, it was alleged, that the honourable reception which he allowed himself to receive from the French statesmen had offended the King. The result of this was the temporary elevation of the late Mr. Wyatt to the President's chair, merely, as I think, because that gentleman was then the royal architect; for it would be difficult to point out the merits which, as an artist, entitled him to that honour. But the election, so far from giving satisfaction in the quarter where it was expected to be the most acceptable, only excited displeasure; and Mr. West was, in due time, restored to his proper seat in the Academy.

This, as a public affair, attracted a good deal of notice at the time; but it was, in its effects, of far less consequence to Mr. West than a private occurrence, originating in circumstances that tend to throw a light on some of the proceedings that were deemed expedient to be adopted during the occasional eclipses of the King's understanding.

For upwards of twenty years Mr. West had received all his orders from the King in person: the prices of the pictures which he painted were adjusted with His Majesty; and the whole embellishment of Windsor Castle, in what related to the scriptural and historical pictures, was concerted between them, without the interference of any third party. But, in the summer of 1801, when the Court was at Weymouth, Mr, Wyatt called on Mr. West, and said, that he was requested by authority to inform him, that the pictures painting for His Majesty's chapel at Windsor should be suspended till further orders.

Mr. West was much surprised at this communication: but, upon interrogating Mr. Wyatt as to his authority, he found that it was not from the King; and he afterwards discovered that the orders were given at Weymouth by the Queen, the late Earl of Roslyn being present. What was the state of His Majesty's health at that time is now a matter of historical curiosity; but this extraordinary proceeding deserves particular notice. It rendered the studies of the best part of the Artist's life useless, and deprived him of that honourable provision, the fruit of his talents and industry, on which he had counted for the repose of his declining years. For some time it affected him deeply, and he was at a loss what steps to take; at last, however, in reflecting on the marked friendship and favour which the King had always shown him, he addressed to His Majesty a letter, of which the following is a copy of the rough draft, being the only one preserved: I give it verbatim:—

"*The following is the Substance of a Letter I had the honour of writing to His Majesty, taken at Weymouth, by the conveyance of Mr. James Wyatt.*

"To the King's Most Excellent Majesty
"Gracious Sire, Newman St.   Sept. 26. 1801.
"On the fifteenth of last month Mr. Wyatt signified to me Your Majesty's pleasure,— 'That the pictures by me now painting for His Majesty's chapel at Windsor, should be suspended until further orders.' I feel it a duty I owe to that communication, to lay before Your Majesty, by the return of Mr. Wyatt to Weymouth, a statement of those pictures which I have painted to add to those for the chapel,

mentioned in the account I had the honour to transmit to Your Majesty in 1797 by the hands of Mr. Gabriel Mathias. Since that period I have finished three pictures, began several others, and composed the remainder of the subjects for the chapel, on the progress of Revealed Religion, from its commencement to its completion; and the whole arranged with that circumspection from the Four Dispensations, into five-and-thirty compositions, that the most scrupulous amongst the various religious sects in this country, about admitting pictures into churches, must acknowledge them as truths, or the Scriptures fabulous. Those are subjects so replete with dignity, character, and expression, as demanded the historian, the commentator, and the accomplished painter, to bring them into view. Your Majesty's gracious complacency and commands for my pencil on that extensive subject stimulated my humble abilities, and I commenced the work with zeal and enthusiasm. Animated by your commands, gracious Sire, I renewed my professional studies, and burnt my midnight lamp to attain and give that polish at the close of Your Majesty's chapel, which has since marked my subsequent scriptural pictures. Your Majesty's known zeal for promoting religion, and the elegant arts, had enrolled your virtues with all the civilized world; and your gracious protection of my pencil had given to it a celebrity throughout Europe, and spread a knowledge of the great work on Revealed Religion, which my pencil was engaged on, under Your Majesty's patronage: it is that work which all Christendom looks with a complacency for its completion.

"Being distinguished by Your Majesty's benignity at an early period as a painter, and chosen by those professors highly endowed in the three branches of the fine arts to fill their highest station, and sanctioned by Your Majesty's signature in their choice;—in that station, I have been, for more than ten years, zealous in promoting merit in those three branches of art, which constitutes the views of Your Majesty's establishment for cultivating their growth. The ingenious artists have received my professional aid, and my galleries and my purse have been open to their studies and their distresses. The breath of envy, nor the whisper of detraction, never defiled my lips, nor the want of morality my character, and, through life, a strict adherer to truth; a zealous admirer of Your Majesty's virtues and goodness of heart, the exalted virtues of Her Majesty the Queen, and the high accomplishments of others of Your Majesty's illustrious family, have been the theme of my delight; and their gracious complacency my greatest pleasure and consolation for many years, with which I was honoured by many instances of friendly notice, and their warm attachment to the fine arts.

"With these feelings of high sensibility, with which my breast has ever been inspired, I feel with great concern the suspension given by Mr. Wyatt to the work on Revealed Religion, my pencil had advanced to adorn Windsor-Castle. If, gracious Sire, this suspension is meant to be permanent, myself and the fine arts have to lament. For to me it will be ruinous, and, to the energetic artist, in the highest branches of his professional pursuits—a damp in the hope of more exalted minds, of patronage in the refined departments in painting. But I have this in store, for the grateful feeling of my heart, that, in the thirty-five years by which my pencil has been honoured by Your Majesty's commands, a great body of historical and scriptural compositions will be found in Your Majesty's possession, in the churches, and in the country. Their professional claims may be humble, but they have been produced by a loyal subject of Your Majesty, which may give them some claim to respect, similar works not having been attained before in this country by a subject; and this I will assert as my claim, that Your Majesty did not bestow your patronage and commands on an ungrateful and a lazy man, but on him who had a high sense of Your Majesty's honours and Your Majesty's interests in all cases, as a loyal and dutiful subject, as well as servant, to Your Majesty's gracious commands; and I humbly beg Your Majesty to be assured that

"I am,
"With profound duty,
"Your Majesty's grateful
"BENJAMIN WEST."

To this letter Mr. West received no answer; but on the return of the Court to Windsor, he went to the Castle, and obtained a private audience of the King on the subject, by which it appeared that His Majesty was not at all acquainted with the communication of which Mr. Wyatt was the bearer, nor had he received Mr. West's letter. However, the result of the interview was, that the King said, "Go on with your work, West: go on with the pictures, and I will take care of you."

This was the last interview that Mr. West was permitted to enjoy with his early, constant, and to him truly royal patron; but he continued to execute the pictures, and in the usual quarterly payments received the thousand pounds *per ann.*. till His Majesty's final superannuation, when, without any intimation whatever, on calling to receive it, he was informed that it had been stopped, and that the intended design of the chapel of Revealed Religion was suspended.

This was a severe stroke of misfortune to the Artist, now far advanced in life, but he submitted to it with resignation. He took no measures, nor employed any influence, either to procure the renewal of the quarterly allowance, or the payment of the balance of his account. But being thus cast off from his best anchor in his old age, he still possessed firmness of mind to think calmly of his situation. He considered that a taste for the fine arts had been greatly diffused by means of the exhibitions of the Royal Academy, and the eclat which the French had given to pictures and statues by making them objects of national conquest; and having thus lost the patronage of the King, he determined to appeal to the public. With this view he resolved to paint several large pictures; and in the prosecution of this determination, he has been amply indemnified for the effects of that poor economy that frustrated the nation from obtaining an honourable monument of the taste of the age, and the liberality of a popular king.

Without imputing motives to any party concerned, or indeed without being at all acquainted with the circumstances that gave rise to it, I should mention that a paper was circulated among the higher classes of society, in which an account was stated of the amount of the money paid by His Majesty, in the course of more than thirty years, to Mr. West. In that paper the interval of time was not at all considered, nor the expense of living, nor the exclusive preference which Mr. West had given to His Majesty's orders, but the total sum;—which, shown by itself, and taken into view without any of these explanatory circumstances, was very large, and calculated to show that Mr. West might really indeed *do* without the thousand pounds a-year. In order, however, to place this proceeding in its true light, I have inserted in the Appendix an account of the works executed and designed by Mr. West for the King, and the prices allowed for them as charged in the audited account, of which the King himself had approved.

Independent of the relation which this paper bears to the subject of these memoirs, it is a curious document, and will be interesting as such, as long as the history of the progress of the arts in this country excites the attention of posterity.

I have now but little to add to these memoirs. But they would be deficient in an important event, were I to omit noticing the death of Mrs. West, which took place on the 6th of December, 1817. The malady with which she had been afflicted for several years smoothed the way for her relief from suffering, and softened the pang of sorrow for her loss. She was in many respects a woman of an elevated character; and her death, after a union of more than half a century, was to her husband one of those irreparable changes in life, for which no equivalent can ever be obtained.

The last illness of Mr. West himself was slow and languishing. It was rather a general decay of nature, than any specific malady; and he continued to enjoy his mental faculties in perfect distinctness upon all subjects as long as the powers of articulation could be exercised. To his merits as an artist and a man I may be deemed partial, nor do I wish to be thought otherwise. I have enjoyed his frankest confidence for many years, and received from his conversation the advantages of a more valuable species of instruction, relative to the arts, than books alone can supply to one who is not an artist. While I therefore admit that the partiality of friendship may tincture my opinion of his character, I am yet confident that the general truth of the estimate will be admitted by all who knew the man, or are capable to appreciate the merits of his works.

In his deportment, Mr. West was mild and considerate: his eye was keen, and his mind apt; but he was slow and methodical in his reflections, and the sedateness of his remarks must often in his younger years have seemed to strangers singularly at variance with the vivacity of his look. That vivacity, however, was not the result of any peculiar animation of temperament; it was rather the illumination of his genius; for when his features were studiously considered, they appeared to resemble those which we find associated with dignity of character in the best productions of art.

As an artist, he will stand in the first rank. His name will be classed with those of Michael Angelo and Raphael; but he possessed little in common with either. As the former has been compared to Homer, and the latter to Virgil, in Shakspeare we shall perhaps find the best likeness to the genius of Mr. West. He undoubtedly possessed, but in a slight degree, that peculiar energy and physical expression of character in which Michael Angelo excelled, and in a still less that serene sublimity which constitutes the charm of Raphael's great productions. But he was their equal in the fulness, the perspicuity, and the propriety of his compositions. In all his great works the scene intended to be brought before the spectator is represented in such a manner that the imagination has nothing to supply. The incident, the time and the place, are there as we think they must have been; and it is this wonderful force of conception which renders the sketches of Mr. West so much more extraordinary than his finished pictures. In the finished pictures we naturally institute comparisons in colouring, and in beauty of figure, and in a thousand details which are never noticed in the sketches of this illustrious artist. But although his powers of conception were so superior,—equal in their excellence to Michael Angelo's energy, or Raphael's grandeur,—still in the inferior departments of drawing and colouring, he was one of the greatest artists of his age; it was not, however, till late in life that he executed any of those works in which he thought the splendour of the Venetian school might be judiciously imitated.

At one time he intended to collect his works together, and to form a general exhibition of them all. Had he accomplished this, the greatness and versatility of his talents would have been established beyond all controversy; for unquestionably he was one of those great men, whose genius cannot be justly estimated by particular works, but only by a collective inspection of the variety, the extent, and the number of their productions.

On the 10th of March Mr. West expired without a struggle, at his house in Newman Street, and on the 29th he was interred with great funeral pomp in St. Paul's Cathedral. An account of the ceremony is inserted in the Appendix.

APPENDIX No. I.

The Account: of Pictures painted by Benjamin West for His Majesty, by his Gracious Commands, from 1768 to 1780. A True Copy from Mr. West's Account Books, with their several Charges and Dates.

When painted.	SUBJECTS.	L.	s.
1769.	1. Regulus, his Departure from Rome	420	0
	2. Hamilcar swearing his Son Hannibal at the Altar	420	0
1771	3. Bayard at the moment of his death receiving the Constable Bourbon	315	0
	4. The Death of Epaminondas	315	0
	5. The Death of General Wolfe	315	0
1772.	6. Cyrus receiving the King of Armenia and family prisoners	157	10
	7. Germanicus receiving Sagastis and his Daughter prisoners	157	10
	8. The portrait of Her Majesty, the Kit-cat size.		
	9. The portrait of His Majesty, the same size, (companion,)	84	0
	10. Six of the Royal Children in one picture, size of life	315	0
	11. Her Majesty and Princess Royal, in one picture	157	0
	12. His R. H. the Prince of Wales and Prince Frederic (Duke of York), in one picture whole length	210	0
	13. A second picture of Ditto, for the Empress of Russia, sent by His Majesty	210	0

		L.	s.
14. A whole-length portrait of His Majesty,--Lord Amherst and the Marquis of Lothian in the back-ground.		262	10
15. A whole-length portrait of Her Majesty, with all the Royal Children in the back-ground		262	10
16. Whole-length portraits of Prince William (Duke of Clarence) and Prince Edward (Duke of Kent), in one picture		262	10
1779. 17. Whole-length portraits of Prince Adolphus and his sisters, in one picture		262	10

From the year 1769 the whole of the above pictures to 1779 were painted and paid for by His Majesty through the hands of Mr. R. Daulton and Mr. G. Mathias.

1780. At this period His Majesty was graciously pleased to sanction my pencil with his commands for a great work on Revealed Religion, from its commencement to its completion, for pictures to embellish his intended New Chapel in Windsor Castle. I arranged the several subjects from the four Dispensations. His Majesty was pleased to approve the arrangement selected, as did several of the Bishops in whose hands he placed them for their consideration, and they highly approved the same.

His Majesty then honoured me with his commands, and did at that time, the better to enable me to carry it into effect, order his deputy privy-purse, Mr. G. Mathias, to pay me one thousand a year by quarterly payments, which was regularly paid as commanded; and the following are the subjects which I have painted from the Four Dispensations, for the Chapel, of various dimensions.

ANTIDELUVIAN DISPENSATION

When painted.	SUBJECTS.	L.	s.
1780.	1. The expulsion of Adam and Eve from Paradise	535	0
	2. The Deluge	525	0
	3. Noah and his Family sacrificing	525	0

DISPENSATION

4. The Call of Abraham going to sacrifice his son Isaac   600   0
5. The Birth of Jacob and Esau   525   0
6. Joseph and his brothers in Egypt, composed, not painted.
7. The Death of Jacob surrounded by his sons in Egypt, ditto.

THE MOSAICAL DISPENSATION

8. The Call of Moses, his Rod turned into a Serpent before the Burning Bush, composed, but not painted.
9. Moses and his brother Aaron before Pharaoh, their Rods turned into Serpents   1050   0
10. Moses destroying Pharaoh said his host in the Red Sea   1050   0
11. Moses receiving the Laws on Mount Sinai   1260   0
12. Moses consecrating Aaron and his sons to the priesthood   1050   0
13. Moses showing the Brazen Serpent to the infirm to be healed   1050   0
14. The Death of Aaron on Mount Hor, composed, but not painted.
15. Moses presenting Joshua to Eleazar the priest, and Congregation, as commanded, composed, but not painted.
16. Moses sees the Promised Land from the top of Mount Abarim, and Death, a sketch in oil colours.
17. Joshua commanding the Ark and Congregation to pass the river into the Promised Land, a sketch in oil colour.

PROPHETS

18. The prophets Isaiah and Jeremiah   525   0

19. The prophet Samuel anointing David the son of Jesse, a sketch.
20. The prophesying of Zacharias at the birth of John his son   525 0
21. The Angels announcing the Birth of our Saviour, a cartoon for a
    painted-glass window, by Mr. Forrest   525 0
22. The Birth of our Saviour, ditto, for painted glass, by ditto   525 0
23. The Wise Man's Offering, a cartoon for ditto   525 0
24. John the Baptist baptizing our Saviour, on whom the Holy
    Ghost descends   1050 0
25. Christ's Temptation and Victory in the Wilderness, a sketch.
26. Christ beginneth to preach at Nazareth, his native place,
    a sketch.
27. Christ healeth the Sick and Blind; &c. in the Temple   1050 0
28. The Last Supper; which picture His Majesty presented to
    St. George's Chapel at Windsor   735 0
29. A Last Supper, painted for the King's Chapel   735 0
30. The Crucifixion, a study in oil colour, for the glass painting by
    Messrs. Jervis and Forrest to colour from, and the cartoon the
    size of the window   1050 0
31. The west end window of St. George's Chapel, 28 feet wide by
    36 high, for them to draw the figures from on the glass   1050 0
32. The Resurrection, a study in oil colour, for glass painting by
    Messrs. Jervis and Forrest to colour from   525 0
33. And the cartoon the size of the window at the east end of St.
    George's Chapel, 28 feet wide by 36 high, to draw
    from on the glass   1050 0
    And two side pictures   525 0
34. The Assumption of our Saviour, for the King's Chapel   1050 0
35. Peter's first Sermon, or the Apostles receiving the Cloven
    Tongues   1050 0
36. Paul and Barnabas rejecting the Jews, and receiving the Gentiles   1050 0

    [Total] L21,705 0

Painted for His Majesty's State Rooms in Windsor Castle the following Pictures from the History of Edward III.

1. Edward III. embracing his Son on the field of battle at Cressy	1365	0
2. The Installation of the most noble Order of the Garter	1365	0
3. Edward the Black Prince receiving John King of France and his son as prisoners	1365	0
4. St. George destroying the Dragon	630	0
5. Queen Philippa defeats David King of Scotland, at Nevil's Cross, and takes him prisoner	525	0
6. Queen Philippa soliciting Edward III. to save St. Pierre and the brave burgesses of Calais	525	0
7. Edward III. forcing the passage of the river Somme in France	630	0
8. Edward III. crowning Ribemont at Calais	525	0
[Total]	L6930	0

By His Majesty's commands I made nine designs for the ceiling in the Queen's Lodge, Windsor, for Mr. Haas to work the ceilings from.
    Viz. 1. Genius inspiring the fine arts to adorn the useful arts and sciences.
        2. Agriculture. 3. Manufactures.
        4. Commerce. 5. Botany. 6. Chemistry.
        7. Celestial Science. 8. Terrestrial Science; and 9. To adorn Empire   525   0

Myself and son, with Mr. Rebecca, for painting
transparent and water coloured pictures to adorn the marble
gallery at a great evening entertainment in the Castle given by
Their Majesties to the nobility   250 0

Painted for His Majesty a whole-length
portrait of Prince Octavius holding the King's sword   73 10

Painted for His Majesty the Apotheosis
of Prince Octavius and Prince Alfred, in one picture, the size of life 315 0

A portrait of Prince Augustus, half length, for the Queen.

A second whole length of Her Majesty, with all the Royal children
in the back-ground, which was placed in Windsor Castle,
but at present in the Queen's Palace, London   262 10

A picture of Peter denying our Saviour,
of which His Majesty honoured me by accepting,
two half-length figures, the size of life.

[Total] L1426 0

    This is a true statement of the numbers of pictures, cartoons, and drawings of designs, and sketches of scripture subjects, as well as historical events, British as well as Greek, Roman, and other nations, with which I had been honoured by the King's commands, from 1768, to 5th January 1801, to paint for His Majesty; and the charges I made for each was by him most graciously acknowledged, when my account was audited and allowed by Mr. G. Mathias, His Majesty's privy purse, who settled for debtor and creditor the whole amount between the above dates.

Benjamin West.

APPENDIX No. II.

A Catalogue of thee Works of Mr. West.

Regulus.
Hanibal.
Epaminondas.
Bayard.
Wolfe, the first and second.
Cyrus and the King of Armenia with his Family, captives.
Germanicus and Segestus with his Daughter, captives.
The Apotheosis of Prince Alfred and Prince Octavius.
The picture of the Damsel accusing Peter.
The Queen, with the Princess Royal, in one picture.
Prince Ernest and Prince Augustus; Princesses Augusta, Elizabeth, and
  Mary, in one picture.
Prince William and Prince Edward, in one picture.
Prince Octavius.
The whole-length portrait of His Majesty in Regimentals, with Lord
  Amherst and the Marquis of Lothian on Horseback, in the back-ground.
The whole-length portrait of Her Majesty, with the fourteen Royal Children.
The same repeated.
The Battle of Cressy, when Edward III. embraced his son.
The Battle of Poitiers, when John King of France is brought prisoner
  to the Prince.
The Institution of the Order of the Garter.
The Battle of Nevil's Cross.
The Burgesses of Calais before Edward III.
Edward III. crossing the Somme.
Edward III. crowning Ribemont, at Calais.

St. George destroying the Dragon.

The design of our Saviour's Resurrection, painted in colours, with the Women going to the Sepulchre; also Peter and John.

The cartoon from the above design, for the east window, painted in the Collegiate Church of Windsor, on glass, 36 feet high by 28 wide.

The design of our Saviour's Crucifixion, painted in colours.

The cartoon from the above design, for the west window in the Collegiate Church, painting on glass, 36 feet by 28.

The cartoon of the Angels appearing to the Shepherds, ditto for ditto.

The cartoon of the Nativity of our Saviour, for ditto, ditto.

The cartoon of the Magi presenting Gifts to our Saviour, for ditto, ditto.

The picture, in water-colours, representing Hymen leading and dancing with the Hours before Peace and and Plenty.

The picture, in water-colours, of Boys with the Insignia of Riches.

The companion, with Boys, and the Insignia of the Fine Arts.

Genius calling forth the Fine Arts to adorn Manufactures and Commerce, and recording the names of eminent men in those pursuits.

Husbandry aided by Arts and Commerce.

Peace and Riches cherishing the Fine Arts.

Manufactory giving support to Industry, in Boys and Girls.

Marine and inland Navigation enriching Britannia.

Printing aided by the Fine Arts.

Astronomy making new discoveries in the Heavens.

The Four Quarters of the World bringing Treasures to the Lap of Britannia.

Civil and Military Architecture defending and adorning Empire.

The Expulsion of Adam and Eve from Paradise.

The Deluge.

Noah sacrificing.

Abraham and his son Isaac going to sacrifice.

The Birth of Jacob and Esau.

The Death of Jacob in Egypt, surrounded by his Twelve Sons.

Moses and Aaron before Pharaoh; their Rods turned into Serpents.

Pharaoh and his Host lost in the Red Sea, while Moses stretches his
  Rod over them.
Moses receiving the Law on Mount Sinai.
Moses consecrateth Aaron and his Sons to the Priesthood.
Moses showeth the Brazen Serpent to the People to be healed.
Moses shown the Promised Land from the top of Mount Pisgah.
Joshua crossing the River Jordan with the Ark.
The Twelve Tribes drawing Lots for the Lands of their Inheritance,
  6 feet by 10.
The Call of Isaiah and Jeremiah, each 5 by 14.
David anointed King, 6 by 10.
Christ's Birth, 6 by 10.
The naming of John; or, the Prophecies of Zacharias, ditto.
The Kings bringing Presents to Christ, 6 by 12.
Christ among the Doctors, 6 by 10.
The Descent of the Holy Ghost on our Saviour at the River Jordan, 10 by 14.
Christ healing the Sick in the Temple, ditto.
Christ's Last Supper, 6 by 10.
Christ's Crucifixion, 16 by 28.
Christ's Ascension, 12 by 18.
The Inspiration of St. Peter, 10 by 14.
Paul and Barnabas rejecting the Jews, and receiving the Gentiles, ditto.
John called to write the Revelation, 6 by 10.
Saints prostrating themselves before the Throne of God.
The opening of the Seven Seals; or, Death on the Pale Horse.
The overthrowing the Old Beast and False Prophet.
The Last Judgment.
The New Jerusalem.
The picture of St. Michael and his Angels fighting and casting out
  the Red Dragon and his Angels.
Do. of the Women clothed in the Sun.
Do. of John called to write the Revelation.
Do. of the Beast rising out of the Sea.

Do. of the Mighty Angel, one Foot upon Sea and the other on Earth.
Do. of St. Anthony of Padua.
Do. of the Madra Dolo Roso.
Do. of Simeon, with the Child in his arms.
A picture of a small Landscape, with a Hunt passing In the back-ground.
Do. of Abraham and Isaac going to sacrifice,
Do. of a whole-length figure of Thomas a Becket, larger than life.
Do. of the Angel in the Sun assembling the Birds of the Air, before the destruction of the Old Beast.
Four half-lengths.
The small picture of the Order of the Garter, differing in composition from the great picture at Windsor.
The picture of the Shunamite's Son raised to Life by the Prophet Elisha.
Do. of Jacob blessing Joseph's Sons.
Do. of the Death of Wolfe, the third picture.
Do. of the Battle of La Hogue.
Do. of the Boyne.
Do. of the Restoration of Charles II.
Do. of Cromwell dissolving the Long Parliament.
A small portrait of General Wolfe, when a Boy.
The Picture of the Golden Age.
The picture of St. Michael chaining the Dragon, in Trinity College, Cambridge, 15 by 8.
Do. of the Angels announcing the Birth of our Saviour, in the Cathedral Church at Rochester, 10 by 6.
Do. of the Death of St. Stephen, in the church of St. Stephen, Walbrook, 10 by 18.
Do. of the Raising of Lazarus, in the Cathedral of Winchester, 10 by 14.
Do. of St. Paul shaking the Viper off his Finger, in the chapel at Greenwich, 27 by 15.
The Supper, over the communion-table in the Collegiate Church at Windsor, 8 by 13.

The Resurrection of our Saviour, in the east window of the Collegiate Church at Windsor, 28 by 32.
The Crucifixion, in the window of ditto, 28 by 36.
The Angel announcing our Saviour's Birth, in ditto, 10 by 14.
The Birth of our Saviour, in ditto, 9 by 16.
The Kings presenting Gifts to our Saviour, in ditto, 9 by 16.
The picture of Peter denying our Saviour, in the chapel of Lord Newark.
The Resurrection of our Saviour, in the church of Barbadoes, 10 by 6.
The picture of Moses with the Law, and John the Baptist, in ditto, as large as life.
The picture of Telemachus and Calypso.
Do. of Angelica and Madora.
Do. of the Damsel and Orlando.
Do. of Cicero at the Tomb of Archimedes.
Do. of St. Paul's Conversion; his Persecution of the Christians; and the Restoration of his Sight, under the hands of Ananias, in one frame, divided in three parts.
Do. of Mr. Hope's Family, containing nine figures as large as life.
Large figures of Faith, Hope, Charity, Innocence, St. Matthew, St. Mark, St. Luke, St. John, St. Matthias, St. Thomas, St. Jude, St. Simon, St James the Major, St. Philip, St. Peter, St. Andrew, St. Bartholomew, St. James the Minor, Malachi, Micah, Zachariah, and Daniel.
Paul shaking the Viper from his Finger.
Paul preaching at Athens.
Elimas the Sorcerer struck blind.
Cornelius and the Angel.
Peter delivered from Prison.
The Conversion of St. Paul.
Paul before Felix.
Two whole-lengths of the late Archbishop of York's two eldest Sons.
A whole-length portrait of the late Lord Grosvenor.
The picture of Jacob drawing Water at the Well for Rachael and her Flock, in the possession of Mrs. Evans.

The picture of the Citizens of London offering the Crown to William the Conqueror.

The Queen soliciting the King to pardon her son John.

Moses showing the brazen Serpent.

John showing the Lamb of God.

Three of the Children of the late Archbishop of York, with the portrait of the Archbishop, half-lengths, in the possession of the Rev. Dr. Drummond.

The Family-picture, half-lengths, of Mrs. Cartwright's Children.

Do. of Sir Edmund Baker, Nephew and Niece, half-length.

Do. of—Lunis, Esq.'s Children, half-lengths.

A Lady leading three Children along the Path of Virtue to the Temple.

A picture of Madora.

The picture of the late Lord Clive receiving the Duannic from the Great Mogul, for Lord Clive.

Christ receiving the Sick and Lame in the Temple, in the Pennsylvanian Hospital, Philadelphia, 11 feet by 18.

The picture of Pylades and Orestes, for Sir George Beaumont.

The original sketch of Cicero at the Tomb of Archimedes, for ditto.

The picture of Leonidas ordering Cleombrotas into Banishment, with his Wife and Children, for W. Smith, Esq.

Do. of the Marys at the Sepulchre, for General Stibert.

Do. of Alexander and his Physician, for ditto.

Do. of Julius Caesar reading the Life of Alexander.

Do. of the Return of the Prodigal Son, for Sir James Earle.

Do. of the Death of Adonis, for—Knight, Esq. Portland Place.

Do. of the Continence of Scipio, ditto.

Do. of Venus and Cupid, oval, for Mr. Steers Temple.

Do. of Alfred dividing his Loaf, presented to Stationers' Hall by Alderman Boydell.

Do. of Helen brought to Paris, in the possession of a family in Kent.

A small sketch of the Shunamite's Son restored, &c.

Cupid stung by a Bee, oval, for—Vesey, Esq. in Ireland.

Agrippina surrounded by her Children, and reclining her Head on the Urn containing the Ashes of Germanicus, ditto.

The Death of Wolfe, the fourth picture, for Lord Bristol.

A do. of do. the fourth picture, in the possession of the Prince of Waldeck.

A small do. of do. the fifth picture, ditto Moncton family.

A small picture of Romeo and Juliet, for the Duke of Courland.

A small picture of King Lear and his Daughters, ditto.

Do. of Belisarius and the Boy, for Sir Francis Baring.

Do. of Sir Francis Baring and part of his Family, containing six figures as large as life, ditto.

Do. of Simeon and the Child, as large as life, for the Provost of Eton.

Do. of the late Lord Clive receiving the Duannic from the Great Mogul, a second picture, for Madras.

The second picture of Philippa soliciting of Edward III. the pardon of the Burgesses of Calais, in the possession of—Willet, Esq.

Do. of Europa on the back of the Bull, at Calcutta.

Do. of the Death of Hyacinthus, painted for Lord Kerry, but now in the National Gallery at Paris.

The picture of Venus presenting the Girdle to Juno, painted for Lord Kerry, and in the National Gallery; figures as large as life in both pictures.

Do. of Rinaldo and Armida, for Caleb Whitford, Esq.

Do. of Pharaoh's Daughter with the Child Moses, for—Park, Esq.: the original painted for General Lawrence.

Do. of the Stolen Kiss, painted for ditto, and in the possession of ditto.

Do. of Angelica and Madora, for ditto, ditto.

Do. of the Woman of Samaria at the Well with Christ, ditto.

Do. of Paetus and Arria, in the possession of Col. Smith, at the Tower.

Do. of Rebecca coming to David, for Sir J. Ashley.

The Drawing respecting Christ's Nativity, for Mr. Tomkins, Doctors' Commons.

Do. of Rebecca receiving the Bracelets at the Well, for the late Lord Buckinghamshire.

The drawing of the Stolen Kiss, ditto.

Do. of Rinaldo and Armida, ditto.
Do. of a Mother and Child, ditto.
The whole-length portrait of Sir Thomas Strange, in the Town-hall of Halifax.
Do. of Sir John Sinclair.
The picture of Agrippina landing at Brundusium, (the first picture,) in the possession of Lord Kinnoul.
Do. of do. for the Earl of Exeter, at Burleigh, second picture.
Do. of do. (third picture,) in the possession of—— Hatch, Esq., in Essex.
A small picture of Jupiter and Semele: the large picture lost at sea.
Hector parting with his Wife and Child at the Sun Gate.
The prophet Elisha raising the Shunamite's son.
The raising of Lazarus.
Edward III. crossing the River Somme.
Queen Philippa at the Battle of Nevil's Cuoss.
The Angels announcing to the Shepherds the Birth of our Saviour.
The Magi bringing Presents to our Saviour.
A view on the River Thames at Hammersmith.
A do. on the banks of the River Susquehanna, in America.
The picture of Tangire Mill, at Eton.
Do. of Chryseis returned to her father Chyses.
Venus and Adonis, large as life.
The sixth picture of the Death of Wolfe.
The first and second picture of the Battle of La Hogue.
The sketch, of Macbeth and the Witches.
The small picture of the Return of Tobias.
The small picture of the Return of the Prodigal Son.
Do. of Ariadne on the Sea-shore.
Do. of the Death of Adonis.
Do. of John King of France brought to the Black Prince.
Do. of Antiochus and Stratonice.
Do, of King Lear and his Daughter.
The picture of Chryses on the Sea-shore.
Do. of Nathan and David:—"Thou art the Man!" as large as life,

Do. of Elijah raising the Widow's Son to Life.
Do. of the Choice of Hercules.
Do. of Venus and Europa.
Do. of Daniel interpreting the Hand-writing on the Wall.
Do. of the Ambassador from Tunis, with his Attendant, as he appeared in England in 1781.
The drawing of Marius on the Ruins of Carthage.
Do. of Cato giving his Daughter in Marriage on his Death, both in the possession of the Archduke Joseph.
Do. of Belisarius brought to his Family.
The large picture of the Stag, or the rescuing of Alexander the Third, for Lord Seaforth, 12 feet by 18.
The picture of Cymon and Iphigenia, and Endymion and Diana, at Wentworth Castle, Yorkshire.
Do. of Cymon and Iphigenia, and Angelica and Madora, in the possession of Mr. Mitton, of Shropshire, painted at Rome.
Small picture of the Battle of Cressy.
Small sketch of the Order of the Garter.
Mr. West's small picture of his Family.
The sketch of Edward the Third with his Queen, and the Citizens of Calais.
Mr. West's small copy from Vandyke's picture of Cardinal Bentivoglio, now in the National Gallery at Paris.
Mr. West's copy from Correggio's celebrated picture at Parma, viz. the St. Girolemo, now in the National Gallery.
The large Landscape from Windsor Forest.
The picture of Mark Antony showing the Robe and Will of Julius Caesar to the People.
Do. of AEgistus viewing the Body of Clytemnestra.
The large sketch of the window at Windsor, of the Magi presenting Gifts to the Infant Christ.
The small sketch of the Battle of Nevil's Cross.
The second small sketch of the Order of the Garter.

The small picture of Ophelia before the King and Queen, with her brother Laertes.
Do. of the Recovery of His Majesty in the year 1789.
Do. from Thomson's Seasons, of Miranda and her Two Companions.
Do. of Edward the Third crowning Ribemont at Calais, a sketch.
The picture of Leonidas taking leave of his Family on his going to Thermopylae.
Do. of a Bacchante, as large as life, half-length.
First sketch of the Battle of Cressy.
The picture of Phaeton soliciting Apollo for the Chariot of the Sun.
The second picture of Cicero at the Tomb of Archimedes.
The small picture of Belisarius and the Boy, different from that in the possession of Sir Francis Baring.
The small picture of the Eagle giving the Vase of Water to Psyche.
Do. of the Death of Adonis, from Anacreon.
Do. of Moonlight and the "Beckoning Ghost," from Pope's Elegy.
Do. of the Angel sitting on the Stone at the Sepulchre.
Second picture of the same, but differing in composition.
A small sketch of ditto.
A sketch of King Lear and his Daughter.
The second picture of Angelica and Madora.
Do. of a Damsel and Orlando.
Mr. West's portrait, half-length.
Sketch of his two Sons, when Children.
Do. when Boys.
Do. when young Men.
Portrait of the Rev.—— Preston.
Picture of the Bacchante Boys.
Do. of the Good Samaritan.
Picture of the Destruction of the Old Beast and False Prophet:—Revelation.
Do. of Christ healing the Sick, Lame, and Blind, in the Tenrple.
Do. of Tintern Abbey.
Do. of Death on the Pale Horse; or, the Opening of the Seals.

Do. of Jason and the Dragon, in imitation of Salvator Rosa.
Do. of Venus and Adonis looking at Cupids bathing.
Do. of Moses and Aaron before Pharaoh.
Do. of the Uxbridge Passage-boat on the Canal.
Do. of St. Paul and Barnabas rejecting the Jews, and turning to the Gentiles.
Picture of the Falling of Trees in the Great Park at Windsor.
Do. of Diomed and his Chariot-horses struck by the Lightning of Jupiter.
Do. of the Milk-woman in St. James's Park.
Do. of King Lear in the Storm at the Hovel.
Do. of the Expulsion of Adam and Eve from Paradise.
Do. of the Order of the Garter.
Do. of Orion on the Dolphin's back.
Do. of Cupid complaining to Venus of a Bee having stung his finger.
Do. of the Deluge.
Do. of Queen Elizabeth's Procession to St. Paul's.
Do. of Christ showing a Little Child as the Emblem of Heaven.
Do. of Harvest-home.
Do. of a View from the east end of Windsor Castle, looking over Datchet.
Do. of Washing of Sheep.
Do. of St. Paul shaking the Viper from his Finger.
Do. of the Sun setting behind a group of Trees on the banks of the Thames at Twickenham.
Do. of the driving of Sheep and Cows to water.
Do. of Cattle drinking at a Watering-place in the Great Park, Windsor, with Mr. West drawing.
Do. of Pharaoh and his Host drowned in the Red Sea.
Do. of Calypso and Telemachus on the Sea-shore; second picture.
Do. of Gentlemen fishing in the Water at Dagenham Breach.
Do. of Moses consecrating Aaron and his Sons to the priesthood.
Picture of the View of Windsor-Castle from Snow-Hill, in the Great Park.
Do. of a Mother inviting her little Boy to come to her through a small Stream of Water.
Do. of the naming of Samuel, and the prophesying of Zacharias.

Do. of the Ascension of our Saviour.
Do of the Birth of Jacob and Esau.
Do. of the Brewer's Porter and Hod Carrier.
Do. of Venus attended by the Graces.
Do. of Samuel, when a Boy, presented to Eli.
Do. of Christ's Last Supper. (In brown colour.)
Do. of the Reaping of Harvest, with Windsor in the back-ground.
Do. of Adonis and his Dog going to the Chace.
Do. of Christ among the Doctors in the Temple.
Do. of Moses shown the Promised Land.
Do. of Joshua crossing the River Jordan with the Ark.
Do. of Christ's Nativity.
Do. of Mothers with their Children, in water,
Do. of Cranford Bridge.
Do, of the sketch of Pyrrhus when a Child, before King Glaucus.
Do. of the Traveller laying his Piece of Bread on t
 he Bridle of the dead Ass. From Sterne.
Do. of the Captivity. From ditto.
Do. of Cupid letting loose Two Pigeons.
Do. of Cupid asleep.
Do. of Children eating Cherries.
Sketch of a Mother and her Child on her Lap.
The small picture of the Eagle bringing the Cup to Psyche.
The picture of St. Anthony of Padua and the Child.
Do. of Jacob, and Laban with his Two Daughters.
Do. of the Women looking into the Sepulchre, and beholding
 Two Angels where the Lord lay.
Do. of the Angel loosening the Chains of St. Peter in Prison.
Do. of the Death of Sir Philip Sydney.
Do. of the Death of Epaminondas.
Do. of the Death of Bayard.
The small sketch of Christ's Ascension.
The sketch of a Group of Legendary Saints. In imitation of Reubens.

The picture of Kosciusco on a Couch, as he appeared in London, 1797.
Do. of the Death of Cephalus.
Do. of Abraham and Isaac:—"Here is the Wood and Fire, but where is the Lamb for Sacrifice."
The sketch of the Bard. From Gray.
Do. of the Pardoning of John by his brother King Henry, at the Solicitation of his Mother.
Do. of St. George and the Dragon.
The picture of Eponina with her Children, giving Bread to her Husband when in Concealment.
The sketch on paper of Christ's Last Supper.
The picture of the Pardoning of John, at his Mother's Solicitation.
Do. of the Death of Lord Chatham.
Do. of the Presentation of the Crown to William the Conqueror.
Do. of Europa crowning the Bull with Flowers.
Do. of Mr. West's Garden, Gallery, and Painting-Room.
Do. of the Cave of Despair. From Spenser.
The picture of Christ's Resurrection.
The sketch of the Destruction of the Spanish Armada.
The picture of Arethusa bathing.
The sketch of Priam soliciting of Achilles the Body of Hector.
The picture of Moonlight. (Small.)
The small sketch of Cupid showing Venus his Finger stung by a Bee.
The drawings of the Two Sides of the intended Chapel at Windsor, with the Arrangement of the Pictures, &c.
The drawing of St. Matthew, with the Angel.
Do. of Alcibiades and Timon of Athens.
Do. of Penn's Treaty.
Do. of Regulus.
Do. of Mark Antony, showing the Robe and Will of Caesar.
Do. of the Birth of Jacob and Esau.
Do. of the Death of Dido.

The large sketch, in oil, (on paper,) of Moses receiving the Laws on Mount Sinai.
The large drawing of the Death of Hippolytus.
The large sketch, in oil, of the Death of St. Stephen. On paper.
The drawing of the Death of Caesar.
Do. of the Swearing of Hannibal.
Do. of the Expulsion of Adam and Eve.
Do. of the Deluge.
The sketch, in oil, of the Landing of Agrippina. On paper.
Do. of Leonidas ordering Cleombrotus into Banishment. On paper.
The drawing of the Death of Epaminondas.
The sketch, in oil, of the Death of Aaron. On paper.
The drawing of the Death of Sir Philip Sydney.
The sketch, in oil, (on paper,) of David prostrate, whilst the destroying Angel sheathes the Sword.
The drawing of the Women looking into the Sepulchre.
Do. of St. John Preaching.
Do. of the Golden Age.
Do. of Antinous and Stratonice.
Do. of the Death of Demosthenes.
The large sketch, in oil, (on paper,) of Death on the Pale Horse.
The drawing of King John and the Barons with Magna Charta.
Do. of La Hogue.
Do. of Jacob and Laban.
The large ditto of the Destruction of the Assyrian Camp by the destroying Angel.
The large sketch, in oil, (on paper,) of Christ raising the Widow's Son.
Do. in ditto, (on paper,) of the Water gushing from the Rock, when s truck by Moses.
The drawing of the Death of Socrates.
Do. of the Boyne.
Do. of the Death of Eustace St. Celaine.

The sketch, in oil, (on paper,) of the Procession of Agrippina with her Children and the Roman Ladies through the Roman Camp, when in Mutiny.
The drawing of the Rescue of Alexander III. of Scotland from the Fury of the Stag.
Do. of the Death of Wolfe.
The sketch, in oil, of King Alfred dividing his Loaf with a Pilgrim.
The sketch, in oil, of the Raising of Lazarus.
The small whole-length of Thomas a Becket, in oil, on canvass.
The small picture of the Death of the Stag.
The drawing of ditto.
Do. of Nathan and David.
Do. of Joseph making himself known to his Brethren.
The drawing of Narcissus in the Fountain.
Do. sketch, in small, of the Duannic received by Lord Clive.
Do. of the Continence of Scipio.
Do. of the Last Judgment, and the Sea giving up its Dead.
Do. of the Bard. From Gray;
Do. of Belisarius and his Family.
The sketch, in oil, of Aaron standing between the Dead and Living to stop the Plague.
Do. on paper, of the Messenger announcing to Samuel the Loss of the Battle.
The drawing of Sir Philip Sydney ordering the Water to be given to the wounded Soldier.
The sketch of Christ Rejected.
The great picture of Christ Rejected.
Do. of Death on the Pale Horse.
The second picture of Christ healing the Sick.
The third great picture of Lord Clive receiving the Duannie.
Portrait of the Duke of Portland.
Portrait of Himself, left unfinished.

N.B. Besides these productions, Mr. West has, in his portfolios, drawings and sketches exceeding two hundred in number.

NATIONAL MONUMENT

[The following letter on an interesting subject is curious, and is inserted here to be preserved.]

Mr. West's Letter to Sir George Beaumont, Bart.

East Cowes Castle, Isle of Wight,
Sept. 30. 1815.

"DEAR SIR GEORGE,
"Your letter to me from Keswick of the thirty-first of last month I have received at this place: in that letter you have honoured me with the communication of 'the Lords Commissioners of His Majesty's Treasury having done you the honour, among others, to inform you of the commands of His Royal Highness the Prince Regent, that measures be forthwith taken for the erection of a monument to commemorate the victory of Waterloo, in pursuance of an address of the House of Commons; and to request you to apply to such artists as you think fit, for designs for this national column;' and you are pleased to say, that you believe at this distance you cannot better forward their views than by applying to me.

"The honourable way in which you have noticed my humble abilities in the arts, by calling on them for a design for a monument, to perpetuate an occurrence of such high military glory and national greatness as that of the victory of Waterloo, demands my warmest acknowledgments, and I also feel a duty and profound respect for the sources of your instructions to procure appropriate designs from the artists. When a monument is to be raised by a great and victorious nation (such as England) in memory of her departed as well as her living heroes, I feel it of the highest importance to her national character, when her arts and her arms stand so high, that they should bear a proud record to posterity of both their powers in such a building as that now under consideration.

"To raise a record to departed virtue in an individual, an obelisk, a column, or a statue, may bear an honourable name to posterity; but a record when thousands have devoted their lives to save their country from a rapacious enemy, as in those victories gained by the Greeks at Thermopylae and Marathon; the English at Blenheim and Trafalgar; and, lastly, that greatest of all, gained by the unsubdued valour and heroism of the armies of the United Kingdom at Waterloo, demands a building of greater magnitude and more national consequence than that of a column.

"Such a design as I have conceived to record that victory I will give to yourself and others for your consideration; but not as a competitor presenting a drawing or model for a decision to be made on it as offered for competition: I therefore give you the following ideas on friendly motives for a dignified building.

"All records to be transmitted, must be by the three means which have been established for that purpose; namely, the pen, the pencil, and the chisel. I therefore propose a building wherein these three may be employed to express the various incidents, and to mark that victory distinct from all others, by applying the several spoils and trophies taken; and to have the building of considerable magnitude. For as the subject is great, so should be its representative: nothing little or mean should be accepted, or permitted to appear in such a work, nothing but what will mark the great features of that event: all of which by dates, names, and sculptured trophies, as well as paintings, may be proclaimed and recorded to distant times.

"The basis of such an erection being intended solely to commemorate the battle of Waterloo, its name should be in capital letters on the four faces, and the trophies of that victory should enrich the sides of the same; and the characters of the various military in British armies made conspicuous by their numbers shown; and on the summit of the lofty pile the sovereign's figure then in power should be placed.

"The plan and dimensions of the building I present to you are as follows:—Its base a square of sixty feet, and its height thirty: this will make each of the four faces of the base a double square on its measurement. From the centre of this base a building to be erected in diameter thirty feet, and in height one hundred and twenty, formed out of the spoils of victory, and diminishing as it rises, and to be surmounted by a figure twelve feet in height, including the pedestal on which it stands, In the centre, over the front face of the great case, to be the equestrian group of the Duke of Wellington, under which, in large letters, WATERLOO to be inscribed; and the four angles of the great base perpendicular tablets, ornamented with military insignia expressive of the British armies, and inscribed on the four tablets the number of each regiment who shared in the glories of that day, and by the four tablets be placed the statues of distinguished generals. Thus I have presented you with the external appearance of my imaginary building in honour of the victory of Waterloo; and the interior of this building to be considered as the place of deposit for preserving the powers of the pen, the pencil, and other gems from perishing by water or by fire: to be built of stone, and all its ornaments to be made of durable metals: all of which to be illustrative of the victory for which such a building was erected.

"The situation of this building should be a populous one, and that within a circus or square of a diameter not less than six hundred and fifty-eight feet. This size of space will give the spectator an opportunity of viewing the erection at double the distance of its elevation, which is the optical distance that pictures, statues, and buildings should always be seen at.

"Should my ideas of a building to commemorate the military achievements of Waterloo be viewed with complacency by yourself and others, I shall feel a satisfaction, as President of the Royal Academy, to have done my duty; and should His Royal Highness the Prince Regent be pleased to signify his approbation, I shall be gratified and honoured. With the sincerity of profound respect,

"I am, "My dear Sir George, "Your obliged and obedient Servant, "BENJAMIN WEST."

* * * * *

Suffolk Lane, 28th Jan,

"MY DEAR SIR,

"Sir Philip Francis's critique on the *Transfiguration* appears very ingenious, so far as it explains the painter's design in representing the Demoniac Boy as the connecting link between the action *on the Mount* and the groupe at the foot of it; but I cannot agree with Sir Philip in supposing the picture to represent the *Ascension* and as you request me to state my reasons for this dissent, I shall briefly endeavour to specify them.

"I have *not* seen the original picture; but in the copy of it by Harlow, which was much admired in Rome, and which one would think must be accurate, at least in regard to so important a point, since it was exhibited beside the original—I say in Harlow's copy the raiment of our Saviour is *white,* not *blue*. The white has, indeed, in the shaded part, a bluish tinge, but the colour is decidedly a *white*, and, therefore, Sir Philip's assumption that it is *blue* appears contrary to the fact.

"The *Transfiguration* was witnessed by *only three* of the Apostles, Peter, James, and John, (see St. Matthew, CHAPTER xvii, v. 1, 2, and 3.) exactly as represented In the picture, 'and (see v. 9.) as they came down from the mountain, Jesus charged them, saying, "Tell the vision to no man, until the Son of Man be risen again from the dead."'

"It maybe as well, to prevent the trouble of an reference, to quote at once from the Evangelist, the description of the subject which it appears to me the painter meant to represent.

CHAPTER xvii. as before.

1. And after six days Jesus taketh Peter, James, and John his brother, and bringeth them up into an high mountain apart,

2. And was transfigured before them: and his face did shine as the sun, and his raiment was white as the light.

3. And, behold, there appeared unto them Moses and Elias talking with him.

6. And when the disciples heard, they fell on their faces, and were sore afraid.

14. And when they were come to the multitudes there came to him a man, kneeling down to him, and saying,

15. Lord, have mercy on my son: for he is lunatic and sore vexed: and oft-times he falleth into the fire, and oft into the water.

16. And I brought him to thy disciples, and they could not cure him, &c.

"Now this is exactly the scene delineated in the picture. There are *on the Mount* the three disciples, fallen on the ground, and shading their faces from the '*bright cloud*' which *overshadows* the transfigured Saviour; and Moses and Elias are the two figures of old men attending the Saviour, or '*talking with him.*'

"At the *foot of the Mount*, there are *the multitude*, the lunatic boy, *his father* holding him, the *disciples* who *could not cure him*; and one of whom appears in the act of attempting to cure him, by addressing or exorcising the demon who is in him. There are also *several women* in the groupe; and it seems that instead of bringing 'different incidents together to constitute one plot,' the painter, on the contrary, has exactly followed the Evangelist, and represented the same instant of time in the action *on* the Mount, among the *multitude* at the foot of it.

"I cannot imagine how Sir Philip Francis could have supposed the picture to represent the *Ascension*, which took place in the presence of the *Eleven Apostles* and of them only, (see St. Luke, last chapter and last paragraph,) as follows:

"And he led them out as far as Bethany, and he lifted up his hands, and he blessed them. And it came to pass, when he blessed them, he was parted from them, and carried up into Heaven."

"This bears no resemblance whatever to the scene represented in the picture, and the opinion given by Sir Philip can only have arisen from an imperfect recollection of the Sacred Writings, and from having neglected to refer to the text.

"I am, "My dear Sir, "Yours truly, S.M'G———."

John Galt, Esq.

THE FUNERAL OF MR. WEST

It would be improper to close this appendix without giving some account of the funeral of Mr. West.

Soon after Mr. West's decease, a deputation from the Council of the Royal Academy waited on his sons and the executors, to apprise them of the intention of that body to honour the remains of their late President., by attending them to his grave, according to the ceremonial adopted on the public interment of the late Sir Joshua Reynolds, in St. Paul's Cathedral. His Majesty having, as Patron of the Royal Academy, given his gracious sanction that similar honours should be paid to the late venerable President, his sons and executors adopted active preparations to carry the arrangement into effect. As the schools of the Royal Academy were closed, and all its functions suspended, by the death of the late President, it was of material importance on this account, and with the view to the usual preparatory arrangements for the annual exhibition, that the funeral should not be delayed; and as early a day as practicable was therefore fixed for the public interment in St. Paul's Cathedral. The obvious consequence, however, of this has been, that owing to the absence from town, at this particular season, of so many noblemen and gentlemen of the highest rank, and the indisposition of several others, many warm admirers and friends of this celebrated artist and amiable man, who have, during his long life, honoured him with their friendship, and who have been particularly desirous of paying their last tribute of respect to his remains, have been precluded attending the funeral. The corpse was privately brought to the Royal Academy on Tuesday evening, attended by the sons and grandson of the deceased, and two intimate friends, Mr. Henderson (one of the trustees and executors of the deceased) and Mr. Hayes (for many years his medical attendant), and was received by the council and officers of the Royal Academy, and their undertaker and his attendants, with every mark of respect. The body was then deposited in the smaller Exhibition-room, on the ground-floor, which was hung on the occasion with black.

About half-past ten yesterday morning, the Academicians, Associates, and Students, assembled in the Great Exhibition-room, and the nobility, gentry, and the deceased's private friends, soon after arrived, and joined the mournful band. The chief mourners were in seclusion in the library of the Academy. About half-past twelve o'clock, the whole of the arrangements having been effected, the Procession moved from Somerset House to St. Paul's Cathedral in the following order:

> Six Constables, by threes.
> Four Marshalmen, two and two.
> City Marshal on horseback.
> Undertaker on horseback.
> Six Cloakmen on horseback, by twos.
> Four Mutes on horseback, by twos.
> Lid of Feathers, with attendant Pages.

Hearse and Six, with rich trappings, feathers, and velvets, attended by Eight Pages.

Two Mourning Coaches and four, with attendant Pages, conveying the Pall-bearers.

Mourning Coach and Four, with attendant Pages, conveying the Sons and Grandson of the deceased, as CHIEF MOURNERS.

Mourning Coach and Four, with attendant Pages, conveying the Family Trustees and Executors of the deceased.

Mourning Coach and Four, with attendant Pages, conveying the Reverends the Vicar of Mary-la-bonne, the Chaplain to the Lord Mayor, and the Medical Attendant of the deceased.

Then followed Sixteen Mourning Coaches and Pairs, with Attendant Pages, conveying the Right Rev. the Chaplain, the Secretary for Foreign Correspondence, and the Members of the Royal Academy and Students.

Twenty Mourning Coaches and Pairs, with attendant Pages, conveying the Mourners and Private Friends of the deceased.

The Procession was closed by above sixty carriages, arranged in rank by the junior City Marshal and Marshalmen—the servants wearing hat-bands and gloves.

The Procession was attended on each side by fifty Constables, to preserve order; and the accesses from Bridge-street, Chancery-lane, the Old Bailey, &c. were stopped. On reaching St. Paul's Cathedral, where the senior City Marshal was in wailing, with several assistants, to arrange the Procession, it entered at the great Western Gate, and was met at the entrance of the Cathedral by the Church Dignitaries, &c. the whole then proceeded to the Choir in the following order:

The two junior Vergers.
The Marshals.
The young Gentlemen of the Choir, two by two.
Their Almoner, or Master.
The Vicars Choral, two by two.
The Sub-Dean and Junior Canons, two by two.
The Feathers, with Attendant Pages and Mutes.
The two Senior Vergers.
Honourable and Rev. Dr. Wellesley.
The Canon residentiary, and the Rev. the Prebendary.

[THE CORPSE]

Pall-bearers.   Pall-bearers.
The Earl of Aberdeen,   Right Honourable Sir

His Excellency the American Ambassador,
Hon. Augustus Phipps,
Sir Thomas Baring.
William Scott,
Honourable Gen. Phipps,
Sir George Beaumont,
Sir Robert Wilson.

CHIEF MOURNERS.

The Sons and Grandson of deceased, namely,
Raphael Lamar West, Esq.
Benjamin West, Esq.
and
Mr. Benjamin West, jun.
followed by
Robert Brunning (the old Servant of deceased)
Henry Fauntleroy, Esq. and James Henry Henderson, Esq. (the Family Trustees and Executors of deceased.)
and
The Rev. Dr. Heslop, Vicar of St. Mary-la-Bonne; the Rev. Mr. Borrodaile, Chaplain to the Lord Mayor; and Joseph Hayes, Esq. Medical Attendant on deceased
(Dr. Baillie being unavoidably absent).

Then followed

The Bishop of Salisbury, (As Chaplain to the Royal Academy; and an Honorary Member).

Prince Hoare, (Secretary for Foreign Correspondence to the Royal Academy.)

The body of Academicians and Associates of the Royal Academy, according to seniority, two by two, Students, two by two.

And the private mourners of the deceased, consisting of—Aldermen Wood and Birch, Rev. —— Est, Rev. Holt Oakes, Henry Bankes, Esq. M.P., William Smith, Esq. M.P., Richard Hart Davies, Esq. M.P., George Watson Taylor, Esq. M.P., Jesse Watts Russell, Esq. M.P., Archibald Hamilton, Esq., Thomas Hope, Esq., Samuel

Boddington, Esq., Richard Payne Knight, Esq., Thomas Lister Parker, Esq., George Hibbert, Esq., John Nash, Esq., John Edwards, Esq., Major Payne, Captain Henry Wolseley, Captain Francis Halliday, James St. Aubyn, Esq., Henry Sansom, Esq., —— Magniac, Esq., George Sheddon, Esq., James Dunlop, Esq., Joseph Ward, Esq., N. Ogle, Esq., George Repton, Esq., William Wadd, Esq., Henry Woodthorpe, jun. Esq., Christ. Hodgson, Esq., —— Cockerell, sen. Esq., —— Cockerell, jun. Esq., Leigh Hunt, Esq., P. Turnerelli, Esq., J. Holloway, Esq., Charles Heath, Esq., Henry Eddridge, Esq., A. Robertson, Esq., W. J. Newton, Esq., John Taylor, Esq., T. Bonney, Esq., —— Muss, Esq., —— Martin, Esq., J. Green, Esq., John Gait, Esq., William Carey, Esq., —— Leslie Esq., —— Behnes, Esq., George Samuel, Esq., John Young, Esq., Christopher Pack, Esq., W, Delamotte, Esq., E. Scriven Esq., J. M. Davis, Esq., C. Smart, Esq., &c.

It being Passion Week, the usual chanting and performance of music in the Cathedral-service could not take place, but an Anthem was, by special permission, allowed to be sung; and the Hon. and Rev. Dr. Wellesley, assisted by the Rev. the Prebendary, performed the solemn service in a very impressive manner. The body was placed in the choir, and at the head were arranged, on chairs, the chief mourners and executors. The pall-bearers were seated on each side of the corpse, and the Members of the Royal Academy, and other mourners, were arranged on each side of the choir. After the Anthem, the body was attended to the vault-door by the pall-bearers, followed by the chief mourners and executors, and was conveyed into the crypt, and placed immediately beneath the perforated brass plate, under the centre of the dome. Dr. Wellesley, with the other canons, and the whole choir, then came under the dome, and the pall-bearers, chief mourners, and executors, stood by them. The Members of the Royal Academy were ranged on the right, and the other mourners on the left, forming a circle, the outside of which was protected by the Marshals and undertaker's attendants. Here the remainder of the service was completed, and the sexton, placed in the crypt below, at the proper period, let fall some earth, as usual, on the coffin. After the funeral-service was ended, the chief mourners and executors, accompanied by most of the other mourners, went into the crypt, and attended the corpse to its grave, which was sunk with brick-work under the pavement at the head of the grave of the late Sir Joshua Reynolds, and adjoining to that of the late Mr. West's intimate and highly-valued friend, Dr. Newton, formerly

Bishop of Bristol, and Dean of St. Paul's, the brick-work of whose grave forms one side of Mr. West's; thus uniting their remains in the silent tomb. Sir Christopher Wren, the great architect, lies interred close by, as well as those eminent artists, the late Mr. Opie and Mr. Barry.

The Members of the Royal Academy, and all the mourners, then returned to Somerset-House, in the like order of procession (with the exception of the hearse and feathers,) where refreshments were provided for them.

The whole of this affecting ceremony was conducted with great solemnity and respect, and was witnessed by an immense concourse of people.

The carriages attending in the Procession were those of the Lord Mayor, the Archbishop of York, the Dukes of Norfolk, Northumberland, and Argyll; the Marquisses of Lansdowne and Stafford; the Earls of Liverpool, Essex, Aberdeen, Carlisle, Dartmouth, Powis, Mulgrave, Darnley, and Carysfort; Viscount Sidmouth; the Bishops of London, Salisbury, Carlisle, and Chester; Admiral Lord Radstock; the Right Honourables Sir William Scott, Charles Manners Sutton, and Charles Long; the American Ambassador; the Hon. General Phipps, Augustus Phipps; Sirs George Beaumont, J. Fleming Leicester, Thomas Baring, and Henry Fletcher; the Solicitor General, Sir Robert Wilson, Dr. Heslop, Dr. Baillie, Aldermen Birch and Wood, Mr. Chamberlain Clarke, Henry Bankes, Esq. M.P., Richard Hart Davies, Esq. M.P., George Watson Taylor, Esq. M.P., Jesse Watts Russell, Esq. M.P., Henry Fauntleroy, Esq., Archibald Hamilton, Esq., Thomas Courts, Esq., John Penn, Esq., Thomas Hope, Esq., Samuel Boddington, Esq., Walter Fawkes, Esq., George Hibbert, Esq., John Yenn, Esq., John Soane, Esq., Francis Chantry, Esq., Henry Sanson, Esq., John Nash, Esq., John Edwards, Esq., George Sheddon, Esq., James Dunlop, Esq., Joseph Ward, Esq., Henry Meux, Esq. &c. &c.

The following is the Inscription upon the Tombstone over the deceased:—

Here lie the Remains of BENJAMIN WEST, Esq., President of the Royal Academy of Painting, Sculpture, and Architecture: born 10th Oct. 1738, at Springfield, in Pennsylvania, in America: died in London, 11th March, 1820.

END OF PART II

www.bookjungle.com *email: sales@bookjungle.com fax: 630-214-0564 mail: Book Jungle PO Box 2226 Champaign, IL 61825*

The Codes Of Hammurabi And Moses
W. W. Davies

QTY

The discovery of the Hammurabi Code is one of the greatest achievements of archaeology, and is of paramount interest, not only to the student of the Bible, but also to all those interested in ancient history...

Religion ISBN: *1-59462-338-4* Pages:132
MSRP $12.95

The Theory of Moral Sentiments
Adam Smith

QTY

This work from 1749. contains original theories of conscience amd moral judgment and it is the foundation for systemof morals.

Philosophy ISBN: *1-59462-777-0* Pages:536
MSRP $19.95

Jessica's First Prayer
Hesba Stretton

QTY

In a screened and secluded corner of one of the many railway-bridges which span the streets of London there could be seen a few years ago, from five o'clock every morning until half past eight, a tidily set-out coffee-stall, consisting of a trestle and board, upon which stood two large tin cans, with a small fire of charcoal burning under each so as to keep the coffee boiling during the early hours of the morning when the work-people were thronging into the city on their way to their daily toil...

Childrens ISBN: *1-59462-373-2* Pages:84
MSRP $9.95

My Life and Work
Henry Ford

QTY

Henry Ford revolutionized the world with his implementation of mass production for the Model T automobile. Gain valuable business insight into his life and work with his own auto-biography... "We have only started on our development of our country we have not as yet, with all our talk of wonderful progress, done more than scratch the surface. The progress has been wonderful enough but..."

Biographies/ ISBN: *1-59462-198-5* Pages:300
MSRP $21.95

www.bookjungle.com *email: sales@bookjungle.com fax: 630-214-0564 mail: Book Jungle PO Box 2226 Champaign, IL 61825*

The Art of Cross-Examination
Francis Wellman

QTY

I presume it is the experience of every author, after his first book is published upon an important subject, to be almost overwhelmed with a wealth of ideas and illustrations which could readily have been included in his book, and which to his own mind, at least, seem to make a second edition inevitable. Such certainly was the case with me; and when the first edition had reached its sixth impression in five months, I rejoiced to learn that it seemed to my publishers that the book had met with a sufficiently favorable reception to justify a second and considerably enlarged edition. ...

Reference   ISBN: *1-59462-647-2*   Pages:412 MSRP *$19.95*

On the Duty of Civil Disobedience
Henry David Thoreau

QTY

Thoreau wrote his famous essay, On the Duty of Civil Disobedience, as a protest against an unjust but popular war and the immoral but popular institution of slave-owning. He did more than write—he declined to pay his taxes, and was hauled off to gaol in consequence. Who can say how much this refusal of his hastened the end of the war and of slavery?

Law   ISBN: *1-59462-747-9*   Pages:48 MSRP *$7.45*

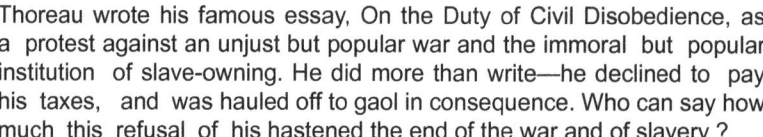

Dream Psychology Psychoanalysis for Beginners
Sigmund Freud

QTY

Sigmund Freud, born Sigismund Schlomo Freud (May 6, 1856 - September 23, 1939), was a Jewish-Austrian neurologist and psychiatrist who co-founded the psychoanalytic school of psychology. Freud is best known for his theories of the unconscious mind, especially involving the mechanism of repression; his redefinition of sexual desire as mobile and directed towards a wide variety of objects; and his therapeutic techniques, especially his understanding of transference in the therapeutic relationship and the presumed value of dreams as sources of insight into unconscious desires.

Psychology   ISBN: *1-59462-905-6*   Pages:196 MSRP *$15.45*

The Miracle of Right Thought
Orison Swett Marden

QTY

Believe with all of your heart that you will do what you were made to do. When the mind has once formed the habit of holding cheerful, happy, prosperous pictures, it will not be easy to form the opposite habit. It does not matter how improbable or how far away this realization may see, or how dark the prospects may be, if we visualize them as best we can, as vividly as possible, hold tenaciously to them and vigorously struggle to attain them, they will gradually become actualized, realized in the life. But a desire, a longing without endeavor, a yearning abandoned or held indifferently will vanish without realization.

Self Help   ISBN: *1-59462-644-8*   Pages:360 MSRP *$25.45*

www.bookjungle.com email: sales@bookjungle.com fax: 630-214-0564 mail: Book Jungle PO Box 2226 Champaign, IL 61825

QTY

☐ **The Rosicrucian Cosmo-Conception Mystic Christianity** by *Max Heindel* ISBN: 1-59462-188-8 **$38.95**
The Rosicrucian Cosmo-conception is not dogmatic, neither does it appeal to any other authority than the reason of the student. It is not controversial, but is: sent forth in the hope that it may help to clear...
New Age/Religion Pages 646

☐ **Abandonment To Divine Providence** by *Jean-Pierre de Caussade* ISBN: 1-59462-228-0 **$25.95**
"The Rev. Jean Pierre de Caussade was one of the most remarkable spiritual writers of the Society of Jesus in France in the 18th Century. His death took place at Toulouse in 1751. His works have gone through many editions and have been republished...
Inspirational/Religion Pages 400

☐ **Mental Chemistry** by *Charles Haanel* ISBN: 1-59462-192-6 **$23.95**
Mental Chemistry allows the change of material conditions by combining and appropriately utilizing the power of the mind. Much like applied chemistry creates something new and unique out of careful combinations of chemicals the mastery of mental chemistry...
New Age Pages 354

☐ **The Letters of Robert Browning and Elizabeth Barret Barrett 1845-1846 vol II** ISBN: 1-59462-193-4 **$35.95**
by *Robert Browning* and *Elizabeth Barrett*
Biographies Pages 596

☐ **Gleanings In Genesis (volume I)** by *Arthur W. Pink* ISBN: 1-59462-130-6 **$27.45**
Appropriately has Genesis been termed "the seed plot of the Bible" for in it we have, in germ form, almost all of the great doctrines which are afterwards fully developed in the books of Scripture which follow...
Religion/Inspirational Pages 420

☐ **The Master Key** by *L. W. de Laurence* ISBN: 1-59462-001-6 **$30.95**
In no branch of human knowledge has there been a more lively increase of the spirit of research during the past few years than in the study of Psychology, Concentration and Mental Discipline. The requests for authentic lessons in Thought Control, Mental Discipline and...
New Age/Business Pages 422

☐ **The Lesser Key Of Solomon Goetia** by *L. W. de Laurence* ISBN: 1-59462-092-X **$9.95**
This translation of the first book of the "Lemegeton" which is now for the first time made accessible to students of Talismanic Magic was done, after careful collation and edition, from numerous Ancient Manuscripts in Hebrew, Latin, and French...
New Age/Occult Pages 92

☐ **Rubaiyat Of Omar Khayyam** by *Edward Fitzgerald* ISBN:1-59462-332-5 **$13.95**
Edward Fitzgerald, whom the world has already learned, in spite of his own efforts to remain within the shadow of anonymity, to look upon as one of the rarest poets of the century, was born at Bredfield, in Suffolk, on the 31st of March, 1809. He was the third son of John Purcell...
Music Pages 172

☐ **Ancient Law** by *Henry Maine* ISBN: 1-59462-128-4 **$29.95**
The chief object of the following pages is to indicate some of the earliest ideas of mankind, as they are reflected in Ancient Law, and to point out the relation of those ideas to modern thought.
Religion/History Pages 452

☐ **Far-Away Stories** by *William J. Locke* ISBN: 1-59462-129-2 **$19.45**
"Good wine needs no bush, but a collection of mixed vintages does. And this book is just such a collection. Some of the stories I do not want to remain buried for ever in the museum files of dead magazine-numbers an author's not unpardonable vanity..."
Fiction Pages 272

☐ **Life of David Crockett** by *David Crockett* ISBN: 1-59462-250-7 **$27.45**
"Colonel David Crockett was one of the most remarkable men of the times in which he lived. Born in humble life, but gifted with a strong will, an indomitable courage, and unremitting perseverance..
Biographies/New Age Pages 424

☐ **Lip-Reading** by *Edward Nitchie* ISBN: 1-59462-206-X **$25.95**
Edward B. Nitchie, founder of the New York School for the Hard of Hearing, now the Nitchie School of Lip-Reading, Inc, wrote "LIP-READING Principles and Practice". The development and perfecting of this meritorious work on lip-reading was an undertaking...
How-to Pages 400

☐ **A Handbook of Suggestive Therapeutics, Applied Hypnotism, Psychic Science** ISBN: 1-59462-214-0 **$24.95**
by *Henry Munro*
Health/New Age/Health/Self-help Pages 376

☐ **A Doll's House: and Two Other Plays** by *Henrik Ibsen* ISBN: 1-59462-112-8 **$19.95**
Henrik Ibsen created this classic when in revolutionary 1848 Rome. Introducing some striking concepts in playwriting for the realist genre, this play has been studied the world over.
Fiction/Classics/Plays 308

☐ **The Light of Asia** by *sir Edwin Arnold* ISBN: 1-59462-204-3 **$13.95**
In this poetic masterpiece, Edwin Arnold describes the life and teachings of Buddha. The man who was to become known as Buddha to the world was born as Prince Gautama of India but he rejected the worldly riches and abandoned the reigns of power when...
Religion/History/Biographies Pages 170

☐ **The Complete Works of Guy de Maupassant** by *Guy de Maupassant* ISBN: 1-59462-157-8 **$16.95**
"For days and days, nights and nights, I had dreamed of that first kiss which was to consecrate our engagement, and I knew not on what spot I should put my lips..."
Fiction/Classics Pages 240

☐ **The Art of Cross-Examination** by *Francis L. Wellman* ISBN: 1-59462-309-0 **$26.95**
Written by a renowned trial lawyer, Wellman imparts his experience and uses case studies to explain how to use psychology to extract desired information through questioning.
How-to/Science/Reference Pages 408

☐ **Answered or Unanswered?** by *Louisa Vaughan* ISBN: 1-59462-248-5 **$10.95**
Miracles of Faith in China
Religion Pages 112

☐ **The Edinburgh Lectures on Mental Science (1909)** by *Thomas* ISBN: 1-59462-008-3 **$11.95**
This book contains the substance of a course of lectures recently given by the writer in the Queen Street Hall, Edinburgh. Its purpose is to indicate the Natural Principles governing the relation between Mental Action and Material Conditions...
New Age/Psychology Pages 148

☐ **Ayesha** by *H. Rider Haggard* ISBN: 1-59462-301-5 **$24.95**
Verily and indeed it is the unexpected that happens! Probably if there was one person upon the earth from whom the Editor of this, and of a certain previous history, did not expect to hear again...
Classics Pages 380

☐ **Ayala's Angel** by *Anthony Trollope* ISBN: 1-59462-352-X **$29.95**
The two girls were both pretty, but Lucy who was twenty-one who supposed to be simple and comparatively unattractive, whereas Ayala was credited, as her Bomb what romantic name might show, with poetic charm and a taste for romance. Ayala when her father died was nineteen...
Fiction Pages 484

☐ **The American Commonwealth** by *James Bryce* ISBN: 1-59462-286-8 **$34.45**
An interpretation of American democratic political theory. It examines political mechanics and society from the perspective of Scotsman James Bryce
Politics Pages 572

☐ **Stories of the Pilgrims** by *Margaret P. Pumphrey* ISBN: 1-59462-116-0 **$17.95**
This book explores pilgrims religious oppression in England as well as their escape to Holland and eventual crossing to America on the Mayflower, and their early days in New England...
History Pages 268

www.bookjungle.com email: sales@bookjungle.com fax: 630-214-0564 mail: Book Jungle PO Box 2226 Champaign, IL 61825

QTY

The Fasting Cure by *Sinclair Upton* ISBN: *1-59462-222-1* **$13.95**
In the Cosmopolitan Magazine for May, 1910, and in the Contemporary Review (London) for April, 1910, I published an article dealing with my experiences in fasting. I have written a great many magazine articles, but never one which attracted so much attention... *New Age/Self Help/Health Pages 164*

Hebrew Astrology by *Sepharial* ISBN: *1-59462-308-2* **$13.45**
In these days of advanced thinking it is a matter of common observation that we have left many of the old landmarks behind and that we are now pressing forward to greater heights and to a wider horizon than that which represented the mind-content of our progenitors... *Astrology Pages 144*

Thought Vibration or The Law of Attraction in the Thought World ISBN: *1-59462-127-6* **$12.95**
by *William Walker Atkinson* *Psychology/Religion Pages 144*

Optimism by *Helen Keller* ISBN: *1-59462-108-X* **$15.95**
Helen Keller was blind, deaf, and mute since 19 months old, yet famously learned how to overcome these handicaps, communicate with the world, and spread her lectures promoting optimism. An inspiring read for everyone... *Biographies/Inspirational Pages 84*

Sara Crewe by *Frances Burnett* ISBN: *1-59462-360-0* **$9.45**
In the first place, Miss Minchin lived in London. Her home was a large, dull, tall one, in a large, dull square, where all the houses were alike, and all the sparrows were alike, and where all the door-knockers made the same heavy sound... *Childrens/Classic Pages 88*

The Autobiography of Benjamin Franklin by *Benjamin Franklin* ISBN: *1-59462-135-7* **$24.95**
The Autobiography of Benjamin Franklin has probably been more extensively read than any other American historical work, and no other book of its kind has had such ups and downs of fortune. Franklin lived for many years in England, where he was agent... *Biographies/History Pages 332*

Name	
Email	
Telephone	
Address	
City, State ZIP	

☐ Credit Card   ☐ Check / Money Order

Credit Card Number	
Expiration Date	
Signature	

Please Mail to: Book Jungle
                  PO Box 2226
                  Champaign, IL 61825
or Fax to: 630-214-0564

ORDERING INFORMATION

web: *www.bookjungle.com*
email: *sales@bookjungle.com*
fax: *630-214-0564*
mail: *Book Jungle PO Box 2226 Champaign, IL 61825*
or PayPal *to sales@bookjungle.com*

Please contact us for bulk discounts

DIRECT-ORDER TERMS

**20% Discount if You Order
Two or More Books**
Free Domestic Shipping!
Accepted: Master Card, Visa,
Discover, American Express

www.ingramcontent.com/pod-product-compliance
Lightning Source LLC
Chambersburg PA
CBHW080501110426
42742CB00017B/2964